THE NINE OLD MEN

THE
NINE OLD MEN

By

DREW PEARSON
and
ROBERT S. ALLEN

DOUBLEDAY, DORAN & COMPANY, INC.
Garden City, New York
1936

PRINTED AT THE *Country Life Press*, GARDEN CITY, N. Y., U. S. A.

To

R. F. *and* L. M.

"When there is muck to be raked, it must be raked, and the public must know of it, that it may mete out justice. . . . Publicity is a great purifier, because it sets in motion the forces of public opinion, and in this country public opinion controls the courses of the nation."

—Charles Evans Hughes.

Speech before the Manufacturers' Association in May 1908, while governor of New York.

"It is a mistake to suppose that the Supreme Court is either honored or helped by being spoken of as beyond criticism. . . . The time is past in the history of the world when any living man or body of men can be set on a pedestal and decorated with a halo."

—Associate Justice Brewer,

of the Supreme Court of the United States, in 1898.

Contents

THE NINE OLD MEN

CHAPTER I

The Taj Mahal

I⊤ was one of the most momentous occasions in the history of the Supreme Court. The highest dignitaries of the nation were assembled. They stood bareheaded, despite a light drizzle, and extolled the mightiness of justice and the magnificence of the building whose cornerstone they were about to lay. They dwelt feelingly on the fact that this new building, this imposing temple of justice, was a symbol of permanence, a constant reminder to the nine justices that they, and they alone, stood as guardians against flexibility in the economic and social life of the nation.

At the climax, President Hoover stepped forward, took a silver trowel with a mahogany handle fashioned from the furniture of the old court chamber, and slapped a little ball of mortar on the cornerstone. Chief Justice Hughes, his silvery beard glistening with raindrops, did likewise, followed by Guy Atwood Thompson, president of the American Bar Association, who added his portion. Then a master mason scraped off their dabs of mortar and spread a skillful smear of his own, while four workmen, uncomfortably dressed up for the occasion, swung a three-and-one-half ton block of Vermont marble into place.

That block of marble sealed into the cornerstone a steel box containing documents sacred to the history of American justice. In it reposed a copy of the Declaration of Independence, famous addresses of famous justices, a photograph of William Howard Taft, a copy of the Constitution of the United States, and finally

—although this august assemblage did not know it—a picture of Fannie, the Supreme Court collie bitch, giving suck to her seven pups.

As deftly as John Marshall once inserted his *Marbury* vs. *Madison* wedge into the Constitution, thereby giving the Court the right to rule on acts of Congress, Ernest A. Cole, watchman of the Supreme Court, had slipped a photograph of Fannie into the steel box of the cornerstone. The learned justices did not know Fannie, but the watchmen loved her. She had come from nowhere, but she was their dog, and this was her big day.

The ceremony was over. Frock-coated justices stepped into their limousines and drove away to tea not knowing that the pictures of Chief Justice Taft and Fannie, the collie bitch, lay side by side, encased in marble as permanent as the system which they, as guardians of the Constitution, sought to perpetuate.

It may be symbolic that the Supreme Court of the United States took its most intransigeant position athwart the path of progress at the very moment it moved into its first permanent abode and surrounded itself with the trappings of Oriental grandeur. Perhaps also it is significant that the Court's migration from pillar to post during its early days of seeking a regular abode corresponded almost identically with a period of flexibility in adjusting its decisions to the needs of the nation.

Commenting upon the statement of Cass Gilbert, court architect, that the proposed temple of justice would "last for all time," the New York *Times* said:

"To raise buildings for all time is to impose ourselves on the future. It denies our posterity the right to express themselves in their own way. It fails to take cognizance of the speed of modern civilization."

But after all, what could be more appropriate than that a Court which fails to take cognizance of the speed of modern civilization in industrial and economic development, and which denies posterity the right to express itself in regard to social and economic reform in its own way, should be housed in a building symbolic of the Court's intransigeance?

This may have been in the minds of three of the Nine Old Men when plans for the new building were under discussion—the same three, incidentally, who fought to fashion the decisions of the Court to the developments of an ever-changing nation.

Justice Holmes gazed at the intricate blueprints spread before him by Chief Justice Taft, plans for a library, three lunchrooms, bookbindery, fountains, eighteen fireplaces, shower baths, a suite of offices for every justice. Then, a little plaintively, he said:

"But will the tourists bother to cross the plaza to look in on the Court?"

Justice Stone was not impressed by the boyish pride of Mr Taft in his blueprints.

"I am very comfortable at home," he said. "I wouldn't move my library if you gave me the whole building to myself."

"But we must think of the future, gentlemen," argued the Chief Justice. "When future generations of justices assume our robes——"

"Future generations of justices," interrupted Justice Brandeis, "will serve the country better if they do not exalt themselves in physical magnificence. Justice is born in the mind."

But when the Chief Justice called for a vote, the result was another six-to-three decision, again in favor of entrenched permanence.

The site chosen for the new temple of justice was a plot of ground directly across the Capitol Plaza. The building on it, originally a tavern, had served the country as its capitol during the hectic months just after the incendiary visitation of the British in 1814, had witnessed the inauguration of Monroe, housed the deathbed of John C. Calhoun, and during the days of the Civil War was used as the Capital Prison. More recently, and more important, at least in the eyes of the ladies in question, it was owned by the National Woman's Party, whose members organized such an effective lobby that they almost defeated the Congressional appropriation for the new building. In fact, it took all of Mr Taft's powerful prestige and genial persuasiveness to push his pet project through Congress.

Thus the Supreme Court of the United States, after a century of nomadic existence in basements, private homes and a tavern, finally broke ground for its sepulchral temple of justice.

Almost invariably throughout the history of the Supreme Court the power which it has exerted over the life of the nation has been reflected in the permanence or lack of permanence of its physical surroundings. When first it dwelt in New York and Philadelphia, appointments to its bench were spurned and appropriations for its expenses curtailed. When it was elevated to an ornate gilded palace it was able to set aside laws affecting the pocketbook of every factory worker and the crop of every farmer.

This progress from poverty to affluence, from insignificance to power, has been long, laborious and fraught with storm.

The first session, held in the Royal Exchange in New York on February 1, 1790, found it without a bench, cases to try and three of its six justices. The Court adjourned to dine with President Washington at his country home, and next day, strengthened by the arrival of two justices from Virginia, went about the business of reading the justices' commissions and fixing a penalty of imprisonment for anyone who broke silence during the reading.

Further attempts to win the respect of the tumultuous young Republic received a setback next day when Justice Cushing, clad in the wig he had worn on the Massachusetts bench, was followed down Broadway by a mob of hooting boys—an incident which contributed to the decision of the Court to follow the admonition of Thomas Jefferson. "For heaven's sake," he said, "discard the monstrous wig which makes the English judges look like rats peeping through bunches of oakum."

Next year, the Court was forced to follow the legislature which appropriated for it to Philadelphia, and ten years later it moved once again to the new capital in Washington, only to find that the highest tribunal of the nation played so small a part in its affairs that designs for the new Capitol Building completely ignored the existence of the Supreme Court. With no chamber provided for them, the justices crept into a humble apartment in the basement beneath the Senate.

The Court arrived in Washington just in time to receive the full force of an attack far more scathing and effective than Franklin Roosevelt's blast against the NRA decision and the return to the horse-and-buggy age. President Jefferson, who already foresaw that the Court was to become the great protector of private property, and who resented President Adams' packing the judiciary with Federalists in the last few hours of his term, set out to abolish the circuit courts and force the Supreme Court to ride circuit again. The debate which followed was bitter and revealing. Thomas Sumter of South Carolina saw in too strong a judiciary "the iron hand of power." George Mason of Virginia warned that the federal courts "may hold the Constitution in one hand and the law in the other, and say to the departments of the government, 'So far shall you go and no further.' This independence of the judiciary may become something like supremacy."

Gouverneur Morris of New York replied that the judiciary was "a check of the first necessity to prevent an invasion of the Constitution . . . to save the people from their most dangerous enemy; to save them from themselves."

"Good God," retorted James Jackson of Georgia, "is it possible that I have heard such a sentiment in this body? Rather should I have expected to have heard it sounded from the despots of Turkey or the deserts of Siberia. I am more afraid of an army of judges than an army of soldiers."

"I did not expect," remonstrated John Breckenridge of Kentucky, "to find the doctrine of the power of the courts to annul the laws of Congress as unconstitutional so seriously insisted upon. I would ask where they got that power, and who checks the courts when they violate the Constitution?"

John Bacon of Massachusetts warned that "the judiciary have no more right to prescribe, direct or control the acts of the other departments of the government than the other departments of

the government have to prescribe or direct those of the judiciary"; while John Randolph of Virginia, calling upon his colleagues in the House not to yield their legislative powers to the
courts, cried:

"For the amusement of the public, we shall retain the right of
debating but not voting!"

In the end, Congress repealed the Judiciary Act and immediately passed another suspending sessions of the Supreme Court
for fourteen months in order to prevent it from declaring the
repeal unconstitutional.

The power of the judiciary was at low ebb. The newly appointed circuit judges were without jobs, the justices of the
Supreme Court were forced to abandon the pleasant atmosphere
of Washington for almost six months of the year and become
itinerant peddlers of justice.

They complained bitterly. Gouverneur Morris chided Jefferson
that in nominating jurists he "must seek less the learning of the
judge than the agility of a post boy." Even as late as 1830 Justice
McLean complained that the roads of Indiana were so deep in
mud that it was impossible to get through, while Justice Mc-
Kinley wrote: "I have never been to Little Rock, the place of
holding the court in Arkansas, but from the best information I
can obtain it could not be conveniently approached in the spring
of the year except by water, and by that route the distance would
be greatly increased."

Moreover, the Court commanded no great prestige as it traveled about the country. Even Chief Justice John Marshall, destined to lay the foundation for the Court's present power, was
unable to get new breeches made when he lost his only pair
while holding court in Raleigh.

"Not a tailor in town could be prevailed upon to work for
me," he wrote his wife, Polly, "and I have the extreme mortifica-
tion to pass the whole time without that important article of
dress which I have mentioned."

No wonder that John Jay, first chief justice, declined further
service, Oliver Ellsworth resigned, Patrick Henry and John

Quincy Adams refused appointments, Robert H. Harrison chose instead to become chancellor of Maryland, while John Rutledge actually resigned from the Court in order to become chief justice of the Supreme Court of South Carolina.

Back in Washington, the physical surroundings of the Court were not much more favorable. It was driven, like a poor-paying tenant, from one abode to another: from the marshal's office to the clerk's office, to the Law Library in the basement, to the clerk's home on Pennsylvania Avenue, thence to the North Wing of the Capitol Building, then back to the Law Library, then to the old Senate Chamber, then to the District of Columbia Committee Room, then to the Judiciary Committee Room, and finally back to the Senate Chamber in which it reposed from 1860 to 1935, when the new temple of justice was ready to receive it.

The most humiliating transfer took place in 1814 after British redcoats had gathered furniture from an adjoining room, piled it high in the court chamber and applied a torch. For the next three years, the justices sat in the home of Elias Boudinot Caldwell, court clerk, despite broken windows and charred timbers, mute testimonial of the British fire.

When the Court returned to the Capitol, it was housed in the North Wing in a room described by a New York newspaperman as "little better than a dungeon." Its sole equipment was "two brown stone pitchers, and a few glasses to furnish speakers with water." Furthermore, the justices were forced to don their black robes in the presence of the spectators, "an awkward procedure, and destroys the effect intended to be produced by assuming the gown."

It was in 1860—after forty years of further wandering—that the Court moved into the old Senate Chamber and at last attained some degree of tranquillity and repose.

This was a chamber which once had reverberated with the debates of Calhoun, Clay and Webster. Once, on its floor, Senator Brooks of South Carolina had belabored Charles Sumner of Massachusetts with his walking stick until that ardent opponent of slavery became unconscious. But with the advent of the Supreme Court, the room became a silent sanctuary, lined with crimson plush, exuding dignity and moth holes. And, for the next seventy-five years, no fist was shaken, no desk pounded, no voice raised in passion or praise. The Old Men, at last, had come to rest; and, with no external cares to worry them, could give their time unreservedly to the entrenchment of their own power and prestige.

Before the new temple of justice was opened to the public, Mrs Brandeis came down with Mrs Woodrow Wilson to inspect the building in which her husband was to work. They were shown the bronze doors of the main entrance costing $50,000, the private retiring room for the wives of the justices, the private elevator, the lofty columns of the courtroom, the garnet curtains of silk velvet behind the bench, the rugs of Wilton and chenille, the drapes of crinkled tapestry and plum damask, and the private dining room where, in Chippendale chairs, the justices were to eat in order of their seniority.

In her husband's three-room office suite, Mrs Brandeis was shown a six-foot mahogany desk, with desk set done in brown leather, electric clock, shower bath, fireplace with an electric fan to draw off the heat, wood paneling in domestic white oak stained gray, and green Venetian blinds at the long windows. Touching the desk, she found no dust on it. She sat at the desk and pulled out one of the drawers. Then she sighed and looked at Mrs Wilson.

"Mercy," she said, "my husband will never use this."

And he doesn't.

In fact only two of the Nine Old Men, Sutherland and Roberts, have moved into their palatial office suites. The other seven prefer to remain at home where they are not afraid to soil the bricks of the fireplace by lighting a genuine fire.

The temple of justice was completed a few months behind schedule despite the fact that the Court, having declared unconstitutional any minimum-wage law, the contractors were able to work their men for as much as an eighty-four-hour stretch, in some cases for twenty dollars a week. Carpenters' and plasterers' strikes, which resulted, were the cause of the delay.

When the temple was finished, some of the court functionaries urged that the transfer from the old Supreme Court chamber to the new be accompanied by a formal ceremony. The United States Senate, they pointed out, in 1859 had marched as a body from its old quarters to the chamber it now occupies. Why should not the nine justices in their black silk robes, preceded by Court Crier Tom Waggaman and followed by book-laden clerks, page boys in knee breeches, and aged Negro messengers, parade across the Capitol Plaza to the new abode?

This idea, it was felt, should make a special appeal to Chief Justice Hughes, who for the first time had organized a special Supreme Court police, in fact had taken a great interest in the matter, selecting the style of uniform, going over the applicants and picking, as captain, Philip H. Crook, a very loyal individual who is educating his two sons to be Supreme Court justices. "It's a steady job," says Crook, "pays good and you certainly can't beat the hours."

But Justice Stone poked fun at the procession idea even before it got started. Looking across the plaza at the massive Corinthian columns, great bronze doors, and the brow and beard of Chief Justice Hughes carved in Dorsett marble above, he remarked: "Whenever I look at that building I feel that the justices should ride to work on elephants."

So in the end it was left to the messengers to parade with the trappings of the old courtroom across the plaza to the new sanctuary of the law. These consisted chiefly of the files, nine old chairs, and two drum-top desks, relics of John Marshall's day.

More dramatic was the Court's opening session, and equally packed with drama has been every session since. The "Standing Room Only" sign would be hung out for every performance were it not for the fact that no one is allowed to stand.

Here is a picture of the drama enacted during court Mondays ever since the temple of justice was built.

From those who are fortunate enough to obtain seats comes a buzz of expectant whispers rivaling any first night on Broadway. In the audience are such notables as Newton D. Baker, former Secretary of War, and John W. Davis, one-time Democratic candidate for President. Senator "Cotton Ed" Smith of South Carolina squeezes into a seat too small for his bulky body. Attorney General Cummings shakes hands with ex-Secretary of State Kellogg.

The stage is a long dais of carefully polished mahogany. The curtain is of red velvet, just beyond. And as the hands of the great gold clock, suspended above, come together at noon, a hushed silence falls over the throng. Behind the velvet curtains nine aged actors wait their cue. They stand abreast, gowned in black. In front of them is a little boy in knee breeches. At a nod from the leading man—a bearded gentleman of stately mien—the boy pushes a buzzer and the Nine Old Men advance abreast through the curtains.

The audience rises.

"The Honorable, the Chief Justice and the Associate Justices of the Supreme Court!" calls the court crier.

The justices take their seats; the Supreme Court of the United States, most powerful judicial body in the world, is now in session.

The chairs in which they sit are the only protest which the venerable gentlemen made against the encroachment of modernity in their new temple of justice. Marble pillars, air-cooling, shower baths, fountains—all were accepted. But at new chairs they balked, insisting that the old leather swivel chairs be brought over from the old Court in the Capitol.

But at the first session in the new chamber, Justice Roberts leaned back, one leg of his chair cracked, and it was only by adroit balancing that he saved himself and the dignity of the honorable Court. After that Frank Green, the court marshal, called in a furniture dealer and was offered thirty-five dollars for the nine old chairs.

But returning to the Court's solemn ritual—Chief Justice

Hughes nods to Justice Cardozo at the extreme left, and Justice Cardozo launches a long opinion on building-and-loan associations. Newsmen stuff messages into pneumatic tubes to be carried to the telegraph room on the floor below. No scurrying messenger boys disturb the supreme serenity.

Like a schoolmaster calling on his pupils, the stately Chief Justice nods to one, then another, of his colleagues. They recite. Audience attention, which lagged during Cardozo's dreary dissertation on mortgages, suddenly snaps back. At the other end of the bench, Owen Roberts, square-jawed and deep-voiced, begins to speak.

"Jeff Bowers was found lying in a grocery store, dying from a gunshot wound."

But the audience is disappointed. Justice Roberts ignores completely the question of who killed Jeff Bowers and launches into a highly technical question of responsibility for paying workmen's compensation. He speaks with full, resonant tones, not once referring to his notes. He is a superb actor, with poor lines. Chief Justice Hughes is the same. But their colleagues mumble into their papers with feeble chords.

Opinion after opinion drones on: Indian property, workmen's compensation, mortgages, garbage disposal. The expectant audience is bored. It is now one-thirty. Suddenly the Court recesses. The first act has been slow. But, as if with a sense of the dramatic, the nine aged actors have kept their best show for the end.

Crackers and milk in the robing room. Justice Brandeis eats two sandwiches, put up in a small box by his wife before he leaves home. Justice McReynolds departs abruptly, seeking solitude and more solid food.

Once again the justices march out on their stage. This time, Stanley Reed, Solicitor General of the Justice Department, stands before them in morning coat and gray-striped trousers. Senator Smith cups one hand behind a large ear. Frank B. Kellogg forgets that he has been bored. Newsmen shoot their messages faster through the pneumatic tubes.

But this time it is the chief actors who appear blasé and bored. Roberts, at the right, leans forward to whisper to Justice Butler, his neighbor. Next to him, McReynolds lets his eyes close and his head drop forward. Justice Sutherland pulls his little beard, scratches his cheek, probes his ear with a finger.

Solicitor Reed talks on.

Suddenly McReynolds snaps to life as if from a deep sleep. But the question that he shoots at Reed indicates that he was not dozing. Butler shoots another question. Then Sutherland, then Brandeis. The nine aged actors have come to life. At last they have reached their climax.

Justices Stone and Roberts are the only members of the Court who regularly attend the theater; the Chief Justice sometimes. But there is no doubt about it—they all appreciate drama.

The first session in their new temple of justice indicated that it had been built more for drama than for utility, at least as far as the chamber is concerned. For Justices Roberts and Cardozo, long deaf to each other where arguments are concerned, now complained that they could not hear the attorneys in front of them; while Justices Butler and Stone, long blind to each other's opinions, complained that they could not see. Also the naked marble of the chamber was cold and damp. The justices complained of drafts.

The acoustic difficulty was remedied by an expert from the Bureau of Standards who placed two screens at the far end of the chamber, while more velvet curtains were hung in the wings to prevent drafts. But this made the lighting even worse. Finally elaborate chandeliers were swung from the ceiling, but they only shone in the justices' eyes. Then a swanky bronze desk lamp was placed before each of them. But Justice Brandeis rebelled, replaced his with an old-fashioned, goosenecked student's lamp, a relic of the early days of Thomas Edison.

Finally it was found that the ceiling was too dark, and a vast expanse of cheesecloth, garishly incongruous alongside carved and gilded columns, was stretched across the very top of the chamber.

But outside the court chamber, the New Deal's severest critics should have been reasonably satisfied, for they found them-selves surrounded by the most ornate and modern equipment enjoyed by any court anywhere in the world. They found, for instance, that when they drove to work their limousines could shoot down inclined driveways to the basement, permitting no drop of rain or snow to touch their grizzled heads. Upstairs they found a law library with a capacity for 106,000 volumes, also a special library accommodating 90,000 volumes more and a "fu-ture" stack room for 150,000 additional volumes, plus a repair shop and a bindery for mending their books. Then there were three lunchrooms, each with its own kitchen, a dozen lavatories and retiring rooms, public and private, the one arranged for the wives of the justices being the most luxurious of them all. And there were eighteen huge fireplaces, each equipped with electric fans to suck off the heat generated by the burning wood; and offices for the Attorney General and the Solicitor General for their convenience on days when they had business before the Court; a robing room, and two magnificent conference rooms, each almost as commodious as the abandoned courtroom in the Capitol.

The only thing the architects neglected were locks on the robing lockers, apparently believing that the justices trusted each other's personal integrity, no matter what they thought of each other's legal reasoning.

And on different sides of the conference rooms, the justices found four elaborately designed courts, each sixty-four feet square and each featuring a fountain splashing rhythmically in the center. Then there was a reading room with seven adjacent nooks, all adorned with paneled and pilastered work, the ceiling finished in color and gilt. The floors of the offices were finished in American quartered white oak, the corridors in Alabama white marble, and around the corridors were pillars of marble dug from the Sienna quarries of Italy, with a base and floor border of Levanto marble and rare marble panels of Brochi Sanguine. Patriotic green-tinted Vermont marble was desired, but it was formally ruled out by the Chief Justice as too suggestive of green-tinted railroad lavatories throughout the United States.

The ensemble was the eighth wonder of the world; two of the others being the pyramids of Egypt and the tomb of King Mausolus.

"Nine million dollars!" sighed the late Huey Long, casting an appraising eye over the columns, the copper, the oak paneling. "A million dollars apiece for those Nine Old Men. And they used to be glad to sit in one room!"

When Chief Justice Taft let the contract for his long-cherished temple, he told Cass Gilbert: "It must conform in design with the Capitol. It should be enduring. And Mrs Taft says it should be easy to keep clean."

The temple of justice is clean, spotlessly, heartlessly clean, even though it must be washed frequently as a result of the soft-coal soot belched upon it by the Methodist building across the street. [Washing, policing and general upkeep cost the nation $1,000 a week.] It is a dead white—colorless, relentless— an atmosphere of austere, Olympian dignity, that yields to no one, that has no soul. Marble, marble, more marble than in any other building in the world. The lines are square, sharp, cold, monotonous. The glare is pitiless, unmerciful. The guards outside wear colored glasses.

The corridor inside is like the entrance to a tomb. The walls are white—flat, dead white, so unrelieved that it is hard to see the niches in which repose the busts of bygone justices. Copper doors along the way appear as entrances to vaults. At the far end is the court chamber itself, again in icy marble, like the ordeal room of the grand inquisitor. The atmosphere, even without artificial air cooling, is damp and chilly. All that is needed to give it the full flavor of a tomb is a catafalque in the very center.

"I wonder," mused Justice Sutherland, "if we will look like the nine beetles in the Temple of Karnak?"

Nine black-gowned beetles, aloof from all reality, meting out a law as inflexible as the massive blocks of marble that surround them in their mausoleum of justice.

CHAPTER II

Supreme Court vs. *New Deal*

Inaugural day, 1933, found the nine justices of the Supreme Court in merry mood. Black-gowned and supposedly sedate, they sat in the front row of the Senate waiting for Vice President Garner to take the oath of office. Before them on the rostrum stood the retiring Vice President, Charles Curtis, who was putting on a special gavel-wielding exhibition in honor of the occasion. The nine justices watched him, fascinated. Mr Curtis had worn out several gavels during his four years of presiding over the Senate, but in this farewell performance he outdid himself.

Suddenly the Clerk of the Senate, who was announcing the arrival of celebrities, appeared in the doorway. Bang, bang, bang, hammered the retiring Vice President. The assemblage rose, craned their necks, expecting Mr Garner. Instead, a meek and diminutive page boy strolled down the aisle. Mr Curtis frowned furiously. The boy was terrified. And the nine justices broke into uncontrollable laughter.

They have been laughing at or fulminating against the New Deal ever since. The question is, who will laugh last?

Franklin Roosevelt really scored the first hit on Inaugural Day by the manner in which he took the oath of office. Even the imperturbable Chief Justice looked surprised. It was not what Mr Roosevelt said which surprised Mr Hughes, but the way he said it. Instead of merely saying "I do" after the Chief Justice stated the oath, Mr Roosevelt replied: "I do solemnly swear that I will faithfully execute the office of President of the United States, and will, to the best of my ability, *preserve, protect* and *defend* the Constitution of the United States."

The new President had learned the oath by heart.

Many times during the months which followed, Chief Justice Hughes and his colleagues were to proclaim that Mr Roosevelt had forgotten the oath that he rattled off so glibly.

There is nothing new about criticism of the Supreme Court, but the New Deal inaugurated a brand-new variety. Thomas Jefferson, when he wanted to let the Seventeen States know what he thought about John Marshall, resorted to such good old-fashioned language as "a crafty Chief Justice who sophisticates the law to his mind by the turn of his own reasoning." Later, the New York *Herald,* whose successor, the *Herald Tribune,* now hails the Nine Old Men as the saviors of the nation, gave vent to the rather frank editorial opinion that their Dred Scott decision deserved no more respect than if it had been made by "a majority of those congregated in any Washington barroom." Abraham Lincoln, also a believer in bare-fisted language, claimed that the Nine Old Men had got the doctrine of democratic government down "as thin as the homeopathic soup made by boiling the shadow of a pigeon that had starved to death"; while Judge Black of the Pennsylvania Supreme Court applied to Chief Justice Taney such gentle epithets as a "mush toad spotted traitor to the Constitution" and a "political turkey buzzard." "Shall he be permitted," Justice Black asked, "to vomit the filthy contents of his stomach on every decent man in the country without having his neck twisted?"

The New Deal, however, has been more subtle than that. Criticism, vituperation, even hatred have raged furiously. But aside from one brief blast after the NRA decision, these were held carefully beneath the surface.

Outwardly all was as calm and amiable as the Roosevelt smile. The President did not rush in, as did that hero of the Republican party, Ulysses S. Grant, with the appointment of friendly justices after the legal-tender decision. Nor did he emulate his fiery cousin Theodore in advocating the recall of judicial decisions. Behind the scenes, these were considered. Behind the scenes, every possible form of attack was debated. But in the end the strategy of punctilious politeness, complete calm and at times—that deadliest of all weapons—ridicule was adopted.

This calm, however, was far more dangerous than the turbulent outspoken days of Jefferson, Jackson, Lincoln and Grant. For beneath the calm was the determination of both sides never to surrender.

To see President Roosevelt greet Justice Sutherland at his annual reception for the judiciary, no outsider would have guessed that the two men were not old and trusted friends perfectly agreed that the salvation of the United States lay in crop curtailment and the complete supremacy of the Blue Eagle. Or to watch the animated expression on Mrs Roosevelt's face as she discussed horseback riding—which they both enjoy—with Justice Roberts, a casual observer would have supposed they had not a difference in the world, not a care to worry them.

Yet both sides knew, and seemed to take a grim sort of joy in that knowledge, that their opposing social and economic philosophies were speeding toward a head-on clash not merely between judiciary and executive, but between the doctrine of omnipotent intransigeance and the thesis that no nation or people can stand still.

Chief Justice Hughes was one of the most inscrutable and delightful actors in this comi-tragedy. He seemed to take real joy in his part. At a dinner which he gave in honor of the Secretary of Agriculture whose Agricultural Adjustment Administration he was to throw into the scrap heap of unconstitutionality, Mr Hughes was debonair and delightful. He lectured the ladies on the value of exercise, told them that he had been doing his standing-squatting exercises regularly for forty-two years, used to do it at night, though now he found it was better in the morning.

"Birth control," said the Chief Justice with a twinkle in his eye, "may be your problem; but girth control is mine."

Then the conversation drifted to fan mail, and with some pride and no little glee he told Mrs Hughes to bring forth his prize possession, a letter from a ladies' church auxiliary in Des Moines, Iowa. That being Henry Wallace's home, Mr Hughes thought the Secretary of Agriculture should see it, and so Mrs Hughes read the letter aloud:

"Dear Mr Chief Justice:

"In order to raise money for the church, our members are making aprons from the shirttails of famous men. We would be so pleased if you could send us one of your shirttails. Please have Mrs Hughes mark them with your initials and also pin a short biography on them giving the famous occasions in which they have been intimately connected with your life."

The Chief Justice had framed the letter in ivory.

The dinner took place just before the announcement of the Supreme Court's decision on the gold clause. Every Monday it had been expected. But every Monday it had been postponed. The stock market waited in breathless suspense. So did the entire New Deal, from the White House down. And it seemed as if the Nine Old Men almost enjoyed that suspense. Certainly the Chief Justice seemed to enjoy it during his dinner to Secretary Wallace.

At one point, however, he did not.

It was shortly after dinner. The men had just rejoined the ladies. Mrs Adolph Miller, wife of one of the oldest members of the Federal Reserve Board and a lady who should have known better, suddenly turned to Mr Hughes:

"Oh, Mr Chief Justice," she said, "when are you going to give the stock market some peace of mind and announce your gold decision?"

The assemblage gasped. The Chief Justice froze. It is the unwritten rule of Washington, more sacred than any matter of precedence or protocol, that no member of the Supreme Court ever is questioned about an advance decision. The silence which followed Mrs Miller's shrill query was stupefying.

Quickly the Argentine ambassadress, one of the cleverest in Washington, came to the rescue.

"Mr Chief Justice," she said, "have you seen that new book, *The American Diplomatic Game?*"

"Yes," he replied, "and did you see where it told about Charley Dawes shaking a broom under my bewhiskered chin?" The Chief Justice wagged his silvery beard after the manner of a billy goat and seemed to enjoy the story hugely.

Charles Evans Hughes has a contagious sense of humor, and he needed it during these days of bitter internecine strife between the Supreme Court and the New Deal.

It seemed a little lacking one evening while talking with Oswaldo Aranha, ambassador of Brazil. Aranha, who wrote the new constitution of Brazil, had asked the Chief Justice regarding the strict interpretation the Court had given to the American Constitution.

"The law," replied Mr Hughes, "is the bulwark of the people."

"But if the law does not solve a difficult problem," suggested the Ambassador, "it should not be applied."

"On the contrary," said the Chief Justice, "it prevents us from going off on tangents. The Constitution has been our cornerstone."

"Constitutional law," philosophized Ambassador Aranha, "is like a virgin. It must be violated to reach its fullest flower."

Not all of Mr Hughes's colleagues have a sense of humor. In fact it was noticeably lacking during the dinner of the Gridiron Club in December 1935—not long before the Court handed down its catastrophic AAA decision. Honored guests were Hughes, Van Devanter, McReynolds, Butler, Stone and Roberts, looking very distinguished and just a little nervous as to what the evening might hold in store for them.

They soon found out. The President of the Gridiron Club began the ceremonies by asking the six jurists to stand up and face the tumultuous banquet hall. All struggled sheepishly to their feet except Van Devanter, who may have had some inkling of what was to come.

Then followed a satire on the highest court of the land which must have warmed the heart of the man who sat one seat removed from the Chief Justice—Franklin Roosevelt.

The scene was the Acropolis. Nine Delphic oracles clad in armor, the first two reverently bearing a scrolled golden box, took possession. They turned out to be such ardent believers in judicial protection for big business as the late James M. Beck; John W. Davis, counsel for J. P. Morgan; ex-Senator David A. Reed, attorney for Andrew W. Mellon; Bainbridge Colby, big gun of William Randolph Hearst; Frank J. Hogan, counsel for Albert B. Fall and Harry F. Sinclair; Thomas N. McCarter, head of the Public Service Corporation of New Jersey; Frederic R. Coudert, Jr; George Wickersham; and last but not least, Jouett Shouse, organizer of the Liberty League.

These nine burst into song:

"Oh it's time to take your places,
   You'll hear the verdict soon;
It's better than the races,
   On a Monday afternoon.

"You'll hear what folks were thinking,
   Back in eighteen hundred ten,
And Latin words a-linking
   What happens now with THEN."

"29 U.S. 398; 210 U.S. 281; 42 Stat. 859 . . ." intoned one of the oracles.

"Wait a minute," broke in a citizen of Athens, "what is this? A football game?"

"Oh, no," sternly reproved the oracle, "I'm handing down a decision."

"O yeah, O yeah," broke in the court crier. "All persons having business with this honorable institution now draw nigh. Writs of certiorari can be obtained at the box office."

"But what is in that box?" asked another citizen, pointing to the golden box.

"The sacred foundation of our being. It tells us what to do and when to do it."

"Could I see it?"

"Of course not," was the answer. "When anyone examines it, it changes color like a chameleon."

"How can one tell what it means?"

"Once a week, revelation is given when wise persons announce what it means—that week."

An attendant stepped forward to the mysterious box.

"Permit me," he said, "to exhibit the historic charter on which our freedom rests. The Contribution List of the Liberty League."

"It is your duty," said the Chief Justice of the Oracles, "to protect this sacred document with your life and uphold it with your cash."

The six justices in the flesh looked on with fixed smiles. Those of Hughes and Stone were genuine. They even contributed several deep belly laughs. But the smiles of Van Devanter, McReynolds and Butler were of that glassy variety developed to perfection by chorus girls, circus clowns and Senator J. Ham Lewis.

The smiles became even more glassy when, at the customary climax of the Gridiron dinner, President Roosevelt took the floor. Once before, after the NRA decision, the President had given vent to a withering horse-and-buggy diatribe against the Court. But this time he changed his tactics. He was the height of good humor. The Rooseveltian smile was at its best. His voice was sheer velvet. For a time he continued, in good-natured vein, the raillery of the evening. Then suddenly he switched to a tone of deadly seriousness.

The constitutionality of the Agricultural Adjustment Act, at that very moment, was being considered by the Court, and while he did not say so in so many words, the President seemed to be actually appealing to the Six Old Men present for their support of the AAA and his New Deal policies.

In doing so he reached back into American history and traced the development of the nation. He showed how each reform, when originally proposed, had aroused the hostility of some part of the people. He showed how this hostility gradually had broken down, until one by one these reforms were enacted. He even pointed to the fact that both the Democratic and Republican parties always had taken up the platform of the Socialist party after the Socialists had done the original crusading.

The income and inheritance tax had been advocated by the Socialists, later adopted into law by Presidents Cleveland, Taft and Wilson. Conservation, the reforestation of waste lands, the building of public works, the abolition of child labor, and social insurance, all originated with the Socialists, subsequently were adopted by Democratic or Republican Presidents. President Harding, by approving the Salt River project, was the first to put into practice the Socialist plank of government-owned power plants. President Hoover followed him with Boulder Dam and the sale of power all over the Southwest.

Then, in an eloquent conclusion, the President said that the genius of the American government lay in its adaptiveness to changing times, that its basic principles were not meant to become rigid formulae, inflexible, resistant to stresses and strains. Out of this give-and-take of opposing forces, he said, does progress come in the United States.

Then occurred the most significant thing of all.

After the President concluded, Chief Justice Hughes, who sat one chair removed, and who himself had coped with many of Roosevelt's problems as a somewhat liberal governor of New

York, leaned across and congratulated the President. And the warmth with which the Chief Justice spoke seemed to indicate that Mr Roosevelt had made at least one convert.

One month later Mr Hughes sat silent in the temple of justice while Mr Roberts read the historic decision killing the AAA. The Chief Justice had changed his mind.

The Roosevelts did their best to look happy and pleased at the Triple A decision, and they succeeded fairly well. Just three days after the fatal decree was handed down they were hosts at the annual White House reception to the judiciary. The date had been set months in advance, and there was no possible way of changing it even if either the Roosevelts or the justices had willed. Whatever gods may guide the New Deal in its devious inclinations must have smiled as they looked down upon Justices Van Devanter, Sutherland, Hughes and Roberts, bitterest foes of the administration, as they greeted the President and his cabinet. The Secret Service, however, did not smile. Ever alert to protect the President, they follow a rule that no outsider shall approach him with hand in pocket or with hand concealed in any manner. This dictum has been handed down ever since an assassin approached President McKinley with bandaged hand concealing a revolver.

Ordinarily this rule is waived for members of the President's administration or those well known to him, and presumably it would apply to members of the Supreme Court. However, as the justices came forward on this particular evening to greet the man whose policies they had stepped upon more than any other President's in history, two Secret Service operators sprang forward and dexterously pulled the hands of two distinguished justices from their pockets.

Probably it was sheer accident, but these two justices happened to be among the most vigorous critics of the New Deal. Red-faced, they continued in the reception line, but soon afterwards got their hats and went home. They were never able to forget the incident.

The incident also caused some discussion among the members of the President's family and his Secret Service staff, some of whom felt that the guards acted unwisely. The Secret Service acts on the rule that the only real danger to the President comes from those of unbalanced mind. Some years ago a newspaperman, confined for a time to an asylum, was the object of much worry to the Secret Service when he attended press conferences. In view of the unbridled tone used by some justices in denouncing Mr Roosevelt's policies, perhaps the Secret Service was right after all.

Meanwhile the surface pleasure of President and Mrs Roosevelt in greeting the gentlemen who were knocking the props from under the chief acts of their administration continued. A few days later they entertained six of the Nine Old Men at the annual White House dinner to the Court. Two judicial enemies of the New Deal, Van Devanter and McReynolds, were absent, the former with the genuine excuse of illness, the latter on the pretense that he never attends social functions, an excuse which did not prevent him attending various debutante parties. Justice Brandeis—ardent friend of the New Deal—also declined. He invariably goes to bed at ten o'clock.

The Roosevelts had invited a varied assortment of guests in Mrs Roosevelt's usual charming and haphazard fashion. They included Bruce Kremer, forced by his lobbying activities to resign as Democratic national committeeman from Montana; W. Forbes Morgan, uncle of Mrs Roosevelt; Thomas J. Watson, president of International Business Machines and a heavy contributor to the Democratic party; Isabella Greenway, Congresswoman from Arizona, a bridesmaid at the Roosevelt wedding; Stanley Reed, the Solicitor General who fainted while presenting the AAA case before the Nine Old Men; Donald Richberg, whose presentation of the Schechter sick-chicken case was emphatically rejected; Raymond P. Brandt, of the St Louis *Post Dispatch,* staunch upholder of the Court; Dr Jacob Viner, Brain Trust adviser to Henry Morgenthau; and the Attorney General himself, who hovered about the justices as if they were his special flock and as if his charm might pave the way for more favorable decisions in the future. Pink carnations, white Buddleia, maidenhair fern and the silver gilt service purchased in the days of James Monroe adorned the table. Fruit filled the tall golden epergnes, while tapers in golden candelabra shed a soft glow over the scene. To have watched the Roosevelts, no one would have dreamed that four of their guests seemed to consider themselves a counterbalance against the economic fallacies of the New Deal, determined to save the country from the social madness of their host.

There were even moments during those hectic days when Mrs Roosevelt appeared blissfully naïve regarding the inability of the justices ever to swallow her husband's social program. On another evening she was attending a White House conference of leaders of the youth movement. The President was there. Also various people not particularly sympathetic to the administration, among them some communist youth leaders whom Mrs Roosevelt seemed to like—perhaps because they were a little fresh and talked back at her. The question drifted round to federal aid to education in some of the more backward states. Some of these states needed federal aid while the industrial states of the Northeast did not, and Mrs Roosevelt expressed herself very emphatically in favor of giving these states government help.

"But, my dear," interrupted her husband, "it's unconstitutional."

"But, Franklin, isn't there some way we can get around it?"

"No, my dear. It was settled when the question of federal aid for good roads came up. The federal government cannot discriminate between states."

"But, Franklin," persisted Mrs Roosevelt, "can't you see the Chief Justice about it?"

The weeks passed, and the outward calm of the New Deal continued. Mr Roosevelt declined to let himself be drawn into any comment, direct or indirect, regarding the devastating barrage of unfavorable decisions thrown in his path by the Court.

Even when a group of Senate progressives called upon him and urged some stand on a constitutional amendment limiting the powers of the Court, he refused to be smoked out.

"Even if the Democrats do not make an issue of the Court in the campaign," reminded Senator Shipstead of Minnesota, "the country is certain to ask you how you propose to continue a liberal program as long as the path is barred by the Court."

The President, however, was noncommittal. He had determined to let the public and the press do the preliminary battling with the Nine Old Men.

Once, however, he took a decisive, though private, step to thwart any court infringement upon his personal prerogative. It was during the suit of the Alabama Power Company to prevent the Public Works Administration from using government funds to help competitive municipal power plants. Newton D. Baker, attorney for the power interests, had asked the Supreme Court of the District of Columbia for the right to subpoena a memo signed "FDR," which the President had sent to PWA Administrator Ickes, and which indicated that the New Deal planned to wage war on all private power companies.

Just before this point was to be argued, Secretary Ickes and Jerome Frank, attorney for PWA, dropped in at the White House to ask the President whether he wanted them to produce the memo. They didn't have to wait long for an answer.

"If the Courts are going to subpoena the confidential memoranda of the President and his cabinet," Mr Roosevelt snapped back, "we will have to spend about all our time on the witness stand. I suppose I write twenty memos a day to cabinet members, and if I had to get on the witness stand to explain them all it would take weeks."

Then he told how, as Assistant Secretary of the Navy, he had received various penciled memos from President Wilson.

"In one case the construction of a battleship was under consideration," Roosevelt explained, "and I got a White House memo which read: 'Go ahead.'—signed 'W. W.' That was all. Now no one would know what that meant unless explained in relation to various other memos and by testimony from the President. And long ago, in the case of *Marbury* vs. *Madison,* it was decided that the President could not be subpoenaed."

John Marshall had tried to subpoena President Jefferson, Roosevelt recalled, but Jefferson refused to answer it. A few years later, he recalled, John Marshall tried to subpoena the papers of General James Wilkinson during the treason trial of Aaron Burr, but Jefferson flatly refused to send them.

"So we'll let Newton Baker whistle for his memo until the cows come home," the President concluded. And he did. This time, at least, the Courts upheld him.

As the weeks passed, gradually it became apparent that the passive-resistance policy of the President was wise strategy. Gradually it could be seen that the relentlessness with which the spotlight of publicity played upon the Nine Old Men was getting under their supposedly imperturbable skin. They even began to hunger for the good old days when they sat in their dark and inconspicuous little chamber in the Capitol, when their decisions were tucked away almost unnoticed in the inside pages of the papers, when they could go out to dinner without having every guest turn and whisper as they entered.

Actually the justices began to lose their sense of humor. They did not appreciate at all the efforts of a group of aesthetic dancers to portray the Court in a series of mask dances, especially the fact that the masks were made by Mr Roosevelt's WPA artists. Justice Roberts' daughter, who attended the performance, should have been shocked—though she wasn't—to see that the biggest laugh of the evening came when the Chief Justice, hovering uncertainly in the center, stepping gingerly toward the Liberals, then toward the Conservatives, finally joined the latter.

Nor did the justices even smile when the editors of the *Harvard Lampoon* hoisted the red flag of Soviet Russia on the eighty-foot pole in front of the mausoleum of justice, where it flopped audaciously in the chiseled marble faces of Taft and Hughes on the fresco of the temple.

Ambassador Troyanovsky, who might have taken offense at

the jibe against his government, was questioned regarding the authors of the prank. "I think," he said, "it must have been the Daughters of the American Revolution."

Even Justice Stone, who for the most part enjoyed being twitted by Alice Longworth for the perversity of his dissenting opinions, complained a little peevishly that the press was quoting his private views.

What he complained about was a statement he had made to a friend after the unfavorable AAA decision in which he said, "I think it will be very difficult to draft an alternative that will meet the objections set forth by the majority. In fact, under the limits laid down by them I do not see how anything that helped the farmers as much as the AAA did can be devised to withstand legal attack."

After this appeared in print, Justice Stone, ordinarily the most convivial member of the Court, drew into his shell. In accepting invitations to dinner he sometimes specified that no newspapermen be present.

Probably the person most incensed by the public's interest in the Court was Mrs Owen J. Roberts, a lady whose attitude toward her husband can be gathered from the fact that she allows him to use their limousine only on those rare occasions when she is not using it. But on one particular afternoon, shortly before this book was written, both Justice and Mrs Roberts motored to the palatial home of Lammot Belin, former Ambassador to Poland and an inheritor of the Du Pont millions, where Justice Roberts happened to let fall the jocular remark: "I'm just one of the Nine Old Men." And then, with a little touch of sadness and a shake of the head, he repeated: "Just one of the Nine Old Men."

"Oh, I wish you'd stop saying that," remarked Mrs Belin in her cheeriest and most consoling voice. "You're not old at all."

This was the cue which Mrs Roberts apparently was waiting for.

"It's that terrible Washington Merry-Go-Round column," she said. "I could wring those boys' necks. They're always calling us the Nine Old Men. And this book they are writing is being talked about, so that everyone uses the phrase. And we're so defenseless. There's nothing we can do about it. We can't answer back. We're the Supreme Court. It wouldn't be dignified."

"Well, you might sue for libel," suggested Constantine Brown, who once had written a book with one of the above-mentioned authors.

"But the things they say aren't libelous. They are very careful to avoid that. They come just within an inch of libel, but never quite go far enough."

"I understand," suggested Mr Brown, "that this book is going to be very favorable to some members of the Supreme Court. I think, for instance, it's going to give a very good break to Justices Cardozo and Brandeis."

"Yes, and you know why," shot back Mrs Roberts, by this time much agitated. "They're being paid by the administration. Mr Roosevelt is getting back at us for what we've done to him. This book is deliberately inspired and paid for by the administration."

Justice Roberts, all this while, had been sitting, silently shaking his head. Obviously he disapproved his wife's indiscretions but did not know how to stop her.

Sensing this situation, Mrs Belin brought the conversation to a close.

"Well, we won't invite Drew around here any more," she said.

The President never was more eloquent than when he delivered his horse-and-buggy tirade against the Supreme Court the day after it had clipped the wings of the Blue Eagle. But he timed his tirade badly. It was one of the few occasions when Franklin Roosevelt rushed out to champion a cause which had already left a sour taste in the public mouth. For months prior to the NRA decision dead cats had filled the air around General Johnson, some of them coming precariously close to the President's desk. For months the little bloc of progressive Senators who always can be relied upon to fight big business had been

allied—during one of those rare occasions in history—with reactionary Republican colleagues in a drive against the NRA.
Bennett Clark of Missouri, one of the President's own party
leaders, had introduced a resolution in the Senate extending the
life of the Blue Eagle for ten months only, and so strong was
sentiment behind the Clark resolution that, in order to give the
NRA any permanency, the President faced an embarrassing cat-
and-dog fight with his own party. And it was precisely at this
moment that the Supreme Court handed down the Schechter
decision unanimously eliminating the casus belli.

In many respects the President should have been relieved. His
leaders were. But so strongly was he convinced that the only
permanent way out of the depression was by the abolition of the
wage-cutting and hour-stretching which had dragged industry
down during Hoover's day, that he cast political discretion to
the winds and went to bat for the Blue Eagle as if it were the
most important plank in his entire program—which, in many respects, it was.

There ensued an immediate tide of public reaction. It was not
only that the Court still was one of the most revered institutions
of the land, but that the Blue Eagle was so widely unpopular.
If Mr Roosevelt had waited until after the demise of the
Agricultural Adjustment Administration to launch his horse-
and-buggy attack, the results might have been different. But he
didn't. And so generally was public sentiment against him that
when R. Walton Moore, solemn Assistant Secretary of State,
criticized the Court during the commencement exercises of
National University he was greeted with deadly silence. Following him a young valedictory speaker upheld the Nine Old Men
and was cheered to the echo.

It was the public reaction to his horse-and-buggy tirade which
dissuaded the President from following the example of Abraham
Lincoln during the Civil War and seeking power to enlarge the
size of the Court. It was also this reaction which warned him to
pull in his horns and let the Nine Old Men dig their own graves,
either literally or on the bosom of public opinion.

Luck has played an important part in molding the legal history of the nation. Some of the most important decisions of the Court have been thrown one way or the other by a sudden twist of fate. The United States would have been saved eighteen years of cumbersome toil in securing a constitutional amendment approving the income tax had not Justice Shiras mysteriously and without a word of explanation reversed himself on the final decision. And if a technicality had not delayed a constitutional test of the Minimum Wage Act until after the ultraconservative Justices Sutherland and Butler were appointed, one of the necessities for the NRA would have been avoided.

Proverbial "Roosevelt luck" has been the envy of both political friends and enemies, but never has it deserted him in so great a time of need as in the case of three of the Nine Old Men. For when Mr Roosevelt was inaugurated, Justices McReynolds, Sutherland and Van Devanter, all ardent reactionaries, were considering retirement. Van Devanter's health had suffered by the shock of his wife's death, and he had written only one opinion the year before Mr Roosevelt took office. Sutherland has pronounced hypochondriacal tendencies and is always talking about his medicines and his ailments. While McReynolds, although in good health, was excessively bored and wore the appearance of perpetual disgust.

But just at the precise moment Mr Roosevelt took office, these three seemed animated by a sudden and hitherto completely concealed regard for the future welfare of the Court. Suddenly it became a sacred symbol of the past, a mighty bulwark against change. And the more the press speculated regarding the prospect of resignations, the greater became their determination to stick to their black silk robes through hell, high water and halitosis.

Let no one insinuate that Mr Roosevelt would have failed to mourn had any one of the five anti-New Deal jurists been called by his Maker. But undoubtedly it was hard for him to understand why these distinguished gentlemen should not take advantage of the $20,000 annual lifelong pension automatically granted after ten years' service at the age of seventy, and retire to havens untroubled by crop control, minimum wages, price-fixing and the regulation of our natural resources.

Congressman Sumners, a loyal Democrat from Texas, even introduced a bill providing that the $20,000 annual pension could never be reduced by subsequent economy acts of Congress. It was recalled that Justice Holmes, when ninety, had his pension cut by the Hoover economy act to $10,000, causing him to remark: "I have always been a prudent man, so this pay cut will not hurt me. But I am distressed that I cannot continue to lay aside for my old age." (When he died he bequeathed $250,000 to the government.)

But nothing, not even immunity from economy cuts, seemed to tempt the justices. There is no doubt that Chief Justice Hughes, although extremely discreet about it, has recognized the difficulty of ladling out a crystal-pure stream of justice when a court is cluttered up with aged reactionaries. In fact, Mr Hughes once gave a series of lectures at the Columbia Law School after he retired as associate justice, in which he used rather emphatic language regarding the incompatability of age and justice.

"Some judges," he said, "have stayed too long on the bench. An unfortunate illustration was that of Justice Grier, who had failed perceptibly at the time of the first announcement of the legal-tender case. As the decision was delayed, he did not participate in it. A committee of the Court waited upon Justice Grier to advise him of the desirability of his retirement and the unfortunate consequences of his being in a position to cast a deciding vote in the important case when he was not able properly to address himself to it.

"Justice Field tarried too long on the bench," Mr Hughes continued. "It is extraordinary how reluctant aged judges are to retire and to give up their accustomed work. They seem to be tenacious of the appearance of adequacy.

"I heard Justice Harlan tell of the anxiety which the Court had felt because of the condition of Justice Field. It occurred to the other members of the Court that Justice Field had served on a committee which waited upon Justice Grier to suggest his retirement, and it was thought that recalling that to his memory might aid him to decide to retire.

"Justice Harlan was deputed to make the suggestion. He went over to Justice Field, who was sitting alone on a settee in the smoking room, apparently oblivious of his surroundings, and after arousing him, gradually approached the question, asking if he did not recall how anxious the Court had become with respect to Justice Grier's condition and the feeling of the other justices that in his own interest and in that of the Court he should give up his work. Justice Harlan asked if Justice Field did not remember what had been said to Justice Grier on that occasion. The old man listened, gradually became alert, and finally, with his eyes blazing with the old fire of youth, he burst out:

"'Yes! and a dirtier day's work I never did in all my life!'

"That was the end of that effort of the brethren of the Court to induce Justice Field's retirement; he did not resign until long after."

When Mr Hughes delivered that lecture, probably he had no idea that the most trying days of his life would be spent presiding over a Court on which three justices, well beyond the retirement age, made no effort to conceal their grim determination to remain on the bench solely to perpetuate the economic system in which they prospered half a century before.

For years the Supreme Court of the United States, outwardly at least, has been the height of decorum. Its chamber is cloaked in an atmosphere of silence and restraint. Voices are pitched low, costumes are somber, the tempo of the drama is that of weighty deliberation. Seldom has any untoward incident ruffled its celestial calm. And of recent years it also has been the height of efficiency. Decisions have rolled sonorously from its bench almost with the precision of a Ford factory; two weeks of argument, two weeks of secret deliberation; between six and seven hundred writs of certiorari rejected; and about two hundred decisions handed down to mold the lives of the people of the United States.

It was the late William Howard Taft who set the Court its standard of efficiency. When he became chief justice he found that the Court was two and three years behind in its docket, and in order to remedy this he asked that the Court be given discretionary power to determine for itself which cases it considered of sufficient importance to review. Under this act, Taft, before he died in 1930, had settled hundreds of long-delayed cases. Chief Justice Hughes has carried this even further. Taft was never able to clear the court docket entirely, but Hughes has developed such a mania for speed that sometimes the docket has been cleared even before the periods set for hearing cases expired.

Mr Hughes's perpetual rush has aroused some resentment on the part of his more meticulous colleagues, and also it has had the distinct disadvantage of cutting down the number of cases the court is willing to hear.

Although there are seven channels through which cases may reach the Supreme Court, by far the most prolific is that of writs of certiorari. Writs of certiorari are orders by a higher court to a lower court to send up the record in a case for review, in order to determine whether the higher court will take jurisdiction. No oral arguments are heard, and the petition for review must be brief. Hundreds of these cases flood the Supreme Court every year, and hundreds of them also are turned down, the total for the 1935–36 term being 717 writs of certiorari rejected out of 990 cases disposed of. A total of 212 decisions were handed down. This is about the average for recent years.

Speed, however, has not deterred the learned justices when some particularly fascinating case comes before them. Thus during the second year of the New Deal a dark-haired, demure young lady named Sally Blue of Clarendon, Virginia, got almost more attention than Honorable Homer Cummings, the Attorney General, when he argued the gold case. Miss Blue was demonstrating a patented device for mending runs in silk hosiery which the attorney for the Stelos Company claimed were "very disquieting to meticulous femininity" and which patent, he claimed, was infringed upon by the Hosiery Motor-Mend Corporation. To prove this point, he distributed to each justice one porcelain egg holder, one magnetic needle and one silk stocking, which Justice McReynolds, a bachelor, held up full length and examined minutely.

"Next," said Henry Gilligan for the Stelos Company, "I will introduce Miss Blue."

"How do you do, Miss Blue," nodded the Chief Justice with a smile calculated to make the young lady feel at home.

Miss Blue, a trifle nervous, did make herself at home on a chair in front of the judicial diadem, crossed her legs, and showed how a few lightning stitches could transform a devastating run into sheer silk.

The Nine Old Men looked on, enthralled.

Every detail about the Supreme Court while in session is calculated to make for efficiency, from the pneumatic tube which carries copies of decisions from the clerk's desk to the press room downstairs, to the stern nod which Chief Justice Hughes gives to the page boy as the Nine Old Men stand behind the crimson curtain ready for the grand entrance. Even the court crier, Thomas Waggaman, who for twenty-five years has been crying "Oyez, oyez, oyez" as the Court enters, has his lines typed in a black leather notebook lest some sudden lapse of memory should leave him speechless.

There was a day when the attorneys appearing before the Supreme Court conducted themselves with an aplomb indicative of equality with, sometimes even superiority to, the gentlemen before whom they argued. In fact Henry Clay, while conducting a case in 1835, once reached forward to where the snuffbox of Justice Bushrod Washington lay open in his hand and calmly and deliberately took a pinch. Then, before the justices could recover from the shock of this transgression, Mr Clay blandly remarked: "I see your honor still sticks to Scotch."

Today, however, guards and Secret Service men are constantly alert to protect the honor and dignity of the Court. Should a gawking visitor from the hinterland dare to level an opera glass at the bench, as sometimes has happened, he is promptly bustled from the chamber. Should a woman rise to ask the justices to take cognizance of her divorce case, as once occurred while Solicitor General Thacher was speaking, a plain-clothes man claps a hand over her mouth, and she is hurried from the august presence.

Today it is those who appear before the Court rather than the justices who sometimes need succor. And no hearing day convenes that Tom Waggaman does not have in his pocket a supply of small, pencil-like bulbs of ammonia, ever ready to bolster an attorney who may keel over while arguing before the Nine Old Men. Six of them folded up during the third year of the New Deal, and an emergency room has now been installed fifty feet from the court chamber for first aid to lawyers. Apparently case-hardened corporation lawyers and prosecutors who can turn a withering fire upon any witness cannot take it when they face the grim gaze of the highest tribunal in the land. For they know they are appealing to a presence more omnipotent than the House of Representatives, the Senate and the President of the United States all combined.

In the early days of the Supreme Court its members were one homogeneous and, on the whole, harmonious family. They did not bring their wives to Washington, but lived together in boarding houses at Dawson's on Capitol Hill, or with the Misses Polk, or at Elliott's on Pennsylvania, regarding which Chief Justice Taney wrote: "You can imagine nothing more abominably filthy." But he hastened to add that the woman in charge had lost her husband and nothing must be said to injure her reputation in Baltimore, for she was doing the best she could. Board and room were cheap, sixteen to seventeen dollars a week —with a wife, forty dollars—which may have been one reason they did not bring their wives to Washington. All the justices ate at the same table, and this intimate association enabled them to come to closer, quicker understanding regarding their decisions.

But as the Court took unto itself more power, was allotted higher salaries, and brought its wives to participate in the social whirl of Washington, this close relationship vanished. Aside from exchanging lengthy and sometimes heated legal views during secret deliberations, some of the justices scarcely ever see each other.

Justice Cardozo, the latest newcomer to join the Court, noticed this especially. He had enjoyed a most congenial relationship with his colleagues on the Court of Appeals in Albany, and found himself almost completely alone in Washington. The one moment when his associates on the Supreme Court were in an informal, human mood was when they adjourned to the washroom just outside the old court chamber in the Capitol Building. Here at least he could exchange an occasional bit of gossip regarding the proceedings of the day.

"But now that we have moved into the new building with its private washrooms," wails the newest justice, "there is no pleasure even in urination any more."

Justice Cardozo had put it very mildly. Actually the Court has been torn asunder. There have been cases of this before, notably in the Dred Scott and legal-tender controversies. Again during the World War espionage cases, the Court was so split that a delegation, including Justices Van Devanter and Day, waited upon Justice Holmes. Knowing that they were coming, Holmes placed his secretary just outside the open door in the next room and told him to take down the conversation. After some preliminary sparring, Justice Day said:

"Wendell, you know your ideas on the law and on civil rights. But these espionage cases go further than the law. They get down to the roots of the nation. Therefore won't you refrain from a minority opinion?"

Even Mrs Holmes had joined the gathering and was inclined to dissuade her husband. But Holmes, a Civil War veteran who detested all things pertaining to war, replied: "You know what my ideas of the law are, and I will not change them."

For some months after that the justices stopped speaking to each other; but it is doubtful whether ever before in history Supreme Court rancor has been more deep-rooted and vitriolic than during the days of the New Deal.

In order properly to appreciate the depth of this rancor it is necessary to know something of how the Supreme Court works.

After hearing oral argument on a case, each justice is given opportunity to study a stenographic report together with the briefs; and with this advance preparation, they meet in their private chamber, usually on Saturdays, to discuss the case. For many years—up until the New Deal days—these were dull and starchy affairs during which the late Justice Holmes sat with his face buried in his hands, elbows on the table. And if one of his colleagues took more than five minutes to present his views on the case, Holmes would uncover his face, turn toward the speaker and grunt:

"Christ!"

Then he returned to the shelter of his hands. But if his colleague insisted on prolonging his discourse, Holmes would emerge again, this time grunting in all too audible a voice:

"God!"

And if by any conceivable chance his colleague did not heed the second warning, Holmes unloosed a flow of profanity that is unprintable.

After a case has been discussed and the vote taken, the Chief Justice assigns one of the majority to write an opinion, although sometimes when the decision is unanimous and creates no important precedent no assignment is made. When the opinion is assigned, the justice writing it may take as much time as he desires. Dissenting opinions are not assigned, but are wholly voluntary statements by the dissenting justices. Sometimes it happens that several justices will dissent on the same case on entirely different grounds, and each will prepare a separate presentation of his views. When the Chief Justice is with the majority, it is customary for him to write the opinion in important cases. In the event of a dissent, the senior justice among the dissenters assigns the opinion.

After the opinions are written, they are sent to the Pearson Printing Company, which has the unique record of handling the Court's work for more than fifty years without a leak. Advance information regarding some decisions would be worth millions to stock-market manipulators, but only once in the history of the Court has there been a leak. This occurred in the office of the late Justice McKenna and was followed by the dismissal of his secretary.

Galley proofs of the opinions are circulated to each of the justices, on the margin of which he marks, "I agree" or "I disagree," or perhaps makes a change which he believes might be made in the opinion. Up until the days of the New Deal changes of this kind were rare, since the opinion already had been thoroughly discussed. Therefore, when the Court met privately on the Saturday prior to announcement of decisions on Monday, the work of passing upon final opinions, in the past, was chiefly one of formality.

Today, however, all that has changed. Saturday after Saturday came and went while the gold clause was under consideration with no agreement in sight. Weeks of secret acrimonious debate took place before the Nine Old Men could harmonize their differences anywhere near enough to reach the semblance of an agreement on the Tennessee Valley and AAA cases. Sixty-eight days dragged by in an unsuccessful attempt to prevent a wide-open breach on the Guffey Coal Act.

And during all these weeks Mr Hughes was like a setting hen trying to get eight unruly chicks under his wing. For him it was a most painful period. For there is no god before whom the Chief Justice prostrates himself more abjectly than before the goddess of harmony. He is the great harmonizer of the Supreme Court.

Justice Butler has been known to become grouchy and irritable. Justice McReynolds, who makes no secret of immense disdain for his liberal associates, has sometimes lost his temper. Justices Van Devanter and Sutherland, hard-boiled reactionaries, remain calm, but absolutely immovable. On the other side, Justices Cardozo and Brandeis are sweet-tempered, serene and equally immovable; while Justice Stone shoots a mixture of acid-tongued jibes and powerful arguments at his reactionary adversaries.

Over them all Mr Hughes remains the cordial, patient, some-times oscillating pacifier. This is a new role for a chief justice. In the past, some chief justices, notably Taft, took great pride in the Court's efficiency, but made no effort to create the impres-sion of harmony. Mr Hughes, however, has become the greatest harmonizer in the Court's history. He hates dissent. And the responsibility of preventing dissent has weighed heavily on his shoulders.

Even before he became Chief Justice, Mr Hughes indicated the importance which he attached to that personage by describ-ing him as "the most important judicial officer in the world."

"While the Chief Justice has only one vote," he said, "the way in which the Court does its work gives him a special opportunity for leadership."

And those who have watched the Chief Justice closely, includ-ing some of his colleagues, cannot escape the impression that, as the years have passed, Mr Hughes has come to give far more consideration to the fact that "dissents," as he once said, "detract from the force of the judgment" than he has to the undesirability of "the sacrifice of conviction."

Certainly Mr Hughes's record as a conformist with the majority would indicate this. Through all the years of the New Deal he has been careful to write only two dissenting opinions, and one—in the Guffey Coal case—sided for the most part with the majority. Furthermore, he has been careful to cast few dis-senting votes. Whereas Stone and Cardozo, leaders of the liberal wing, have averaged twelve and thirteen dissents every year during the past four, and whereas Butler, on the opposite wing, has averaged eight, the Chief Justice has averaged only three.

Here, at one glance, is the line-up of dissenting votes during the years of the New Deal:

	1932–33	1933–34	1934–35	1935–36
HUGHES	3	4	3	2
VAN DEVANTER	3	3	5	2
MCREYNOLDS	8	9	5	3
BRANDEIS	11	9	10	13
SUTHERLAND	5	5	5	5
BUTLER	10	9	7	4
STONE	14	13	11	13
ROBERTS	3	4	3	4
CARDOZO	13	11	11	14

But in the court year 1935–36, not even the beatific influence of Mr Hughes could prevent the Supreme Court from setting its all-time record for internal strife. All attempt at harmony, all attempt to save the prestige of the Court was cast to the winds. There was a time when the minority would hold its nose on minor points and go along with the majority just for the sake of outward appearances. But no more. Today intercourt rancor is such that the minority flays away at its dissents with no thought of retreat or compromise. And during the third year of the New Deal a total of twenty-two dissenting opinions—the greatest number in history—was handed down by the minority.

After the demise of the Agricultural Adjustment Act even the Chief Justice abandoned all attempt at an outward semblance of harmony. When the justices assembled for secret discussion on the first Saturday after the case was argued, there was not the slightest doubt in the minds of the liberal members that the AAA would be upheld. Solicitor General Reed had put up a masterful argument pointing out the power of Congress to levy taxes, expend money, and to organize agencies for the lending of money to farmers. Furthermore it seemed inconceivable to the liberal justices, as it did to many legal authorities throughout the country, that even the most reactionary members of the

Court could undo a system of benefit crop payments which had become so interwoven with the agricultural fabric of the nation.

In registering the private opinion of the Court it is customary for the Chief Justice to call upon the most recent appointee—now Justice Cardozo—and then the other justices in reverse order of their seniority. Each justice states his view and the arguments for supporting it. Opportunity is given for interchange of ideas and, on occasion, hot and protracted debate. After this, a vote is taken—unless, as so frequently has happened during the days of the New Deal, there was such irreconcilable disagreement that a vote was postponed.

In the final voting, the Chief Justice votes first. And perhaps taking advantage of the trend of the preceding debate, Mr Hughes has shown a decided inclination to throw his weight with the majority.

But during the confidential debate on the AAA, Mr Hughes at first appeared to be with the minority. McReynolds, Van Devanter, Sutherland, Butler and Roberts, much to the amazement of the liberals, were unalterably opposed to the AAA. Not for one moment did they entertain the slightest doubt regarding its unconstitutionality. In fact, it almost appeared that they had been waiting this opportunity to quash one of the most important and popular planks in the New Deal platform. Nothing could budge them. Inner council debate dragged out for one month. On the last Saturday before the decision was announced, the usual sightseers and newspapermen loitered in the marble corridor outside the court chamber. As always, a guard stood thirty feet from the door to prevent eavesdropping. But the muffled thunder of high-pitched argument could be heard inside. Suddenly above all the others' came the strident voice of the Chief Justice:

"Gentlemen! You are not only ruining this country, you are ruining this Court!"

When the decision was announced, a few days later, it was found that Mr Hughes had been able to convince himself of the unconstitutionality of the Agricultural Adjustment Act. The vote was 6 to 3. The prestige of the Court—for the moment—had been saved.

A few days after that, Justice Stone bumped into Professor Henry Schulman of Yale, one of his former students, who said he had a very indiscreet question to ask regarding the AAA decision.

"It's not contempt of Court to ask a question," Stone replied.

"Well, to be blunt, Mr Justice," Schulman said, "did Hughes change his decision in the Triple A case?"

"While I can't answer that," replied Stone with a twinkle in his eye, "if that were stated as a fact, I should be unable to prove the contrary."

One New Deal enterprise after another was knocked down after that, until one day Justice Stone again met one of his students, now a government lawyer.

"How are you getting on, John?" inquired Stone.

"Pretty good, Mr Justice," the young man replied. "I was with the legal division of the NRA last year, then I transferred to the AAA, and now I am in the legal division of the Securities and Exchange Commission."

Justice Stone smiled.

"I see," he said, "keeping just one jump ahead of us."

A few days later, Justice Stone's conservative colleagues handed down a decision restricting the powers of the Securities and Exchange Commission.

"Legislation in the United States," remarked Sir Wilmott Lewis, of the London *Times,* "is a digestive process by Congress with frequent regurgitations by the Supreme Court."

CHAPTER III

The Lord High Executioners

T HERE have been three periods of tension between the Supreme Court and the executive-legislative branches of the government which have molded American history. There was the dispute between Thomas Jefferson and John Marshall over the attempt of the Federalists to increase the power of the judiciary. There was the Dred Scott decision which led to the Civil War. And there was the long period of accumulating power under the Fourteenth Amendment which led to the present clash between the Court and the administration of Franklin D. Roosevelt.

There have been other cases of serious dispute, as Andrew Jackson's frequent flouting of the Court, President Grant's controversy over the Legal Tender Act, and the bitterness which the Court incurred in vetoing the constitutionality of the income tax. But none of these pulled at the roots of the nation and had such important effects upon subsequent history as did the early dispute between Jefferson and Madison, and the Dred Scott decision. Nor did they so deeply affect the varied walks of life as the present conflict between the Court and the so-called New Deal.

It is too early to know what the outcome of the present clash may be or to know what afteraffects it may have upon the course of the nation. But with the Court denying the right of state and federal governments to control the production of such

vital raw materials as oil and coal and of agriculture, to co-
operate with industry in establishing codes for hours, wages and
fair trade practice, to modify farm mortgages, to co-operate with
the railroads in establishing a system of pensions, and to permit
municipalities to go into bankruptcy, the present conflict may
be the most important in history.

Probably it is not an overstatement to say that upon the outcome of the present clash between the Supreme Court and the
administration will depend the ability of the United States to
avoid such internal conflicts as now grip parts of Europe.

That which follows is an attempt to set forth the history of
the most important conflicts between the Court and the executive-legislative branches of the government.

The political setting of the first clash—between Marshall and
Jefferson—was not unlike that of today. Not long after the
adoption of the Constitution, the country had divided itself into
two political camps, the Federalists, representing the industrial
and commercial interests of the Atlantic seaboard and New
England on the one hand, and the anti-Federalists or Republicans
(actually the beginning of the Democratic party), representing
the agricultural interests of the South and West on the other.
The anti-Federalists, led by Thomas Jefferson, had spent the
four years prior to the elections of 1800 storming against the high-
tariff and centralized-government policies of John Adams, who,
according to his friend Alexander Hamilton, was elected only
"by a miracle."

Particularly they stormed against the Alien and Sedition acts
and against the highhanded sentences meted out by the judiciary,
which already had become a storm center of the early republic.
Many of the judges were British born, and since the common
law of the new states had not been codified, the judges fell back
upon English law, much to the resentment of those who recently
had fought against the yoke of England. Some of the sentences
handed down by the judiciary were severe in the extreme. In
April 1800 Justice Samuel Chase of the Supreme Court decreed

that John Fries, who had resisted paying the Federalist land tax in Pennsylvania, "shall be hanged by the neck until dead." The sentence caused such an uproar from Jefferson's anti-Federalists that President Adams pardoned Fries. Undoubtedly, it was one of the factors which swept Jefferson into office later in that same year.

Again the same Justice Chase learned of a treatise written by James Thompson Callender in which he described President Adams as a "professional aristocrat" who "had proved faithful and serviceable to the British interest." Chase swore that he would take Callender's book with him to Richmond, and "if Virginia was not too depraved" to furnish a jury of respectable men, he would sentence Callender for libel. "It is a pity," he said, "that they had not hanged the rascal." And deriding Callender's attorneys as "beardless young gentlemen," Chase sentenced Callender to nine months' imprisonment and a fine of two hundred dollars.

These and many other instances of highhandedness on the part of the courts added to the general unpopularity of the Federalist party, and in November 1800 swept Thomas Jefferson and the Republicans (later Democrats) into power. It was an overwhelming victory. John Quincy Adams, son of the defeated President, wrote: "Whatever the merits or the demerits of the former administrations may have been, there never was a system of measures more completely and irrevocably abandoned and rejected by the popular voice. It [the administration of his father and the Federalists] can and never will be revived . . . and to attempt the restoration would be as absurd as to undertake the resurrection of a carcass seven years in the grave."

Nevertheless, an attempt to prolong the authority of the carcass was exactly what his father and the Federalists now attempted to do. Congress and the presidency had been lost, but there remained one stronghold—the judiciary. Between elections in November and the inauguration in March, President Adams worked feverishly, rushing through his lame-duck Congress a new judiciary act creating sixteen new circuit courts. These

new judgeships Adams now filled with lame-duck Federalists—
for life. And while President-elect Jefferson sat irate and helpless, Adams secured the resignation of Chief Justice Ellsworth
and appointed in his place John Marshall of Virginia, thus
thwarting Jefferson's known intention of making his close
friend, Spencer Roane of Virginia, chief justice of the Supreme
Court.

Adams worked until midnight of March 3, appointing new
judges. When he finished, the Federalists, although defeated at
the polls, were in a position, through life-term appointments to
the Court, to thwart the radical doctrines of Thomas Jefferson
for many years to come.

Some time before their defeat, the Federalists had advocated
the right of the Supreme Court to hold acts of Congress unconstitutional. Actually, the Constitutional Convention had rejected
this thesis only thirteen years before. Four times during the debates in Philadelphia, on June 5 and 6, July 21 and August 15,
James Madison and James Wilson, the latter to become an associate justice of the Supreme Court, proposed that the Constitution contain a provision giving the judiciary the right to
pass on the constitutionality of acts of Congress. And four
times their proposal was rejected. Never did it receive the votes
of more than three states.

In the end, not only did the convention categorically fail to
enthrone the judiciary, but it wrote into the Constitution an
explicit veto power for the President and equally specific provisions permitting the Congress to override him. This negative
action against the judiciary, coupled with the positive action in
regard to the President and Congress, indicated that there was
no doubt whatsoever in the minds of the founding fathers that
the Supreme Court was given no power to pass upon the constitutionality of acts of Congress.

Nevertheless it was only a short time after the Constitution
was written that the Federalists claimed the power for the
Court. And undoubtedly this question was uppermost in
the minds of both Federalists and anti-Federalists during the

Jefferson–Aaron Burr electoral contest. According to Jefferson himself all the evils accomplished by the "aristocrats have been solitary inconsequential, timid things in comparison with the audacious, barefaced and sweeping pretension to a system of law for the United States without the adoption of their legislature and so infinitely beyond their power to adopt."

Immediately after his inauguration, therefore, Jefferson set about the demolition of the Federalist stronghold—the judiciary. On January 8, 1802, his henchmen in Congress moved to remove from the statute books Adams' last-minute judiciary law, and after three months of the most acrimonious debate so far held in the halls of the new Congress this was passed. Adams' "midnight judges" were unbenched. But then, for fear the Supreme Court, meeting a few months later, might declare the law unconstitutional, Jefferson's anti-Federalists went further and passed an act whereby Supreme Court sessions were suspended for fourteen months. Seldom has the Court been more vigorously squelched.

When the Court convened after its long recess in 1803, Chief Justice John Marshall nursed the ambition, not only for himself but for his fellow Federalists, to reinstate the shorn power of the judiciary.

There was no doubt at all where John Marshall stood in the matter. On the morning of Jefferson's inauguration he wrote to his friend, Charles Cotesworth Pinckney: "The Democrats [anti-Federalists] are divided into speculative theorists and absolute terrorists. With the latter I am disposed to class Mr Jefferson. If he ranges himself with them it is not difficult to foresee that much difficulty is in store for our country—if he does not, they will soon become his enemies and calumniators."

Marshall and Jefferson were distant cousins, but it would be impossible to say which despised the other more. The foremost attorney in Richmond, Marshall had become a man of some wealth and in 1793 joined his brother, who was the son-in-law of the tremendously wealthy Robert Morris, in buying the estates of Lord Fairfax, comprising 160,000 acres of some of the

best land in Virginia. He had served beside Washington during
the agony of Valley Forge and later became ambassador to
France. He admitted quite frankly that he no longer "idealized
democracy" as he did during the early struggle for independence, and that he was determined to make the Supreme
Court the stabilizing force of the nation. Also he was worried
over the health of his associates on the bench, all of whom were
old and feeble and might drop off, thereby giving Jefferson a
chance to fill the vacancies with friends of his own.

Marshall, therefore, was looking for some way to put across
his thesis that the Court could pass upon the constitutionality
of laws—and of putting it across as soon as possible. A case of
this kind had presented itself very early in the Jefferson administration when James Madison, Jefferson's Secretary of State,
refused to issue commissions to seventeen justices of the peace
for the District of Columbia appointed by Adams during the
closing hours of his administration. The appointees had been
confirmed by the Senate, but Madison, acting upon instructions
from Jefferson, refused to deliver the commissions, and four of
the gentlemen thus appointed—including William Marbury—
applied to the Supreme Court for a writ of mandamus to compel Madison to deliver their commissions. The other thirteen
did not consider their pending positions as justices of the
peace important enough to worry about and dropped the
matter.

John Marshall now scrutinized the case of William Marbury
and his three associates as a vehicle to put across his thesis,
now almost an obsession on his part, that the Supreme Court
must have final power to pass upon the constitutionality of acts
of Congress.

The fact was that Marshall himself was largely responsible
for the case of *Marbury* vs. *Madison*. Still acting as Secretary of
State during the late hours of the Adams administration, he had
gone off to Richmond leaving the commissions, with customary
negligence, on his desk. His excuse was that he had loaned his
clerk to President Adams and forgot to mail them himself.

It required a long stretch of the imagination to read any importance into the case other than a political one. Also, Jefferson's action in suspending sessions of the Court delayed the case, and *Marbury* vs. *Madison* did not come before Marshall until 1803, two years after the failure to deliver the commissions. Even if they were now delivered, the justices of the peace would have but a very short time to serve.

However, the feud between Jefferson and the judiciary continued. Early in 1803 his anti-Federalists in Congress impeached John Pickering, judge of the United States District Court in New Hampshire; also had announced its intention of impeaching Supreme Court Justice Chase for his highhanded sentences in enforcing the Sedition Act, and threatened to impeach Marshall himself if he ruled in favor of judicial supremacy over legislative law in the case of *Marbury* vs. *Madison*. However, this supremacy was just as firm a conviction in the mind of John Marshall as the opposite was prevalent in the minds of the public. Chief Justice Jay and his associates had complained that the Judiciary Act of 1789 was unconstitutional, but they lacked the nerve to oppose public opinion by saying so officially. Now, however, Marshall set about to put his Court on record despite the threat of impeachment.

The general public, including the anti-Federalists in Congress and Jefferson himself, believed that only one of two courses was open to Marshall. Either he could disavow the power of the Supreme Court over the Executive and dismiss the plea of Marbury, or he could command Secretary of State Madison to deliver the commissions.

But Marshall knew what he faced in the latter event. His Court had no power to compel Madison to deliver the commissions, and he would become the laughingstock of the country. So he persuaded his associate justices—all of them Federalists— to rule that Madison had violated the law in refusing to deliver the now famous commissions. But then he turned around and also persuaded them that the Supreme Court could do nothing about it, since the Judiciary Act of 1789 was unconstitutional.

Marshall's associate justices were quite prepared to hold the Judicial Act of 1789 unconstitutional on the ground that it required them to travel over the undeveloped roads of the country to sit as circuit judges, but hitherto they were not prepared to hold it unconstitutional for the novel reason now put forward by their Chief Justice, namely, that the act gave them too much power. He claimed that Section 13 of the Judiciary Act was unconstitutional because it gave the Supreme Court the power to issue writs of mandamus. The Constitution, he pointed out, provided that cases could come before the Court only in two ways, namely, on appeal or through original jurisdiction in controversies between states, ambassadors or public ministers. The Constitution having thus defined the powers of the Court, Marshall argued that Congress had no power to give it the additional right to issue writs of mandamus. Therefore the entire Judiciary Act of 1789 was unconstitutional. Since Congress lacked this power, the Supreme Court could not issue a writ of mandamus against Secretary of State Madison on behalf of Marbury, he concluded, and the case was dismissed.

It was one of the most adroit politico-legal maneuvers in history.

Marshall had very neatly sidestepped the wrath of the anti-Federalists and his own impeachment by refusing to take action against Madison. Yet simultaneously he had reached out and taken for his Court the power to declare acts of Congress unconstitutional. But, his eye always upon the political storm clouds, he had taken this power on the grounds that Congress had given his Court too much power.

In other words, by throwing back to Congress the insignificant crumb of writs of mandamus, Marshall took for the Supreme Court the right to rule on the whole loaf of congressional power in the future.

All of this Marshall wrapped in about ten thousand words of such involved legal verbiage that the general public did not immediately catch its significance. Jefferson did, however, and issued a scathing denunciation of the opinion as an "obiter dissertation of the Chief Justice" and an attempt to foist upon the nation a "dangerous doctrine, one which would place us under the despotism of an oligarchy."

"If this opinion be sound," he declared, "then indeed is our Constitution a complete felo-de-se. For, intending to establish three departments, co-ordinate and independent, that they might check and balance one another, it has given, according to this opinion, to one of them alone, the right to prescribe rules for the government of the others, and to that one, too, which is un-elected by and independent of the nation. The Constitution on this hypothesis is a mere thing of wax in the hands of the judiciary which the judges may twist and shape into any form they please."

John Marshall had inserted his wedge. Thereafter he was content to rest. The next test between the Court and the Executive was to plunge the country into the fearful conflagration of the Civil War. But now, during the thirty-two years that Marshall remained chief justice of the United States, not once did he dare raise the issue of Supreme Court supremacy over acts of Congress. And for twenty years after his death—a total of fifty-two years—the Court carefully refrained from challenging the executive or legislative branches of the federal government.

There was a very good reason for this submission.

Jefferson's defiant words were echoed by succeeding Presidents, by members of Congress, state legislatures, and from a thousand political platforms. Even judges joined in the dissent. In 1815 Justice Gibson of the Pennsylvania Supreme Court handed down his famous opinion in the case of *Eakin* vs. *Raub* emphatically refuting Marshall's dictum; while twenty-eight years later the same court, in the case of *Sharpless* vs. *The Mayor,* reaffirmed this view in a notable opinion by Chief Justice Jeremiah S. Black. In Congress feeling against the judiciary reached such a pitch that in 1804, one year after the *Marbury* vs. *Madison* decision, Justice Chase was impeached for making a political attack on proposals to curb the courts, Judge Pinckney was convicted, while several state judges in Kentucky, Ohio and Pennsylvania also were impeached, though not convicted.

When Jefferson finally retired from the presidency he sent a letter to Judge Tyler, continuing the battle: "We have long enough suffered under the base prostitution of law by party passions in one judge and the imbecility of another," he said. "In their hands the law is nothing more than an ambiguous text, to be explained by their personal malice. There is not a word in the Constitution that gives the power of final interpretation to the judges rather than to the executive and legislative branches."

Andrew Jackson took up the battle after his election in 1828, and in the case of *Worcester* vs. *State of Georgia,* he struck at the Court's power to pass upon state laws. The Supreme Court had reversed the Georgia Supreme Court by ruling that the Creek Indians were not required to adhere to the jurisdiction of Georgia law, because of a prior treaty with the federal government.

The decision was like waving a red flag at a bull. Jackson flatly refused to enforce the decree.

"John Marshall has handed down his decision," he said, "now let him enforce it."

Georgia long had been a hotbed of fierce opposition to the Court, and the Indian decision fanned this deep-rooted hostility to fever pitch. Jackson's sympathetic attitude was all that was necessary to spur the state into open revolt. Georgia officials refused to accede to the Court's order and defiantly put their outlawed state act into effect by force.

This defiance was typical of the first part of the half-century which elapsed between the *Marbury* vs. *Madison* decision in 1803 and the Dred Scott decision in 1857. During fully half of that period the Court sank to near impotence and was repeatedly overridden by both the Executive and Congress. During this period of impotence the justices who controlled the Court continued to be the Federalists appointed when that party was in its heyday. They were old, had been reared in a past generation and were thoroughly out of sympathy with the "heretical" views of the Democratic party which had fallen heir to Jefferson's anti-Federalists. And yet they dared not oppose those heretical views. The country had shown all too clearly what would be the result.

One by one these aged justices dropped out. Justice Story was the last to go. He had served on the Supreme Court for thirty-four years. He had seen the United States grow from a struggling handful of colonies huddled along the Atlantic seaboard unconnected save by road and river boat, until in 1845 it extended almost to the Pacific Coast and was connected in part by railroad and steamboat. When he resigned in that year, Justice Story issued this lament:

"I have long been convinced that the doctrines and opinions of the 'old court' were daily losing ground, and especially those on great constitutional questions. New men and new opinions have succeeded. I am the last member now living of the old court, and I cannot consent to remain where I can no longer hope to see these doctrines recognized and enforced."

As these aged justices dropped out and were replaced by younger men more in tune with the political ideas of that day, the Supreme Court began to gather new strength. In fact, as Jackson, Van Buren and Polk built up favorable representation on the Court by appointing loyal Democrats, it was natural that they should give the Court more confidence and support. Gradually, therefore, it became a helpful adjunct and stamp of approval for the acts and policies of the Democratic party just as it had been on the Federalist party.

And since the dominant doctrine of the Democratic party of that day—from which the Democratic party of today has strayed—favored states' rights, the Supreme Court also became the champion of states' rights and issued many a clarion call for a hands-off policy in regard to state legislation. By and large the justices interpreted the law as lawyers and did not attempt to become legislators.

Roger B. Taney, whom Jackson elevated to the chief justice-

ship in 1836, during his fight with the United States Bank, was
the son of a large slaveholder in southern Maryland, and won
his first fame as a young lawyer by championing John Gooding,
a notorious Baltimore slave smuggler, apprehended while trying
to bring 290 Africans into the United States. Young Taney defended him, fought the case to the Supreme Court, where he
won an acquittal on the grounds that the wording of the
indictment was "fatally defective." Taney married the sister of
Francis Scott Key, author of "The Star-Spangled Banner," also
a descendant of slaveowning families, and soon built up a reputation as the shrewdest defender of slaveholders in the South.

His conservatism, however, was confined to this one point.
On questions not relating to slavery, Taney took a progressive
stand and was an ardent believer in a hands-off policy by the
Supreme Court—at least until age dulled his perspective.

"This tribunal," asserted Taney when called upon to inter-
vene in Dorr's Rebellion in Rhode Island, "should be the last
to overstep the boundaries which limit its own jurisdiction. And
while it should always be ready to meet any question confided
to it by the Constitution, it is equally its duty not to pass beyond its appropriate sphere of action, and to take care not to
involve itself in discussions which properly belong to other
forums."

Rhode Island and its insurrectionists were forced to settle
their dispute between themselves.

As the nation passed the middle of the century, and as the
Democratic party continued an almost unbroken line of Presidents in the White House, it became not the troop of "radical
heretics" as in Jefferson's day, but the party of reaction. More
and more it came to represent the big plantation owners of the
South and those whose prosperity was bound up in the con-
tinuation of slavery. More and more, also, the justices of the
Supreme Court, most of them from the slaveholding states and
well advanced in years, came to reflect the views of the party
which appointed them.

It was at this point—1856—that the Dred Scott case came before the Supreme Court. Dred Scott, a Negro slave, was taken by his master from Missouri, a slave state, to what is now Minnesota, where for four years he lived in territory that was free by the terms of the Missouri Compromise of 1820. Upon returning to Missouri, Scott claimed that previous residence in a free territory made him a free man. He sued for his freedom, won in the lower courts, was reversed in the Missouri Supreme Court and finally appealed to the United States Supreme Court.

Charles Evans Hughes attaches importance to the statement of Van Hoest that "it had been the systematic and conscientious aim of the South to make the Supreme Court a citadel of slavocracy and that the Dred Scott decision was to witness the success of their efforts." The entire country now awaited the decision. The South particularly demanded that the Court now decide the question of slavery's extension to the new territories being opened in the West. So intense was the interest in it that, although the case was argued before the Supreme Court just prior to the elections of 1856, Chief Justice Taney held up the final verdict until after the inauguration of James Polk, newly elected Democratic President, in March 1857.

Chief reason for the delay undoubtedly was the desire of the Democratic party not to lose votes by the turbulent reaction bound to follow the Court's announcement, whichever way the decision went. But there was another reason for the delay.

Originally Taney planned to dodge the question of slavery's extension to the new territories and to treat the case merely as a local matter. In fact, Justice Samuel Nelson, New York Democrat who supported slavery, prepared an opinion along this line.

But sometimes the most important judicial decisions turn upon luck or the eccentricity of man, and in this case it was discovered that Justice John McLean of Ohio, a staunch opponent of slavery, planned to write a dissenting opinion, burning up the Southern slave leaders and maintaining that Congress had the power to abolish slavery in the territories. Behind McLean's proposed fireworks was the fact that he was a candidate for the Republican nomination, in fact received 196 votes at the convention that year and a number of votes at the Chicago convention which nominated Lincoln. His dissent was good politics as far as his presidential ambitions were concerned, but it was not good politics for the Court's majority. They saw themselves the butt of criticism throughout their own party if they dodged the slavery issue while McLean came out with his scathing rebuke.

Meanwhile there had been other developments. The interval which followed the argument in the case in the autumn gave time for a tremendous slave lobby to be formed in Washington. Slaveholding by this time had come to be a major industry. It was as important to one half the United States at that time as the power industry now is to the entire country. Thirty thousand slaves a year were bought and sold in the South. The slave population was 3,000,000 persons, owned, according to Senator William H. Seward of New York, by only 347,000 overlords, who in turn possessed nearly all the real estate between the banks of the Delaware and the banks of the Rio Grande.

The lobby which this industry now mobilized in Washington was comparable—for that day—with the more recent lobby which endeavored to emasculate President Roosevelt's Holding Corporation Bill, or to prevent the power-trust investigation during the Coolidge administration. The effort of the slave lobby was to get the proslavery Supreme Court to settle the extension of slavery to the western United States once and for all. At dinners, receptions, and on every conceivable occasion they importuned the aged justices to put the question of the hour at rest forever.

Leader of this campaign was Alexander H. Stevens, a Southern politician and later vice president of the Confederacy. Subsequent publication of confidential letters showed that he had an intimate knowledge of everything that was going on inside the Court down to the last detail. President Buchanan, it was discovered later, also had been in communication with the Court. Justice Catron of Tennessee wrote to him on February

19, 1857, just thirteen days before his inauguration, informing him that the constitutionality of the Missouri Compromise was to be decided and asked him to use his influence with Justice Grier, who, like Buchanan, was a Pennsylvanian. Justice Grier was so senile that Charles Evans Hughes tells how a committee of his fellow justices eventually asked him to retire. In the papers of President Buchanan is a letter from Justice Grier in reply to one from Buchanan, informing him on February 23, nine days before inauguration, that the Missouri Compromise would be held invalid.

Safely assured on this point, Buchanan cheerfully referred to the Dred Scott case in his inaugural address and announced his intention of submitting to the decision, "whatever this may be."

When the decision was announced two days later it was easy to understand why he had been so cheerful about it. It was so savage that it left the North gasping. Chief Justice Taney, who delivered the opinion himself, declared: "The Negro race is regarded as so far inferior that it has no rights . . . The Negro might lawfully and justly be reduced to slavery for the white man's benefit."

By a 7–2 vote the Supreme Court dragged in the constitutional issue by the forelock and declared that Congress was without power to abolish slavery in the federal territories. In doing so, it reached back to the precedent so quietly wedged into the court record by John Marshall in the case of *Marbury* vs. *Madison,* namely, that the Supreme Court had the power to pass upon the constitutionality of acts of Congress. Marshall, the arch-Federalist, had inserted the wedge. Now the Democratic party, which defeated his party and which had done its best to humiliate him, even threatening impeachment, made the most of it.

Both Marshall, the Tory landowner, and the Democrat representatives of Southern plantation owners on the Supreme Court used it for one and the same thing: the protection of property.

The Civil War was fought because the South, by this decision, indicated its ability to spread its economic system, its theory of human property, into all the territories, both north and south. Taney, who had risen from a Maryland slavery attorney to chief justice of the United States, died at eighty-seven, penniless and broken, in the last year of the bloody carnage he helped to start.

The Dred Scott decision marked the second eclipse of the Supreme Court. The next twenty years were to see it more impotent, more openly derided than during the period immediately following John Marshall's quarrel with Jefferson.

Charles Evans Hughes, now sitting in the exalted position once held by Taney, has described the opinion handed down by his predecessor as a "public calamity."

"The decision was greeted by antislavery papers in the North with derision and contempt," Hughes continued. "The widespread and bitter attacks upon the judges who joined in the decision undermined confidence in the Court. False and scurrilous comments upon the traits and character of the judges supplemented hostile analysis of Chief Justice Taney's opinion. . . . It was many years before the Court, even under new judges, was able to retrieve its reputation."

As war broke out, the Supreme Court either was completely ignored or else deliberately flouted. Time after time Lincoln threw its decisions into the scrap basket. Once, when called upon by Taney to release a prisoner at Fort McHenry, Baltimore, the President answered with a proclamation which contained more venom than Roosevelt's horse-and-buggy diatribe: ". . . the judicial machinery," he said, "seems as if it had been designed not to sustain the government, but to embarrass and betray it."

And the founding fathers of the Republican party, drawing up their convention platform for the re-election of Lincoln, adopted a blistering plank far different from that drafted by their heirs at Cleveland in 1936.

And when the Supreme Court considered the case of Mc-
Cardle, a Mississippi newspaper editor, imprisoned for printing
incendiary articles, the Republican Congress passed an act de-
priving the Supreme Court of jurisdiction, before which Chief
Justice Salmon P. Chase meekly bowed. "We are not at liberty,"
he said, "to inquire into the motives of the legislature. We can
only examine into its power under the Constitution; and the
power to make exceptions to the appellate jurisdiction of this
Court is given in express words."

"It was during this period," according to Charles Evans
Hughes, "when the Court was still suffering from lack of a satis-
factory measure of public confidence, that another decision was
rendered which brought the Court into disesteem."

Mr Hughes referred to the legal-tender cases, decided in 1870,
by which the Court declared unconstitutional the greenback currency act of the Union government to finance the war. The act
had been upheld by the lower courts, and what particularly in-
furiated the country was that Chief Justice Chase, administrator
of the wartime currency measure as Secretary of the Treasury,
now joined in the 4–3 majority opinion attacking the act as
invalid. (Chase, at that time, aspired to the Democratic nomination for the presidency.)

Whereupon President Grant promptly appointed two staunch
Republicans to fill two vacancies on the Court, and next year
they reversed Chase's ruling by a 5–4 decision.

"The overruling in such a short time, and by one vote, of the
previous decision shook popular respect for the Court," remarked Charles Evans Hughes in later years.

Mr Hughes put it very mildly. For more than ten years the
Court had been booted and kicked about until its prestige had
sunk to a level certainly not so low since the days of Thomas
Jefferson. Republicans on the floor of the House openly boasted
that at last they had "subdued the Supreme Court."

Their boasts, however, were premature. For even while this
oratory was reverberating on the floor of Congress, these same

Republicans unwittingly were writing into the Constitution an amendment by which the Supreme Court would attain a power never dreamed of, either by them or by the founding fathers.

It was the Fourteenth Amendment.

The purpose of the Thirteenth, Fourteenth and Fifteenth amendments was to abolish slavery, safeguard the freed slaves, also to strengthen the control of Congress over the states. The last thought of Thaddeus Stevens, author of the amendments and fiery defender of Negro rights, was that they should strengthen the hand of the judiciary. In fact, Stevens, one of the bitterest critics of the Supreme Court, once had warned: "The Court should recollect that it has had bad luck with its political decisions. The people of this country thus far have preferred to govern the country themselves and let the Court attend to its law business."

But tucked away in Section 1 of the Fourteenth Amendment was this sentence:

"No State shall make or enforce any law which shall abridge the privileges and immunities of citizens of the United States; nor shall any State deprive any person of life, liberty, or property without due process of law; nor deny to any person within its jurisdiction the equal protection of the laws."

On these half-dozen lines, the Supreme Court was to build the all-dominant power it exercises today.

Less than fifty cases involving discrimination against Negroes have come before the Court. But these lines, inserted in the Constitution as a charter for human liberty, have been metamorphosed into an impregnable bulwark of property. Instead of protecting the Negro race, they have been used to ensure long and gruelling factory hours for both white and colored, to block legislation which would preserve wage standards for both white and colored, to continue the employment of children, both white and colored, to delay the adoption of an income tax against the representatives of wealth and property, and to crush every important social and economic reform attempted by federal and state governments in the last half-century.

This domination, however, did not come to the Supreme Court immediately. It was built up carefully and deliberately during the quarter-century following the Civil War.

The first important case came when the Louisiana legislature, controlled by carpetbaggers and Negroes, passed an act giving to the Crescent City Slaughter House Company a monopoly of the butchering business of New Orleans. The avowed purpose of the act was to "improve health conditions" in the city of New Orleans, but reliable reports of bribes to susceptible legislators, coupled with the fact that one thousand butchers were thrown out of work in New Orleans, caused an unfavorable surge of public opinion.

The New Orleans butchers immediately sued, and retained, as their attorney, John Archibald Campbell, a former justice of the Supreme Court who had resigned shortly after the outbreak of the Civil War in order to return to his native Alabama and aid the Confederacy. Campbell had lost all his property during the war, and undoubtedly the slaughterhouse case appealed to him because it typified the legislation then being railroaded through carpetbagger-controlled Southern legislatures at the expense of the old landed aristocracy of the South.

In order to find a legal loophole which might serve as a bulwark against the threatened supremacy of the liberated slaves, Campbell locked himself up for three days. Finally, he hit upon the innocuous sentence in the Fourteenth Amendment, "nor shall any state deprive any person of life, liberty, or property without due process of law."

These words, inserted in the Constitution for the protection of the Negro, Campbell now turned round for the benefit of Southern whites, and, appearing before his former colleagues of the Supreme Court in 1873, he asked the question:

"What are life, liberty and property?"

They are the right of a man to earn a living, he argued, the right of a man to his job, the right of the butchers of New

Orleans to their jobs. This is a right, he claimed, that is guaranteed by the Constitution under the Fourteenth Amendment, and which could not be taken away by the Louisiana slaughterhouse monopoly without due process of law.

It was a magnificent presentation and made a profound effect upon Campbell's ex-colleagues. And it came within one vote of winning him a favorable decision. However, the Court too recently had suffered the drubbing of the Civil War and the legal-tender cases. It was not looking for another immediate fight. Also, both Lincoln and Grant had packed the Court with sympathetic Northerners until there was not, at that time, one Southerner on the Supreme bench. Finally, the most dynamic member of the Court was Justice Samuel F. Miller, an ardent abolitionist even before the Civil War, who had moved from Kentucky to Iowa because of his strong disapproval of slavery.

Justice Miller it was who wrote the opinion for the majority in the slaughterhouse case. It was a ringing opinion, championing the rights of the oppressed Negro race and upholding the right of the Louisiana legislature to create a butchering monopoly in New Orleans.

"No one," he said, "can fail to be impressed with the one pervading purpose found in them all [Thirteenth, Fourteenth and Fifteenth amendments], lying at the foundation of each, and without which none of them would have been suggested; we mean the freedom of the slave race, the security and firm establishment of that freedom, and the protection of the newly made freemen and citizens from the oppressions of those who had formerly exercised unlimited dominion over them. . . . We doubt very much whether any action . . . not directed by way of discrimination against the Negroes as a class, or on account of their race, will ever be held to come within the purview of this provision."

Strong as were the Northern sympathies of the Supreme Court, four other justices on the bench were more interested in property than in the rights of slaves. Justices Bradley of New Jersey, Swayne of Ohio, and Field of California all were former railroad attorneys and corporation lawyers. And they all issued strong dissents. Chief Justice Chase also dissented, but did not write a minority opinion. He was afflicted with paralysis at the time and died shortly thereafter.

The dissents in this case proved more important than the majority opinion. They were expanded and enlarged upon little by little during the next ten years until gradually they became the opinion of the majority and contrary to the intention of the supreme law of the land.

From the milestone marked in the slaughterhouse case in 1873, the Supreme Court now went off on two tangents, both contrary to the original intent of the Thirteenth, Fourteenth and Fifteenth amendments. One was to wipe out all of the benefits intended to be given the Negro. The other was to transfer, not to the white man, but to the corporations which the white man created, all the protection originally intended for his black brother.

Justice Miller had begun to age by this time. No longer did he pen stentorian opinions upholding the rights of the colored race. Their only champion on the Court was now Justice Harlan, a mint-julep-drinking gentleman from Kentucky who once had owned slaves, but who had fought in the Union army and was a militant dissenter from the Court's roughshod treatment of the Negro. The two justices who seemed to take greatest glee in distorting the original intention of the Thirteenth, Fourteenth and Fifteenth amendments were the two ex-corporation lawyers, Bradley and Field.

First—in 1876 in *United States* vs. *Reese*—they led the Court in trampling on an act to punish state officers who prevented Negroes from voting. Then—in 1883 in *United States* vs. *Harris* —they declared unconstitutional an Act of Congress protecting Negroes from the terrorism of the Ku Klux Klan. Again, in 1883, Justice Bradley wrote the majority opinion in the civil-rights case in which he declared unconstitutional Senator Sumner's act giving equal privileges to Negroes in "inns, public conveyances and theaters."

This marked the death of the Fourteenth Amendment as far as rights for Negroes were concerned, and Justice Harlan wrote a blistering dissent against his Northern colleagues who had fought a war to free the Negro and now withdrew that freedom.

"Constitutional provisions," he said, "adopted in the interest of liberty, and for the purpose of securing liberty . . . have been so construed as to defeat the ends the people desired to accomplish, and which they supposed they had accomplished by changes in their fundamental law. . . .

"It is for Congress, not the judiciary, to say what legislation is appropriate. . . . The judiciary may not, with safety to our institutions, enter the domain of legislative discretion and dictate the means which Congress shall employ in the exercise of its granted power.

"The right of a colored person to use an improved highway upon the terms accorded to freemen of other races, is as fundamental in the state of freedom established in this country, as are the rights which my brethren concede to be so far fundamental as to be deemed the essence of civil liberty."

Despite that burning dissent, Justice Harlan's "brethren" continued their interpretation of the Fourteenth Amendment, making a complete mockery of its original intent. In 1885 they followed with a decision in *Soon Hing* vs. *Crowley* upholding a city ordinance prohibiting laundry work at night, obviously aimed against the Chinese. And Justice Field of California, who had championed the right of white New Orleans butchers to their jobs, now wrote the majority opinion denying that same privilege to yellow-skinned laundrymen despite the guarantee, "nor shall any State deprive any person of life, liberty or property without due process of law."

Thus did the Supreme Court not only obliterate the acts of Congress passed to carry out the results of the Civil War, but also the Civil War amendments, passed over the hurdle of two thirds of the state legislatures and representing the opinion of the allegedly sovereign people of the United States.

Meanwhile the Court had started on its second tangent of

building up the Fourteenth Amendment as the bulwark of corporate property. This tangent did not become fully developed until there came an almost complete change in the personnel of the Court. The old Court of Civil War days was still dominated by the states'-rights inheritance of Jackson's day and the philosophy of "the people rule." Also, Justice Miller was determined to preserve the stand he had taken for the freedom of state legislatures in the slaughterhouse case.

Therefore when the state of Illinois passed a law licensing grain elevators, the majority of the Court still stood by the old Jacksonian theory, and its new chief justice, Morrison R. Waite of Ohio, advised the elevator operators in *Munn* vs. *Illinois, 1873,* to "resort to the polls, not to the courts."

However—and this was important—he did discuss in great detail the contention of the elevator operators that the Illinois law deprived them of property "without due process of law." He did not agree with their contention, but he did discuss it, and by this very discussion he helped to open the way for the much broader interpretation to come.

Simultaneously, Justice Field, who that same year so vigorously opposed the protection of Negroes under the Fourteenth Amendment in *United States* vs. *Reese,* wrote a scathing dissent branding the majority opinion as "subversive to the rights of private property, heretofore believed to be protected by constitutional guarantees against legislative interference."

After the case of *Munn* vs. *Illinois* in 1876, there occurred in short succession, four important changes in the personnel of the Court. Justices Strong, Clifford, Swayne and Hunt, all remnants of the Civil War days and inheritors of the Jacksonian states'-rights theory, either died or resigned. They were replaced by William B. Woods, a Georgia politician and supine worshiper of vested interests; Stanley Matthews, a director in the Knoxville & Ohio Railroad and chief attorney for Jay Gould's railway interests; Horace Gray, an affluent Massachusetts judge; and Sam Blatchford, a New York railroad lawyer.

These four changed the entire viewpoint of the Court. They

represented a new era in the history of the United States, the
era of the promoter, the exploiter, the entrepreneur, the de-
mander of high protective tariffs, the organizer of monopolies
and trusts. The cry of that era was for unrestricted competition,
for a hands-off policy by state and federal governments. And
when the states did step in to regulate, the economic rulers of
the day turned, not to the polls, but to the Supreme Court,
and after the appointment of these four new justices they did
not turn in vain.

These four represented the viewpoint already so dynamically
expressed by Stephen J. Field, chief court champion of big business. He was typical of that land-grabbing, railroad-building,
monopoly-rampant era which believed that to the victor belong
the spoils. Born in Connecticut, he moved to California with
the gold rush of '49, became a powerful legal figure in the new
state and was appointed to the Supreme Court by Lincoln during the heat of the Civil War. He remained on the Court nearly
thirty-five years, during part of which he became so eccentric
and senile that, according to Charles Evans Hughes, a committee of fellow justices asked him to resign. Long before this,
however, one of his opinions caused such a furor that in 1889
he was assaulted in a California railroad station by Judge David
S. Terry, who was shot and killed by a deputy marshal appointed to defend Field. In that same year his nephew, David
J. Brewer, was appointed to the Supreme Court. Brewer had
studied law in his uncle's office and worshiped the ground the
old Justice walked on. In fact, while a United States district
judge in Kansas, Brewer actually refuted the Supreme Court's
majority opinion in *Munn* vs. *Illinois* and handed down opinions conforming to the minority dissent of his uncle. Brewer's
appointment to the Supreme Court, therefore, meant that for
ten years Field exercised two votes instead of one.

It was in 1885, a few years after these four important personnel changes had taken place, that the Court first narrowed its
decree—in *Munn* vs. *Illinois*—that the states had the power to
regulate utilities. Mississippi had established a commission to

regulate railroad rates, and the carriers immediately rushed to the Supreme Court, invoking, as their defense, Justice Field's dissent in *Munn* vs. *Illinois*. They lost their case, but won a victory for corporate interests in general. For Chief Justice Waite now junked the "resort to the polls" principle he had enunciated nine years before and laid down the dictum that while the states did have the right to enact laws regulating utilities, there were good regulatory measures and bad regulatory measures, and the Court—not the ballot—would decide which was which.

From this it was but a short jump to another expansion of the Fourteenth Amendment and of the Court's power. That same year the Southern Pacific Railroad sued to set aside a new California law taxing corporations at a higher rate than individuals, and ex-Senator Roscoe Conkling, famous Tammany politician, appearing before the Supreme Court in defense of the railroad, argued that a corporation also was a person and that the civil rights of persons guaranteed by the Fourteenth Amendment also extended to the property rights of corporations. He even said—although it appeared to be a very tardy inspiration —that, as a member of Congress when the Fourteenth Amendment was drafted, he had helped insert the due-process clause as a protection of corporate property.

The Court accepted his thesis.

From that milestone in 1885, the next step was the historic decision in *Chicago, Milwaukee & St. Paul Railroad* vs. *Minnesota* in 1890. Between those years, however, Chief Justice Waite had died, being replaced by Chief Justice Melville W. Fuller of Chicago. Justice Miller, the ardent abolitionist who still sat upon the Court, once said: "It is vain to contend with judges who have been the advocates of railroad companies, and all the forms of associated capital, when they are called upon to decide cases where such interests are in contest. All their training, all their feelings are from the start in favor of those who need no such influence."

The new Chief Justice who succeeded Waite was the former attorney of Marshall Field, of the Armour meat-packing company and, most important of all, the Burlington Railroad. Also, just before the important *Chicago, Milwaukee & St. Paul Railroad* vs. *Minnesota* case came up, Justice Brewer, nephew of Field, was appointed associate justice.

So the Court now reversed its decision in *Munn* vs. *Illinois* and declared unconstitutional the Minnesota act regulating railroads —justifying its move once more by the Fourteenth Amendment.

It had taken twenty-two years to do it, but decision by decision the rights of men slowly had been commuted into the rights of corporations to resist legislation. "Liberty," as interpreted by the Supreme Court, now had become property. "Due process of law" had come to mean the approval of the Nine Old Men.

But this trampling on the legislative power, handed down by Justice Blatchford, an ex-railroad attorney, was too much even for Justice Bradley to swallow. Bradley himself once had been director of the United Railway Companies of New Jersey. But now he handed down a dissent reeking with indignation.

"I cannot agree to the decision of the Court," he wrote. "It practically overruled *Munn* vs. *Illinois* and the several railroad cases that were decided at that time. The governing principle of those cases was that the regulation and settlement of the fares of railroads and other public accommodations is a legislative prerogative and not a judicial one. This is a principle which I regard as of great importance. We declare, in effect, that the judiciary, and not the legislature, is the final arbiter in the regulation of fares and freights of railroads and the charges of other public accommodations. It is an assumption of authority on the part of the judiciary which, it seems to me, with all due respect to my brethren, it has no right to make."

Having completely distorted the Fourteenth Amendment, the Court now set up in its stead its own omniscient wisdom. And having already swallowed the Constitution, it became a body of experts, which from 1890 legislated as such, its decisions determined not by law but by what the economic views and prejudices of a majority of the Court happen to be on that particular issue.

Thus the Supreme Court, created by the founding fathers as a tribunal of law, has spent its latter days in deciding whether acts regulating Chinese laundries, Johnson grass on railroad rights of way, the manufacture and sale of oleomargarine, unripe lemons, bird shooting by aliens, oyster planting by non-residents, stock exchanges, private schools, trading stamps, cemeteries, ticket scalping in New York, kosher meat, boric acid, window screens in soft-drink emporiums, street-car fares, railroad rates, utility profits, chain stores, junk dealers, prostitutes in New Orleans, chiropractors, sheep grazing in Idaho, importation of Texas cattle into Missouri, the size of bread in Chicago, Greek-letter fraternities, and hundreds of other similar measures, are sound economic practice.

During thirty years between 1890, when the Fourteenth Amendment was completely emasculated, and 1920, more than seven hundred state and federal acts were declared unconstitutional in the holy name of "due process."

And as the years have passed, the pace of the Court in declaring federal laws unconstitutional has accelerated. During the first seventy-five years of its history and up until the last part of the Civil War in 1864 only two federal statutes were declared unconstitutional. During the next sixty years, up until 1924, the pace jumped to fifty-three, or an average of almost one a year. But during the twelve years from 1924 to 1936 the appetite of the Nine Old Men became insatiable, and the number of federal acts which went down the maw of unconstitutionality increased to twenty-three or an average of almost two a year. And during the two vital years of the Roosevelt administration, a total of twelve state and federal acts either sponsored by or in tune with New Deal policies were scuttled by the Supreme Court.

As the appetite of the Nine Old Men became more insatiable, their taste became more demanding. No longer were they content with biting off laws regulating Johnson grass on railroad rights of way, or the location of a children's home in Seattle, or railroad side tracks and switches in Nebraska. Their appetite reached out for laws extending to the vitals of the nation. Child-labor laws, pension laws, workmen's-compensation laws, minimum-wage and maximum-hour laws, laws to curb utility rates and profits, to prevent monopoly, to tax corporate interests, to protect investors from fraud and deception, to ensure honest weight and purity of product, to safeguard the health and lives of users of public conveyances, to succor agriculture from a disastrous depression and to secure for labor the right to organize collectively—all went down the ravenous maw of the Nine Old Men.

They had become legislators, not jurists. They had taken into their own hands the right of self-government for which our colonial ancestors fought a long-drawn-out war against Great Britain; and while no British court can supersede an act of Parliament, the descendants of those who once fought Britain for legislative liberty have found that liberty deftly stolen from their hands.

"When I look at the work of Congress," remarked Justice Cardozo, whose great-uncle administered the oath of office to George Washington, "and when I compare it with the decrees of the Supreme Court at times when its members have tried to act as legislators, I cannot but be impressed that Congress was right every time."

Conditions have changed since the Dred Scott decision in 1857. At that time the conservative forces of the nation were in the South. Slavery was the great vested property of that period. The Republican party represented the radical forces of the North, and the Supreme Court, packed by Jackson and overwhelmingly Democratic, was the guardian of the Southern reaction.

Today the stronghold of conservatism and wealth lies in the industrial North and East. That area has profited by a high protective tariff as the South once prospered through the protection of slavery.

And today the Supreme Court has become the protector of

the industrial overlords. Its staunchest supporters are the Du Ponts, the Morgans, the Mellons, the Rockefellers, Alfred E. Smith, John W. Davis, Herbert Hoover, the United States Chamber of Commerce, the National Manufacturers' Association, all representatives of an industrial oligarchy, all laboring to deify the judiciary, the doctrine of judicial autocracy; all striving to block legislation to redistribute the wealth of the nation, to remedy the forces which catapulted the country into the last depression.

The war over the protection of Southern slavery is a thing of the past. But, remembering the three wounds he received fighting its battles, and thinking, no doubt, of the possibility of war over the protection of industrial slavery, Oliver Wendell Holmes once told Tom Corcoran, his secretary:

"A shoemaker must stick to his last, sonny, a lawyer must stick to the law. When we try to be legislators we get into trouble.

"I saw what those fools took us into in the Civil War, and I don't want to go through that hell ever again."

CHAPTER IV

The Man on the Flying Trapeze

Shortly after Chief Justice Taft died, the late Joseph P. Cotton, Undersecretary of State, was called to the White House by Mr Hoover for advice as to whom he should appoint as Taft's successor. Hoover, who leaned heavily upon Cotton in all important matters, told him that he wanted to elevate his old friend Justice Stone to that office, but considered himself under obligation to Charles Evans Hughes, who had campaigned most effectively in his behalf, and who, he felt, carried great prestige throughout the nation.

Cotton agreed emphatically that Stone was the man for the chief justiceship, and mentioned the idea of elevating Judge Learned Hand, of the United States Circuit Court in New York, as a successor to Stone as associate justice.

"What I would like to do," said Hoover, "is to offer Hughes the appointment but make sure that he will turn it down."

"That's very simple," suggested Cotton. "Hughes's son, Charles Evans, Junior, is Solicitor General and argues the government's cases before the Supreme Court. If his father became chief justice he would have to resign, and I'm sure Hughes wouldn't have him do that. Hughes is almost seventy years old. He has lived his life. He has received almost every honor there is to receive. He doesn't need the job, while being Solicitor General means a great deal to his son who is just at the start of his public career. So you can offer Hughes the appointment and be sure that he will turn it down."

Hoover thought this was sound reasoning and got Mr Hughes on the long-distance telephone immediately.

"Mr Hughes," he said, "I would like to offer you the chief justiceship of the Supreme Court."

Without a moment's hesitation, Hughes replied:

"Mr President, this is a very great honor indeed. I accept."

Hoover and Cotton looked at each other in astonishment. Then the latter exploded:

"Well, I'll be damned! Can you beat that? The old codger never even thought of his son."

Charles Evans Hughes is the No. 1 high-aerial acrobat of Big Top politics.

He has swung back and forth from liberalism to economic stultification with greater ease than the daring young man on the flying trapeze; and it is only now, at the zenith of his career, that he shows signs of losing his nerve and his balance.

He swung from the family of a poor Baptist preacher into a prosperous New York law firm; then to the academic atmosphere of a professorship at Cornell and after two years back to New York and corporate law again; then from the crusading attorney for New York's investigation of the gas and insurance rackets to governor of the state; then from one of the most liberal dissenters on the Supreme Court to a dull and inept Republican candidate for the presidency; then, after more New York law fees, he swung into the State Department and a record as one of the most outstanding and forthright Secretaries of State in recent history; then, after six years in which he raked in lush law fees from almost anyone who would hold out his hand, Charles Evans Hughes swung into the chief justiceship of the Supreme Court.

Only one star has guided these oscillations between the service of corporate interests and service of the public. It is the manner in which Mr Hughes best could serve himself.

As chief justice, Mr Hughes has run back and forth so frantically between the liberals on one side and the reactionaries on the other in an effort to preserve harmony that he has lost the respect of both. And at this, the climax of his life, having lived three quarters of a century, he finds his treasured court more bitterly torn asunder than at any time since the Civil War.

Despite his stately bearing, Charles Evans Hughes today is the most pathetic figure on the Supreme Court.

Mr Hughes was born in Glens Falls, New York, as the Civil War reached its second bitter year. From the age of three, there was little doubt that he was destined for bigger and better things. He learned to read between the ages of three and four and, shortly after he was five, laid before his father an original plan of study, including Herodotus, Homer and Virgil. After that, young Charles was taken from kindergarten and tutored by his mother, a woman of considerable brilliance and of Scotch-Irish, English and Dutch descent. Hughes's father was a Baptist preacher of pure Welsh descent, and the family led an itinerant life, seldom more than four years with one church flock. At the age of eight, Charles was reading Shakespeare, and the Bible from the Greek. The family lived in Newark, N. J., at that time, then moved to New York City, where Charles graduated from high school at eleven, and at thirteen tried to enter Colgate University, at that time known as Hamilton College.

Young Hughes's life did not appear to be a very happy one. He was timid, slight, definitely the bookworm type and had few friends. Undoubtedly his retiring youth had something to do with the great difficulty he experienced in making a popular campaign for the presidency. He had promised his father that he would not read a novel until he had finished college, and perhaps it was this pledge which inspired him, at the age of thirteen, to write two essays on "The Evils of Light Literature" and "The Limitations of the Human Mind."

So Charles read his Bible, his Latin and his Greek, graduated from Brown University—to which he had transferred—at the age of nineteen, and after one year of teaching at the Delaware

Academy, Delhi, N. Y., he entered the Columbia Law School, from which he graduated with highest honors plus a prize of $500 annually for three years.

During the next three years young Hughes grubbed as a clerk in the firm of Chamberlain, Carter & Hornblower by day and taught at Columbia at night. It was a drab and dreary life, as testified by his pallid face and none too robust health. But in the middle of it he met Antoinette Carter. Antoinette was the daughter of Walter S. Carter, a partner in Hughes's firm. In 1888 he married Antoinette, and simultaneously her father left his old firm to form a new partnership with his son-in-law and Paul D. Cravath, for many years the attorney and confidential agent for Thomas F. Ryan, notorious for the corruption of state legislature and city councils in behalf of his utility and insurance interests.

Hughes was then twenty-six years old and a partner in one of New York's leading law firms. From a pecuniary point of view, his legal career was made. Big corporation clients began to come his way, among them the United States Illuminating Company and the Mount Morris Electric Light Company, for whom Hughes secured an injunction to prevent Mayor Grant of New York City from forcing the companies to put their electric wires underground. "An invasion of the rights of property" was what Hughes termed Mayor Grant's attempted action, which brought a scathing rebuke from the presiding judge. Another client was the New York, Westchester & Boston Railway, suspected of being the secret subsidiary of the Morgan-controlled New Haven road, which desired terminal facilities in Manhattan. Hughes got the terminal.

Hughes worked as hard for his corporate clients as he did on his books at Brown and Columbia, with the result that he approached a physical breakdown. His doctors advised him to give up the practice of law, and he turned to a professorship at Cornell. Two years later, however, the financial crash of 1893 proved a heyday for the legal profession and brought him hustling back to New York. For the next twelve years he concentrated on making money and building up a reputation as an able and hard-working attorney. Then in 1905 the New York Legislature created the Stevens Commission to investigate gas rates; and Henry W. Taft, brother of the late President and a warm admirer of Hughes, secured his appointment as counsel for the commission.

Next to his marriage to Antoinette Carter, this was one of the most important events in Hughes's life. Overnight he found himself catapulted from the position of a successful but relatively obscure New York lawyer to the center of one of the most dramatic and spotlighted investigations ever held in New York State. Hughes threw himself into it with all the zeal and resourcefulness which he had given to his corporation clients and, in a series of sensational hearings, revealed that the Consolidated Gas Company had a monopoly of New York gas business and was charging extortionate rates based on a huge watered-stock valuation. Hughes forced a rate reduction from $1.00 to 80¢ and was acclaimed as a fighting liberal. The Republican leaders of New York, desiring to capitalize on his popularity, offered him the mayoralty nomination, but he declined. Next year Hughes once again headed a New York State investigation, this time of insurance companies, and again his sensational exposures rocked the country—although for some reason the probe did not prevent a group of insiders from obtaining control of the big companies. The House of Morgan emerged with the New York Life in its grip. Harriman gained dominance over Mutual Life, and Ryan secured possession of the $470,000,000 of Equitable's assets for a song.

Hughes, however, was sitting on top of the world. Only forty-four years old, he was the most prominent figure in New York. Again the Republican bosses made an offer, this time of the gubernatorial nomination; and this time he accepted.

Despite the bombardment he had just given big business, Wall Street ladled out generously for his war chest. Hughes's opponents charged that his friend and former partner Cravath had assured the big boys that Hughes was a "safe man." Hughes's friends, on the other hand, contended that the financial interests feared him and were trying to curry his favor. Whatever the reason, their contributions flowed freely, amounting to $313,923. J. P. Morgan & Co. and Levi P. Morton each gave $20,000; Andrew Carnegie and J. D. Rockefeller, Jr, $5,000 each; Harvey Fisk & Sons, Chauncey M. Depew, J. and W. Seligman & Co., Kuhn, Loeb & Co., $2,500 each; and Charles Schwab, Edward Gould, Jacob Schiff and several others chipped in one to two thousand dollars.

As governor, Hughes reflected both his strict Baptist background and his apprenticeship in representing big business. With a great clatter of moral indignation he attacked race-track gambling and had it banned from the state. He also sponsored and put through some mild reforms in insurance-company regulations, plus a direct-primary act—the latter after a noisy tussle with party leaders. But while stepping on the toes of the political bosses, the economic rulers of New York could make no real complaint. Hughes vetoed a two-cent railroad rate bill and strongly opposed the constitutional amendment for an income tax. And when Manhattan civic leaders petitioned him to take legal action against District Attorney Jerome for failing to prosecute Thomas F. Ryan—client of Hughes's ex-law partner—for looting the traction company, the Governor sidestepped and appointed a commissioner to "investigate." The investigator gave the District Attorney a clean bill of health—despite damaging admissions by him—and Hughes dismissed the case.

On the whole, Hughes's gubernatorial record fell short of the expectations aroused by his crusading investigations. It was a mixed picture, however, and he was regarded as such a Frankenstein monster by the Republican bosses who made him that President Taft was openly accused of conspiring with the bosses just at the time Hughes was pushing a regulation-of-utilities bill, by offering him an appointment to the Supreme Court.

Whatever the motive may have been, Mr Hughes lost no time in accepting, with the result that the bill was shelved. Whereupon friends who had furthered the crusading portions of his career sighed regretfully and observed: "Well, that's the end of Hughes."

The politicians and his old friends in Wall Street also sighed, but with relief. They would have been wiser, however, had they saved their breath. For no sooner did Hughes reach the cloistered chamber of the Supreme Court than he threw aside the restraint that had featured his years as governor and swung back to the militancy which featured his days as investigator for the Stevens and Armstrong committees. He upheld social, labor and anti-trust measures. He championed the right of federal and state governments to regulate utilities, railroads and industry. In the six years that he served on the Court, he voted with the liberal wing 51 times, with the conservatives only 10 times, as against a record for Justice Holmes of 37 votes on the liberal side and 32 on the conservative.

Furthermore, when Wilson named Brandeis to the Court early in 1916, Hughes did everything he could privately to assist his confirmation and, when the Senate finally voted approval, was the first to extend the hand of welcome to his new colleague.

Had Hughes continued on the Court, no doubt he would have hewn out a name as lustrous as that of any jurist in American history. But he was still young, still ambitious, still had his eye riveted on the main chance. And in 1916 the clamor of the Republican party—which had healed the wounds of the Bull Moose split in 1912—offered a chance which the once poverty-stricken son of a Baptist preacher could not pass up.

Prospects for a Republican victory appeared bright, and Hughes's name soon began to figure prominently as a nomination possibility. Fifty-four years old, in vigorous health and with an aura of liberalism about him, he appealed to the G. O. P. bosses as just the man to oppose the lofty Democratic President. At first Hughes was aloof and chilly, refusing to declare whether he would accept the nomination. But as the drive to "Draft Hughes" gained momentum, a storm of criticism arose against involving the Supreme Court in party politics, so finally Hughes issued a statement categorically denying that he was a candidate.

"Under no circumstances," he said, "will I permit my name to be used, and if used I will not accept the nomination."

Republican leaders, however, took these words in their stride and continued to line up delegates for him. They knew their man. A little later the Republican convention nominated Hughes as its standard bearer. That same day he resigned from the Court and telegraphed his acceptance.

The campaign which followed was issueless and inept. Mr Hughes's years on the bench had dulled his never too keen political sense. He continued to be the Judge, austere, magisterial, far above the realm of politics and its dross. He ducked everything savoring of controversy and was the acme of self-confidence and political ignorance. On one matter, however, he was adamant. He insisted on touring the country.

Angus McSween, veteran political writer of the now extinct Philadelphia *North American,* Hughes's ablest adviser, strongly counseled against this plan. He urged him to stay in New York and shun a swing around the circuit.

"No one has ever been elected who toured the country as against a candidate who stayed at home," McSween argued.

Hughes refused to be convinced.

"I've led a cloistered life," he contended. "The people know me as a name but not personally. I feel that I have to get out among them, show myself, talk to them."

"Well, what will you talk about?" McSween asked.

"Why . . . the *Titanic,* and the necessity of reorganizing the Coast and Geodetic Survey to prevent similar disasters."

"All right. What else?"

"I think I shall also talk on the importance of the Civil Service."

McSween mopped his brow, but continued:

"What else?"

"I have not thought that out yet, but probably I can repeat some of these speeches."

McSween pointed out that in the modern days of telegraph and newspapers, repetition was impossible. He also pointed to the factional fights within the Republican party as a result of the 1912 split, into which Hughes would be dragged.

"I am a candidate for the presidency, not for state office," replied Hughes with all his dignity.

But exactly what McSween predicted took place. Hughes found it next to impossible, despite his tremendous energy, to maintain a sufficient freshness in his speeches. The Old Guard Republicans took charge of his train, refusing to let the remnants of Roosevelt's Bull Moosers get near him. Hughes was made the goat and lost four out of five states he visited.

On election night, however, Hughes retired believing himself the next President of the United States. A little after midnight a newspaper man called at his house to tell him that California was in doubt.

"The President cannot be disturbed," announced young Charles Hughes, Jr.

The newspaper man persisted.

"You will have to come back in the morning; the President cannot be disturbed."

"Well, when he wakes up just tell him that he isn't President," the reporter replied.

Hughes never got over that defeat. At first he could not believe that he had been defeated and waited several days before sending the customary telegram of congratulations to President Wilson. The telegram was worded in such unsportsmanlike language that it shocked the country. Several years later he repeated this partisanship, when Wilson, early in 1918, appointed Hughes as special federal investigator of the wartime aviation industry which the United States was heavily subsidizing. Wilson had named Hughes with the hope of getting an impartial and non-partisan investigation, but for months Hughes conducted his inquiry in secret, carefully holding up his findings until November 1, when, on the eve of crucial congressional elections, he made public a report of a most damaging nature politically. He charged Colonel Deeds, chief government representative in the aviation industry, with "highly improper conduct" and recommended court-martial. In substantiation of his accusation, Hughes quoted four telegrams exchanged between Deeds and former business associates.

Two months later the War Department, after investigating Hughes's charges, completely vindicated Colonel Deeds and disclosed the fact that, in publishing four telegrams, Hughes suppressed a fifth which would have exonerated the aviation officer.

After his defeat for the presidency, the Hughes trapeze swung back to corporate law practice. The one-time crusader against big business became the darling of Wall Street, and his first case was in defense of a notorious Tammany graft contract.

Hughes made money, but at the same time he kept his eye on the political arena and brought his sonorous oratory and prepossessing appearance into full play on behalf of Warren Gamaliel Harding in 1920, with the result that he was appointed Secretary of State. As such he sat for several years alongside Harry M. Daugherty, Albert B. Fall, and Edwin Denby, never raising his voice against their depredations.

He did raise his voice, however, to prevent an attempt at an investigation proposed by Senator Couzens of Michigan into the administration of the tax laws under Secretary of the Treasury Mellon. Hughes wrote a secret brief in which he expounded the startling theory that Congress had no constitutional right to investigate a department of the executive branch of the government, and Harding sent the document to Capitol Hill as a special message over his signature. Judging by the tax-evasion suits subsequently brought against Charles E. Mitchell, Pierre S. Du Pont, Thomas S. Lamont and Mr Mellon himself, the investigation was more than justified.

But, compared with his contemporaries, Hughes was an excellent Secretary of State. He was vigorous, forceful, with an amazingly efficient command of all the details of his vast office. At times he even showed flashes of the old liberalism which made him such a powerful dissenter during his early days on the Supreme Court.

But again his strict Baptist background clashed with a life-time of private practice for big corporations. Hughes pushed the principle of peace at the Washington Arms Conference and in many negotiations with Latin-American countries, withdrawing the Marines from Santo Domingo and Nicaragua. At the same time he waged a stupendous battle for the programs of big corporations abroad, especially the oil interests, and in Turkey was charged by the American-owned Turkish Petroleum Company with discrimination in favor of the Standard Oil interests which later retained him as attorney.

Hughes performed an excellent but little-noticed job in dispelling much of the bitterness which Latin-American nations had harbored against the "Colossus of the North." He took this mission most seriously and, in 1924, made a good-will pilgrimage to Rio de Janeiro to open the Brazilian Exposition and to dedicate the laying of the cornerstone of a monument given the city of Rio by the American colony.

Since leaving the State Department, Hughes has given unsparingly of his time and energy to aid Pan-American friendship. He spent two months at the sixth Pan-American Conference in Havana in 1928, where he served as chief of the American delegation and steered a reasonably harmonious course through the multitudinous pitfalls of Pan-American politics. Again, in 1929, he abandoned his law practice to serve on the Pan-American Arbitration Conference and helped to draft the fairest arbitration and conciliation treaties ever approved by the Senate. Again, in 1932, he acted as neutral arbitrator for the long-smoldering boundary dispute between Guatemala and Honduras and remained in Washington through most of the summer's heat, working on the case. For this and similar services he refused to take any honorarium, informing the State Department, which offered to remunerate him:

"The justices of the Supreme Court should take care of these little judicial jobs as a patriotic duty."

It was while attending one of these Pan-American conferences

four years after his trip to Rio de Janeiro that Franklin Adams
of the Pan-American Union approached Mr Hughes with a sad
tale of woe.

Mr Hughes, at that time, was looking exceptionally pleased
with himself, having just scored a diplomatic victory for the
United States.

"Mr Hughes, do you remember that good-will pilgrimage of
yours down to Rio de Janeiro?" Mr Adams asked.

"Of course," replied Mr Hughes, looking even more pleased.
"I have a distinct recollection of that event. It was a great
occasion. It did much to promote harmony between the United
States and Latin America. There should be other such occasions."

"And do you remember, Mr Hughes, the cornerstone you laid
for the monument to be erected by the American colony in
honor of Brazilian-American friendship?"

"Ah, I do indeed," replied Mr Hughes, almost bursting with
pride. "That also was a great occasion. Other Secretaries of State
should go south and get acquainted with our Latin-American
neighbors and dedicate more monuments to our friendship."

"But do you know what's happened to that monument?"

"No. I trust nothing of an untoward nature."

"It's still in a warehouse waiting to be erected, and all the
Brazilians are wondering what's become of it," replied Adams.
"You see, you only laid the cornerstone, and afterward the
American colony found they would have to spend $30,000 on a
marble pedestal which they had forgotten about. But about that
time the price fell out of the coffee market, and they have never
been able to finish it."

So Mr Hughes, perpetual apostle of Pan-American peace, dug
down into his jeans and helped contribute toward the cost of
finishing the monument which he had dedicated to Brazilian-
American friendship.

Charles Evans Hughes resigned from the State Department on
the excuse that he had to recoup his personal fortune. It was
true that the money he had raked in as attorney for big business

had dwindled almost to the vanishing point, but he recouped with astonishing celerity. Along with John W. Davis, former American ambassador to the Court of St. James's, Hughes was singled out as the chief Supreme Court attorney of the country. Scores of cases flocked to his office, including that of Truman H. Newberry, convicted of spending $178,000 to become senator from Michigan, whereas the Corrupt Practices Act permitted only $10,000. Hughes turned down none of them and lost most of them. This, of course, was to be expected. Most of the cases which came his way already were lost and were put in his hands on the last lone chance that a man with his prestige as former justice of the Supreme Court and a former Secretary of State could win.

Hughes developed a reputation at this time for being slipshod and careless in his legal preparation. This was not, perhaps, entirely his fault. He handled so many cases that obviously it was a physical impossibility for him to be thoroughly familiar with all of them, and his delivery gave the appearance of having taken a brief handed him by an underling in his law office and memorizing it on the train en route from New York.

Hughes has a photographic mind which can grasp and retain every detail with a few minutes' glance, after which his delivery is as automatic as a phonograph. If a member of the Court knocked him off the beaten track of his speech with a question, Hughes came right back to the exact word and sentence where he deviated from the text, and, without looking at the manuscript or even having it in his hand, picked up the sequence again. This photographic mind, his persuasive voice, his beard, his prepossessing appearance combined to make Hughes a powerful pleader before any court, and once Justice Cardozo, then on the New York Court of Appeals, remarked of Hughes: "When I am listening to that man I say to myself: how can I ever decide against him?"

But as a special pleader before the Supreme Court after his resignation from the State Department, Hughes got distinctly in wrong with his former colleagues. They felt that he was taking advantage of his former position on the bench, that he was not giving enough attention to the legal points of his cases, and as a result his former colleagues appeared to go out of their way to pick up and challenge every slip he made. And there was one occasion when Mr Hughes stood flushed and embarrassed while an attorney, arguing a case in which Hughes's clients were interested, said:

"I have ten minutes of my time left, and if it please your honors I should like to relinquish this to Mr Charles Evans Hughes whose clients share our position."

"We will proceed to the next case," ruled Chief Justice Taft, looking straight through the bearded gentleman he once appointed to the Supreme Court.

On another occasion Hughes was representing New York's Interborough subway before the Court, and in the course of his argument was interrupted by Justice McReynolds, who asked a question.

"That is immaterial," snapped back Hughes, who once sat beside Justice McReynolds on the Supreme bench.

Those in the court chamber blinked in astonishment. McReynolds glared, but said nothing. Hughes calmly continued with his dissertation.

Some time later, the Court handed down its decision—written by McReynolds. It was against the Interborough.

In 1928 Hughes returned once again to the political arena, sharing honors with William E. Borah as the chief campaign mouthpiece for Herbert Hoover. It was a weird alliance, as demonstrated eighteen months later when Borah publicly denounced his former campaign partner and voted against his confirmation as chief justice.

The fight in the Senate over Hughes's appointment lasted four days and was one of the most notable in history. It was the only case since the appointment of Roger B. Taney in which the confirmation of a chief justice has been seriously contested. The character and extent of the opposition was as surprising as it was unexpected. Tories such as Senator Carter Glass of Virginia joined liberals in the attack. Glass accused Hughes of being guilty of a "shocking lack of sensibility." Norris reviewed Hughes's career in detail, listing among his clients Swift & Company, General Electric, Victor Talking Machine, Beech-Nut Packing Company, United States Industrial Chemical Company, Wabash Railroad and the Anaconda Copper Company.

"No man in public life," declared the Senator from Nebraska, "so exemplifies the influence of powerful combinations in the political and financial world as does Mr Hughes. During the last five years he has appeared in fifty-four cases before the Supreme Court. Almost invariably he has represented corporations of almost untold wealth. His viewpoint is clouded. He looks through glasses contaminated by the influence of monopoly as it seeks to get favors by means which are denied the common, ordinary citizen."

In the end, Hughes was confirmed. But it was a sour victory. Twenty-six votes were rolled up against him, and Republican senators in the privacy of the cloakrooms said that had they been free to do so they would have voted against the appointment.

This bare-knuckle manhandling had a chastening effect on the new Chief Justice—for a short time.

In his first term he sided with the liberal justices in upholding a New Jersey act regulating fire-insurance rates and an Indiana tax on chain stores; in demanding a fair trial for a Negro in the District of Columbia; in throwing out a vicious Minnesota newspaper-gag law and a moronic California red-flag statute. He also joined with the liberals in dissenting in the famous MacIntosh case in which a Canadian-born professor of philosophy at Yale was denied citizenship because he refused to take the oath to bear arms in the event of any war.

But it is significant that most of these were civil-liberties cases. On the basic economic questions of control of wealth, it was to be another story. And one court term after his appointment, Hughes had forgotten all about the salutary warning issued by the Senate and was planting his large and heavy feet almost as squarely in the path of progress as his four irreconcilable colleagues.

Age has mellowed Hughes considerably. He has now learned what might have elected him President in 1916—the art of being human. The austerity inherited from the schoolboy days when he was an aloof Latin grind has melted now, and few members of the Court are as charming, as sociable, and have such a delightful sense of humor. Hughes learned the art of unbending chiefly when he was Secretary of State. When he puts his mind to mastering anything, Hughes can do it, and as Secretary of State he deliberately set himself the task of banishing the icy manner which once caused him to be known as "Chilly Charlie" and the "Baptist Savonarola." As Secretary of State, Hughes's press conference set a precedent for straightforward information plus good-natured bantering which has not been equaled by a Secretary of State since.

The Chief Justice also has been much more tolerant of criticism than some of his colleagues on the Supreme bench—even more tolerant, perhaps, than the liberal Stone. As governor of New York in 1908, Hughes once told the New York Manufacturers' Association: "When there is muck to be raked, it must be raked, and the public must know of it, that it may mete out justice. . . . Publicity is a great purifier," he continued, "because it sets in motion the forces of public opinion, and in this country public opinion controls the courses of the nation."

As chief justice, Mr Hughes must have winced when the spotlight of publicity was none too kind to him. He could not, for instance, have been enthusiastic over the Chace Dancing School rhythmical interpretation of the Court, in which the three minority justices dance together on one side, the five majority members on the other, with Mr Hughes hovering uncertainly between. But whatever his reactions were, he was wise enough not to let anyone know them.

In fact Mr Hughes even displayed a certain sense of humor regarding the relentless pounding the Court received from some representatives of the press and public. One of the most formidable judicial assemblies in the country is the annual conference of the senior federal circuit of judges, held in Washington just before the opening of the fall court term and presided over by the Chief Justice. In the fall of 1935, when criticism of the Court's New Deal decisions was rampant, Mr Hughes opened this annual meeting with the following grave observation:

"Gentlemen, I have noticed with much satisfaction the great amount of public interest in the proceedings of the Supreme Court this past year. I am glad that our citizens are so attentive, for there was a time, not so long ago, when I thought we were in danger of being overlooked.

"As an earnest example of this reawakened public interest, I hold in my hand a letter recently received. It is addressed to John Marshall, Chief Justice of the United States."

With continued gravity Mr Hughes added:

"I have been in a quandary as to where I should forward this letter, as I do not know the ultimate destination of our distinguished predecessor."

On another occasion, the Kansas City Terminal case was before the Court, and Attorney Frank H. Towner was engaged in a lengthy explanation of what the case involved, when Chief Justice Hughes interrupted.

"Young man," he said, "aren't you ever going to get down to the law in this case?"

"Yes, your honor," replied Towner, "but I wanted to give the Court some atmosphere."

"This Court has already got enough atmosphere," shot back Hughes. And then, nudging Justice Van Devanter on his right, he gave him a broad smile and a knowing wink.

The Chief Justice's family life is extremely happy. He and Mrs Hughes are real comrades, and she has contributed a great deal to his success, not merely in the early days when her allowance was far greater than his meager income, but also in advice, inspiration and sympathetic understanding.

Mr Hughes is still something of an old-fashioned Baptist puritan, though he does not give the time to the church that he did in New York, where he organized the famous Bible class later turned over to John D. Rockefeller, Jr.

It was with real conviction that Hughes, as Secretary of State, negotiated the rum-running treaties by which the United States was permitted to seize and search foreign vessels outside the three-mile limit, provided they were within one hour's sailing distance from shore. Shortly after he became chief justice during the Hoover administration, the case of the captured rum-runner *Mazel Tov* came before the Supreme Court, and Solicitor General Thacher, pointing out the impossibility of ascertaining one hour's sailing distance from shore, told the Court:

"These treaties are unenforceable, impossible and never should have been written."

The Chief Justice stroked his chin thoughtfully.

Mr Hughes is a prodigious worker and does all of his work at home. Every morning after breakfast, a Supreme Court delivery truck dumps a pile of mail at the Hughes home, and the Chief Justice answers it religiously, especially letters criticizing him or the Court. This is no insignificant task, for next to the White House and Senator Huey Long, when he was alive, Mr Hughes receives the largest amount of fan mail in Washington.

Hughes works until a moderately late hour almost every night and lets nothing interfere with his health or his work. He enjoys a dinner party in the evening but, except on state occasions, seldom goes out except on Saturdays, which are booked far in advance for the entire year. In case an ambassador desires to invite the Chief Justice to dinner, he sends him a letter to that effect, and receives word as to which night, if any, the Hugheses will be free.

Mr Hughes also writes his opinions at home. He is extremely conscientious about them, but no member of the Court pours forth more prolix word torrents. They are dull, ponderous, and wade through reams of ambiguous language before coming to the conclusions. Sometimes it is impossible to tell which way a Hughes opinion is going until the final paragraphs, and this was what led the Associated Press to send out an erroneous flash in the gold cases to the effect that the government had lost.

Hughes used to get a little nettled when people stared at him on the street, and once while walking down Fifth Avenue, as Secretary of State, Charley MacArthur, famous playwright, saw him, and began walking just behind, repeating over and over again: "I know you, Mr Secretary of State, I know you, Mr Secretary of State, I know you, Mr Secretary of State."

Finally Hughes jumped into a passing taxi and fled.

The Chief Justice's striking appearance still causes him to be the object of all eyes wherever he goes, but he is more philosophic about it. Once a letter reached him which bore no name or address, only a pencil sketch of the Chief Justice. It was a perfect likeness, and the post office delivered it immediately to its proper destination. Hughes kept the envelope as a great joke on himself.

One of his favorite stories is how he was walking down Connecticut Avenue one morning and noticed a rather shabbily dressed stranger keeping pace with him on one side and staring in unabashed curiosity. The Chief Justice paid no attention, but the man continued to walk almost abreast of him. Finally, summoning up his courage, the stranger said:

"Pardon me, brother, but you certainly are a dead ringer for Chief Justice Hughes."

"Really," laughed the Chief Justice.

"Yes, I should think a lot of people would take you for him."

"Well, I am Chief Justice Hughes."

"Oh, g'wan and quit kidding."

Hughes has a slight touch of vanity about his appearance, just enough to make him take great pride in preserving his figure and to like the fact that his bust, featuring bare breast and beard after the manner of the ancient Greeks, is chiseled in the frieze of the new temple of justice, for all posterity to revere.

He is extremely careful about his exercise and his diet, a fact which undoubtedly contributes to his excellent physique at the age of seventy-five. During his younger days as an associate justice, he walked from his house on Sixteenth Street to the Capitol every day. Now he walks part way occasionally, but, rain or shine, he takes his setting-up exercises every morning, or, as he calls it, "girth control." His menu at lunch invariably is two poached eggs, two pieces of toast and lemon juice. On his seventy-fourth birthday he put in a full day's work and then took Mrs Hughes to see *Tobacco Road* at a downtown theater.

Many years ago Hughes declared that judges should retire when they reach the age of seventy-five. But now, as he reaches that milestone, it seems almost as if he were fighting to prevent the years from meaning what they should. Justice Holmes did just the opposite. He was always subjecting himself to soul-raking scrutiny to make sure that he was not slipping, and he would have resigned long before he did, had not his friends and colleagues dissuaded him.

To outward appearances Hughes has not aged. His once red and flaming beard is white now, but he is as erect, as hale and hearty as ever. It is only when you examine Hughes's perspectives that you realize how fast he is slipping.

Many things connected with Hughes's past have come back to haunt him in these latter years, among them his advice to Cuba as Secretary of State to plow under its sugar fields. Charley Michelson, campaign strategist of the Democratic National Committee, dug this up about the time the Chief Justice sided with the court conservatives in vetoing the AAA and crop control. Then there was the arms-embargo resolution of 1922 which Congress passed at his behest, by which the President was given the power to place an embargo against shipments of arms to Latin-American countries in case of revolution. But when Congress passed a much more restricted resolution at the behest of President Roosevelt limiting arms shipments to Bolivia and Paraguay, the lower courts threw it out on the basis of Mr Hughes's and his colleagues' ruling in the hot-oil and sick-chicken cases. But no act of his early life could have embarrassed Mr Hughes more than the statement he made as governor of New York, "The Constitution is what the judges say it is," or the book he wrote regarding the Supreme Court shortly after he retired as associate justice. Since the beginning of the feud between the judiciary and the New Deal there have been more demands for this book than for almost any other at the Library of Congress.

Mr Hughes made many sage observations in that book, and both he and the Court would be better off today had he followed them.

"In truth," he observed in discussing minority opinions, "the judges will have their convictions, and it is of the essence of the appropriate exercise of judicial power that these should be independently expressed. Divisions on close questions cannot be prevented."

But during recent years it almost seemed that Mr Hughes was solely concerned with throwing all the weight of his powerful personality to prevent too sharp dissent among his colleagues.

The climax came with the bitter-fought decision on the Agricultural Adjustment Act where all the evidence points to a last-minute switch on the part of the Chief Justice. The original alignment of the Court was 5 to 4 against the act. But Mr Hughes, once a candidate for the presidency, knew the force of public opinion in the farm belt, the bitterness of that opinion if the Supreme Court should throw out its AAA by a majority of only one vote. And also he once had written, in that fatal book of his, that "stability in judicial opinions is of no little importance in maintaining respect for the Court's work."

And so the final vote on the AAA was 6 to 3, one vote closer to Mr Hughes's coveted stability.

Following the howl of public protest against the AAA decision, Mr Hughes swung the Court back to an 8–1 vote in favor of the generally popular Tennessee Valley Authority, though in order to do it he yielded to the reactionary wing and extended the Court's powers further than ever before, claiming for it the right to review the grievances of minority stockholders in all-important questions of the constitutionality of acts of Congress.

In a decision limiting the power of the Securities and Exchange Commission to protect the investing public, Hughes was back on the side of the conservatives again; then with the liberals on the constitutionality of the Municipal Bankruptcy Acts; and finally, on the Guffey Coal Act, he neatly contrived to stay with the liberals on the question of price fixing, but voted with the reactionary majority to throw out the entire law on the grounds that minimum wages and maximum hours are unconstitutional.

Long before this, however, Hughes had lost the very thing which he sought to preserve—the prestige of his Court. Discussing the degree to which the Court lost prestige by its Dred Scott decision, Hughes wrote in his book:

"Twenty-five years later when the Court had recovered its prestige, its action in the income tax cases gave occasion for a bitter assault. . . . There can be no objection to a conscientious judge changing his vote," he continued, in discussing the income tax decision, "but the decision of such an important case by a majority of one, after one judge had changed his vote, aroused a criticism of the Court which never has been entirely stilled. At the time, the most bitter attacks were made upon Justice Shiras, who was popularly supposed to have changed his vote."

The bitter attacks upon Chief Justice Hughes came not only from the press and public, but from within the Court.

"No member of the Supreme Court is under any illusion as to the mental equipment of his brethren," according to Mr Hughes, and as case after case came up for intense and angry argument, the feeling against the Chief Justice increased. The majority distrusted him, felt that they could never depend on him. The liberals had difficulty in concealing their active dislike. And partly because of this resentment they threw to the winds all attempt at saving the prestige of Mr Hughes's Court and took definite deliberate delight in injecting additional vitriol into their dissents.

And the Chief Justice, an old man now, with warped and jaded perspective, tried to be the same proud and powerful Charles Evans Hughes of the days when he ran for President, or when he steered the postwar foreign relations of the United States. He did not realize that he was old. But he did realize and is bitterly disappointed at his tragic failure as chief justice of the United States.

That failure probably is the most tragic in contemporary history. Hughes has been an acrobatic liberal, deserting his convictions when pushed by the other side; riding into power by investigating the insurance companies and the gas monopoly, then turning round to make himself wealthy on their pay roll; swinging from private practice to public office, not for the good of the people, but to satisfy the ambition welling up within his breast.

Hughes's failure is all the more tragic because his qualifications and experience are greater than those of any other member of the Court. Little could be expected from Butler, the corporation lawyer. Or from Van Devanter and Sutherland, still living back in the days of the cowboy, the buffalo and the frontier. Or from McReynolds, who has become more prejudiced than any other member of the Court.

But Hughes was qualified more than any other member of the Court to grasp and act upon the problems of the present emergency. No other member of the bench had had previous experience on the Court—nor could be prouder of his record. No other member had held such high public office. He knew what it was to run a government. Twenty years out of his forty years of active adult life he had spent in government service. He knew the trials and tribulations of the governor of a state, the conflict of federal and state jurisdictions. And as highest member of the Harding-Coolidge cabinet, he knew the stress and strain of working with these forty-eight heterogeneous

United States on any constructive program. He knew; and he sympathized with President Roosevelt.

And yet in the crisis he lacked the courage to stand by his convictions.

Despite his vast experience, his unusual background, his powerful personality, his imposing figure, Charles Evans Hughes became a weak-kneed oscillator between the two wings of the Court, until he fell, discredited and exhausted, in the middle.

Across from the Chief Justice's home on R Street lives Mrs Howell Moorehead, a wealthy supporter of the Foreign Policy Association. Returning from a dinner one evening at about eleven-thirty, she discovered that she had forgotten her key. Ringing the doorbell several times, she was unable to arouse the servants, and one of the friends who had escorted her home began sounding his horn in order to awaken them.

Suddenly a window was thrown up across the street and an amazing apparition appeared. It was the Chief Justice of the United States, bareheaded, fist clenched, his snow-white beard set off by an even whiter old-fashioned nightgown.

"What do you mean by raising such a disturbance at this hour of the night?" he thundered. "If you do not desist, I shall summon the police."

Mrs Moorehead was so overcome by the awesome spectacle that she had her friends take her to a hotel, where she spent the night.

Poor lady! She did not know that all she had to do was argue back and the Chief Justice would have reversed himself.

CHAPTER V

Hoover's Pal

Dᴜʀɪɴɢ those cold damp mornings when Harlan Fiske Stone got up at six-thirty to play medicine ball with the President of the United States, probably neither of them dreamed that during a Republican National Convention in Cleveland several years later Mr Hoover was to thank God for the conservative majority on the Supreme Court which Justice Stone opposed, and inferentially damn his old medicine-ball partner as among those who sought to bring grief and destruction to the nation.

Nor, probably, did Herbert Hoover realize, when he delivered that speech, that the old friend whom he reviled still remained just as good a friend, just as staunch a Republican as during the days when they played medicine ball together—which illustrates one great difference between Herbert Hoover and Harlan Fiske Stone. For the latter does not let his personal likes or dislikes influence his judgment. After Mr Hoover's blast at Cleveland, Mr Stone did not take from the prize position on his desk the silver medicine ball on which is inscribed the signature of the former President of the United States. Nor did he, during the days when case after case vital to the New Deal came before him, ever let the fact that he was being urged as Republican nominee for the presidency influence his decision. Reports that he was definite presidential timber were not mere whispers in those days. Various emissaries high in Republican ranks came to him with what they said was a definite promise of nomination.

No one who is human can turn down a suggestion of this kind without serious consideration, and Stone is very human. But whatever his personal emotions may have been, no trace of them crept into his conduct on the bench. It would have been a relatively simple matter for Stone to slip over to the conservative majority on one or two of the borderline cases. It would have been easy for him to pull the punches of his historic dissent on the Agricultural Adjustment Act. Or it would have been easy not to have written the dissent at all. One or two slight shifts on his part might have enhanced his political position immeasurably, would have struck disastrously at the New Deal, of much of which he definitely disapproved.

But Harlan Stone has worked out his own philosophy regarding the functions of the courts and the Executive, and so he handed President Roosevelt a better campaign document than even his famous Brain Trust could have concocted. Casting aside all personal political ambition—if he ever had it—he declared:

"The courts are concerned only with the power to enact statutes, not with their wisdom. . . . For the removal of unwise laws from the statute books appeal lies not to the courts but to the ballot."

And then, without looking at his colleagues who had so obstinately blocked New Deal legislation, he said:

"While unconstitutional exercise of power by the executive and legislative branches of the government is subject to judicial restraint, the only check upon our own exercise of power is our own self-restraint. . . . Courts are not the only agency of government that must be assumed to have capacity to govern."

After that, all whispers of Justice Stone as presidential timber stopped.

To those who were boosting him, it was a tragic blow. But they should have been prepared for it. For Harlan Stone has been disappointing his old New York friends ever since he took his seat on the highest bench. To those who commuted with him every evening to Englewood, N. J., where he was a neighbor of Dwight W. Morrow, Thomas W. Lamont and other Morgan partners, and to those who knew him as a law partner of Herbert Satterlee, son-in-law of the elder J. P. Morgan, there was nothing in his make-up to indicate that he would become a traitor to his class. Harlan Stone in those days was considered a conservative, hard-working, solid sort of person, willing on occasion to champion the rights of mankind, but safe nevertheless. His articles in the *Columbia Law Review* were brilliant pieces of word juggling, but none of his law deviated from the accepted theories; and if today you removed the name from those early dissertations and his recent opinions no one would ever know they had been written by the same man.

But if, through some psychic power, Stone's downtown friends had known he was to be appointed to the Supreme Court and had sought to block his nomination, they would have found, had they searched carefully enough, the seeds of revolt against "his own class." They might have attached some significance, had they been interested, to the fact that Stone opposed A. Mitchell Palmer's "Red Raids," befriended Professor McKeen Cattell when he and Professor Henry Wadsworth Longfellow Dana were ousted from Columbia for pacifist preaching, and secured for Cattell a substantial settlement of his $115,000 libel suit against Nicholas Murray Butler. They might also have considered significant the fact that when Stone first was invited to become dean of the Columbia Law School, he accepted only on condition that the dictatorial Mr Butler, for whom Stone cherished no great love, should make no appointments without first consulting the law faculty. And when Mr Butler immediately went over his head with the appointment of Harry Alonzo Cushing, Stone resigned even before launching on his new duties. It was not until three years later, 1910— Stone then being only thirty-eight—that a group of professors and graduates of the Columbia Law School again forced Butler to draft Stone, this time with an agreement on professorial appointments which Butler carefully honored.

Another thing which Stone's Wall Street friends might have been squeamish about was the group of liberal professors which surrounded him. Thomas Reed Powell at that time led a little coterie of liberals on the Columbia law faculty, with whom Stone enjoyed a good natural argument. The group included Herman Oliphant, now counsel to Secretary of the Treasury Morgenthau, and Underhill Moore, now professor of law at Yale. The three made up a hard-boiled, rough-and-tumble group of liberals who kidded Dean Stone incessantly about his Wall Street connections and undoubtedly laid the foundation— though they never dreamed it at the time—for some of the most liberal philosophy ever to be handed down from the Supreme Court. Stone seemed to enjoy their company almost more than that of his dilettante Englewood neighbors, although the professors always looked at him a little askance. They could not quite get over the fact that he was a director in many of the big corporations whose practices they were always prating about, and the fact that sometimes he had defended such high-binders of finance as the Morgans.

One of these, subsequently aired in the Senate, was a case in which the heirs of the late J. P. Morgan, Senior, secured a writ of attachment against the mining property of Colonel James A. Ownbey of Boulder, Colorado, alleging that they found in the dead Morgan's assets claims against Ownbey for $200,168. In order to collect the alleged debt, Harlan Stone and Willard Saulsbury, attorneys for the Morgans, secured a writ of attachment against 3,000 shares of Ownbey's stock in the Wootten Land & Fuel Company, a very valuable property. No notice was given to Ownbey of the action, and when he learned of it in January 1916, he came to Wilmington, Delaware, where the company was incorporated, only to find that Stone and Saulsbury had written into the decree a provision that it could not be set aside without a $200,000 deposit by Ownbey. This the court granted. Ownbey, therefore, found himself unable to get the restraining order removed from his stock unless he put up $200,000, and he could not put up $200,000 for the simple reason that the Morgans' shrewd attorneys had taken the precaution of throwing Ownbey's Wootten Land & Fuel Company into receivership. Naturally, no bank was anxious to loan him money on the stock of a company in receivership.

In various petitions to the courts, Ownbey prayed for a fair and full trial, but the Supreme Court of Delaware remained closed to him unless he first put up the $200,000. Eventually he got the Supreme Court of the United States to review the question of whether or not he was entitled to a hearing on the merits of the case, at which time Stone appeared for the Morgans and made a lengthy plea before his future colleagues to the effect that, if Ownbey wanted the case to be heard on its merits, all he had to do was put up the $200,000 as the lower court had directed. In the end, Justice Pitney wrote an opinion for the majority of the Court citing the right to attach a defendant's property under the "Custom of London," and finding for Stone and the Morgans. Chief Justice White and Justice Clarke dissented.

As a result of all this, Stone's professorial colleagues were so skeptical about his legal fundamentalism and his social perambulations with the Morgans, the Morrows and the Coolidges that when he was elevated to the Supreme Court one of them gave Stone this introduction to Justice Brandeis: "For ten years, Mr Justice, I've been trying to educate him and have failed miserably. I wish you better luck."

Justice Brandeis did play an important part in the education of Harlan Stone. But he had a receptive field in which to work. The most outstanding characteristic of Harlan Stone up to that time was a broad, sympathetic understanding of mankind. Had he shut his mind to all save one narrow vista as did Van Devanter, had he come to the Court unalterably prejudiced as did Pierce Butler, then no amount of teaching at the feet of those two great philosophers, Holmes and Brandeis, could have changed him. But when Stone came to the bench he was still learning. That was in 1925, and he was only fifty-three. Today at sixty-four he is still tolerant, still open-minded, still able to learn.

But in 1925 he was groping. When he became Attorney General in 1924, supplanting the notorious Harry M. Daugherty, Stone did not immediately turn out the "Ohio Gang." It was not until he had been in office some months that he ousted the red-baiting William J. Burns as head of the Bureau of Investigation and selected in his place J. Edgar Hoover. And it was not until approximately one year of feeling his way as Attorney General that Stone was ready to open his guns against the aluminum trust for violation of the anti-trust laws—a move, incidentally, which caused his old college friend, Mr Coolidge, to act with unprecedented alacrity in boosting him upstairs into the Supreme Court.

It was typical of Stone, therefore, that he should move cautiously when first he reached the rarefied heights of the Nine Old Men. It was said of him during those early days that he was "always right the second time." His first reaction usually was toward the conservatism of his Englewood–Wall Street days. But his sturdy open-mindedness, his scrupulous fairness and broad humanitarian outlook eventually brought him round to the other side.

The fact that he was young, the fact that he developed slowly, made Stone all the more apt a pupil of Holmes and Brandeis. From the latter he got his economics (Holmes sometimes could be an arch Tory when it came to finance); and from Holmes he got his social philosophy. Stone's words today have much the same ring as those of Brandeis when he wrote *Other People's Money* many years ago—a ring which Franklin Roosevelt re-echoed in his acceptance speech at Franklin Field in June 1936. Stone has cracked down especially hard on his old associates on Wall Street, upon the "corporate officers who award to themselves large bonuses from corporate funds without the assent or even the knowledge of their stockholders"; upon the "reorganization committees created to serve the interests of others than those whose securities they control"; upon "those who serve nominally as trustees, but relieved, by clever legal devices, from the obligation to protect those interests they purport to represent"; and finally upon "the towering edifice of business and industry . . . that seemed to be the impregnable fortress of a boasted civilization, but which has developed unsuspected weaknesses."

In these words are the sting of the old lash which Brandeis used to wield; now wielded with even greater sting in the clenched fists of a pupil sixteen years his junior, just as fearless, far more energetic. Brandeis is eighty now and fading, but he taught well. His pupil will carry on for many years to come.

Oliver Wendell Holmes is gone now, but he too taught well, perhaps laid a more basic philosophy than did Brandeis. On one occasion Stone is reported to have asked the aged justice what guiding principle he had worked out during his ninety-odd years which molded his decisions. To this Holmes replied:

"Young man" (Stone was then sixty-one), "about seventy-five years ago I learned that I was not God. And so, when the people of the various states want to do something I can't find anything in the Constitution expressly forbidding them to do it, I say, whether I like it or not, 'Goddam it, let 'em do it.'"

Undoubtedly these words still were ringing in the ear of Harlan Stone when, in his historic AAA dissent, he said: "Courts are concerned only with the power to enact statutes, not with their wisdom."

You have only to look at Justice Stone to see that, whether sitting with his colleagues on the bench, or bantering with Alice Longworth at a White House reception, he enjoys his life in Washington. On the bench, however, he seems restless and bored. He is inattentive, like an outdoors man who cannot endure confinement. There is nothing classic about his features, which are pudgy and heavy-set. Head resting on his chin, he sits like a middle-aged athlete anxious to be elsewhere.

Stone began enjoying life as a husky youngster, nicknamed, because of his bulk and deviltry, "Slug" Stone. Born at Chesterfield, New Hampshire, in 1872, his father had moved the family to Amherst, Massachusetts, when Harlan was two in order that the eldest son might attend the new agricultural college on the edge of town. Here Harlan also entered after only two years of high school—which was sufficient preparation for an agricultural institution—and immediately distinguished himself as instigator of every ducking party, nightshirt parade and chapel rush which featured college life in those days. One of these proved his undoing. Stories differ as to what happened, but apparently during one chapel rush a professor grabbed young Stone by the nape of the neck, and Stone, failing to respect professorial immunity, was promptly expelled.

So Harlan went back to the prosaic task of helping his father on the farm on the edge of Amherst. His father was one of those proverbial Yankees whose shrewd understanding of human nature must have been passed on in considerable degree to the man who now sits on the Supreme Court. He had come to Amherst a landless trader. He died just one year before his son became Attorney General, the biggest taxpayer in town. He had amassed his fortune through horse swapping, cattle buying, farming, and doing anything by which he could turn a dollar, including the employment of young Calvin Coolidge as his lawyer.

Coolidge graduated from Amherst in 1895, just one year after Stone, who had persuaded the authorities to admit him despite only two years of high school and his record in the agricultural college. At Amherst, Stone harnessed his exuberance and put it to work tutoring, selling insurance, peddling typewriters, and by excelling in almost everything he did. He served for three years as president of his class, attained Phi Beta Kappa in his junior year, managed the *Amherst Student,* delivered the class oration, was voted the "man who would become most famous," and despite the protests of his father, who frowned on football, played a star game at right guard on the famous Amherst team of 1892 which defeated Williams 60 to 0. When members of his class answered the college-yearbook question: "What is the best thing the town has given to Amherst?" many of them replied: "Slug Stone."

Only once during those more mature years in Amherst did the harlequin streak in Stone crop out again. During his senior year he led a raid on a Boston express office, stealing Sabrina, goddess of Amherst men, away from alumni guardians and sending her to a barn in Chesterfield, N. H. A few years later, having worked his way through Columbia Law School by teaching, Stone married Agnes Harvey, whose father owned that barn.

The mischief in the heart of Harlan Stone bubbles up occasionally even now when he is supposed to be a sedate justice of the most dignified and powerful court in the world. He loves the theater, enjoys a good movie, is never happier than when fishing, and still is a small boy at heart.

Arriving one evening to dine with the Irish minister, Michael MacWhite, Stone stood in the doorway, glanced round at the sea of Gaelic faces, then whispered to the butler who was making the announcements: "Justice and Mrs O'Stonegal." On another occasion he attended a dinner of the New York Bar Association at which Morris Ernst took several jibes at the corporation lawyers then arguing anti-New Deal cases before the Supreme Court. Afterward several members of the New York Bar protested against Ernst's lèse majesté, and Ernst sent the protests on to Justice Stone. He received this reply: "I do not like these stuffed shirts in our profession any better than you do."

In Justice Stone's home is the fulfillment of every small boy's dream—a secret button which will cause a bookcase to swing to one side, revealing a hidden door between his study and the dining room of his house. On the walls of his study, which is a long rectangle, is a collection of etchings and caricatures, some being of his own colleagues on the bench; while at the extreme end is a neatly arranged balcony which provides a second escape into the house proper if Stone's secretary is occupied with callers in the anteroom. The house was designed by the Stones themselves, and in the attic is a studio where Mrs Stone dabbles among her water colors on those occasions when she is not too

busy keeping abreast of Washington. It is in the summer, however, that Stone really gets back to his youth. The first week
after the Court recesses in the spring finds him on the Isle au
Haut off the coast of Maine, where he mows the lawn, drives
a dilapidated old car and pulls a fishing dory between the island
and the mainland.

In Washington the Stones entertain moderately and dine out
perhaps a little more than the other justices, with the exception
of Roberts and Butler. Like his liberal colleagues, Stone delights
in the company of young people and has two sons, of whom
Marshall, the elder, is a professor of mathematics at Harvard,
while Lausen is a member of a downtown New York law firm.
There are few Mondays during the court term that Mrs Stone's
weekly "at homes" are not crowded with young people, most of
them gathered around the Justice. Stone is especially interested
in young artists and musicians and is a great devotee of the Washington municipal orchestra. Once after listening to the young
violinist, Yehudi Menuhin, he dropped in on his old friend
Justice Holmes—then ninety-two—and told him how a gangling
youth of seventeen had come before the audience, awkward, ill
at ease, lifted his bow and held three thousand people spell-
bound.

"Ah," said Holmes with a sigh, after the younger jurist had
finished, "what a triumph! I sometimes think that I would
give ten years of my life to be able to play like that."

"Yes," replied Justice Stone, "but some of us would give ten
years of our lives to be able to write opinions like yours."

Justice Holmes brightened, showed that he enjoyed the praise,
then, with a twinkle in his eye, he said:

"My boy,"—Stone was then sixty-two—"God sees through all
this modesty."

Stone's most outstanding quality is his humanness, his ability
to understand people. The groundwork for this was laid at
Columbia, where he was never too busy to see even the most
insignificant of his students; and this holds true of him today.
One day, at Columbia, W. O. Douglas, now one of the out-

standing commissioners on the Securities and Exchange Commission, was encountering rough financial sledding in his efforts to finish his course and, not knowing which way to turn, called at the Dean's office. Stone at that time was probably the busiest man at Columbia. He was a member of a downtown law firm; he also taught several classes and, as dean, had a hundred and one administrative details to handle. Douglas at that time was an unknown law student who had come East from Yakima, Washington, with hardly a cent in his pocket. Stone had no idea who he was, but nevertheless saw him immediately. Most big executives would have given a youngster of Douglas' type five minutes, if that much. They would have been constantly looking at their watch, and finally would have passed him off to an assistant. But Stone dropped everything and talked for two hours. He went over the advantages of part-time work while continuing in school, or of dropping out completely until he could recoup his finances, citing his own experience as a student in law school, when he also was broke and had to go back to teaching in Vermont until he could save enough money to return.

In the end, Douglas decided to follow Stone's example and found a teaching position in a Plainfield, New Jersey, high school. Just before leaving, however, he dropped into the Columbia Employment Bureau as a matter of routine, as he had hundreds of times before, and found an application for a ghost writer to help write a book on law. Douglas got the job, which paid him $600 and enabled him to continue at Columbia. A few years later, he was earning $18,000 at Yale, the highest-priced law professor in the country.

Stone follows the precedent set by Justice Brandeis of taking on a new law graduate every year to act as his secretary, except that Stone drafts his men from Columbia rather than Harvard. This practice is a definite inconvenience, since it is necessary to break in a new man every year. But, in compensation, both Stone and Brandeis have helped to launch some of the finest young lawyers in the country. The system has an additional disadvantage which those outside the inner court circle do not realize. For many of the justices do not write their own opinions. Stone, for instance, writes the general outline of his opinion on a pad of paper, using a thick pencil and in handwriting which almost no one can read. Then, reading his own notes, he dictates the facts and arguments in the case, a stenographer being present. Using this as a basis, the secretary whips the opinion into shape, and Stone, if necessary, revises it. The main thought is Stone's. He knows exactly what he wants to say, but is notoriously bad at expressing himself on paper. Hence his opinions during one year will be masterpieces of clarity, and the next will be long and wordy, depending upon his secretary's capacity for expression.

Professors who really get a grip on the hearts of their students are rare in our modern, highly mechanized universities. But especially are they rare in Columbia. There, a highly sophisticated, hard-boiled element adopts an attitude of "get" the professor or else he "gets" the class. The result is a sarcastic alertness on the part of the teaching staff to keep the class in its place. Student razzing by the professor has been the accepted method at Columbia—except for Dean Stone.

Stone stood before his class, twirling his eyeglasses on a black silk ribbon, never opening a book, never razzing, never raising his voice above a conversational tone. For one hour he talked, always twirling his eyeglasses. And there was something about the kindliness of his manner, his desire to meet his class more than halfway, the sense of fairness permeating everything he did, which made Stone loved and revered perhaps more than any other Columbia professor of that day. And when finally he resigned to give all his time to Sullivan & Cromwell, there were members of his class who actually wept, while the staff of the *Columbia Law Review* gathered in an atmosphere of deep dejection to speculate on how they "could carry on with this guy gone." One year later when Stone came back to address the *Law Review* dinner, he got a reception which was indescribable.

Several years after that he came back as a justice of the Supreme Court to another *Law Review* dinner. By this time a new generation had come in which had not known Stone personally. Stone's reception was enthusiastic, but his own performance was pathetic. When he arose to speak, he stammered, fumbled, looked at his notes, and finally, with a look of utter helplessness, he said: "I didn't have time to prepare a speech, but wrote out some notes coming up on the train. Now I can't even read my own notes. It proves, I suppose, what I have always said, that a man should stick to his own knitting. I hope you will forgive me." He sat down.

And indicative of the imprint Stone had left even upon a new generation was the feeling of sympathy which swept the audience.

No justice of the Supreme Court has been as close to three Presidents as Harlan Stone. Although he was one class ahead of Calvin Coolidge in Amherst, the two men did not become intimate until afterward, when young Coolidge did some legal jobs for Stone's father. As a member of the cabinet, Stone was probably as intimate as anyone could be with Calvin Coolidge, at least intimate enough to take with good-natured skepticism his promotion from a crusading Attorney General to the isolated dignity of the Supreme Court, and to warn his chief in the White House that the worst panic since 1873 was in store for him.

Stone is on moderately good terms with Roosevelt, though he does not approve of many New Deal policies; in fact, was once quoted as saying: "If the damn fools want to go to hell, it's not our duty to stop them if that's what they want to do."

It was with Hoover, however, that Stone was really intimate. The intimacy began when both were members of the Coolidge cabinet, in the days when Hoover was classed as something of a liberal. The two families lived not far from each other, frequently dined together, and a bond of friendship grew up between the two men which never weakened even during the hectic days of the depression when Stone was quite frank in favoring a large-scale public-works and relief program, subsequently adopted by Roosevelt and at that time urged upon Hoover by Dwight Morrow, Colonel Arthur Wood and others.

Hoover consulted his friend on various problems during their early-morning jousts with the medicine ball. Stone never volunteered advice. But when Hoover asked his opinion, Stone gave it frankly, and it was his warm recommendation which clinched the appointment of Justice Cardozo.

On the surface, Stone is on good terms with all of his court colleagues except McReynolds, whose rudeness he cannot tolerate. Beneath the surface, however, there is no great love lost between Stone and both Hughes and Roberts.

For the Chief Justice, Stone has no great regard, either in respect to his law or his constant efforts at compromise. Hughes's opinions he frequently regards as verbose and circuitous, and after the Chief Justice devoted twenty-two pages to upholding the constitutionality of the Harbor Workers' Compensation Act—which was not involved—and then, in the last two pages, stabbed the administrative features of the act so as to make it inoperative, Stone remarked:

"The Chief Justice is getting concise. Whenever I read one of his opinions, I feel as if I'd been through a cyclone with everything but the kitchen stove flying in my face."

This remark, published in 1932 in *More Merry-Go-Round,* did not help the co-operative endeavors of the two men, and in 1936 Mr Hughes's feverish efforts to prevent sharp diversion on New Deal legislation further vexed the straight-from-the-shoulder Stone.

Most Supreme Court justices get so afraid to open their mouths lest some hint of a future decision fall forth that they go around with a hermetically sealed expression on their faces. But Stone continues frank and outspoken, though, once or twice, remarks he has dropped to close friends, supposedly in confidence, have burst into print, causing him no end of embarrassment. One such remark was Stone's view that the Court's massacre of the Agricultural Adjustment Act made it "very difficult to draft an alternative that will meet the objections set forth by the majority. In fact," Stone added, "under the limits laid down by them I do not see how anything that helped the farmers as much as the AAA did can be devised to withstand legal attack."

After that the Justice intimated to hostesses, on occasion, that he would prefer not to have newspapermen present.

While one important decision was pending, he happened to praise the eggnog of his hostess and was informed that it was made by a secret formula.

"Can't I persuade you to let me in on the secret?" he asked.

"I'll tell you what I'll do," she replied. "I'll tell you my secret if you'll tell me yours."

One secret which did leak out, however, was Stone's relationship with Justice Roberts. Few people know it, but Stone was chiefly responsible for Roberts' elevation to the Supreme bench. When Justice Sanford died, Stone had warned Hoover against the appointment of John J. Parker, and when Parker failed of Senate confirmation it was natural that he should turn to his medicine-ball friend for advice. Stone then called attention to the work of Owen J. Roberts, who had just finished a brilliant prosecution of the Teapot Dome Oil scandals, and whom Stone had known favorably as a lawyer. As a result of this, plus the lobbying of George Wharton Pepper, Roberts was appointed. Since then no two men on the Court have written more opposing opinions. Roberts started by leaning toward the liberal side, then turned sharply to the right. And he has been the spearhead of the reactionary wing ever since. Privately, Stone feels rather bitterly about his old friend—probably as bitterly as Mr Hoover sometimes feels about his own medicine-ball partner.

Harlan Stone's basic philosophy comes into clearest relief during the private chamber sessions of the Court. More forceful than the aging Brandeis at whose feet he listened, more direct than the aesthetic Cardozo, who seems alone and isolated, Stone is the bulwark of the liberal minority. He is a shrewd, canny fighter. No military leader ever planned his moves more carefully than Stone maps his legal strategy. He watches precedents like a hawk. Other members of the Court also are alive to the importance of building up precedents which will support their own pet theses, but none are as wide awake as Stone. Long in advance of the others, he has foreseen points which might arise and worked them innocuously into the majority opinions in order to pick them up at some later date and use them to substantiate his own thesis. Particularly does he watch the decisions handed down by the Court without written opinions. These pass almost unnoticed, sometimes even by the justices themselves, since usually they are unanimous. But they contain important points of law which Stone subsequently has picked up and flaunted in the face of the reactionary majority.

Probably it was in the St Paul case in 1930 that Stone first definitely emerged from the groping period and assumed the role of one of the forthright members of the Court. The Chicago, Milwaukee & St Paul Railroad had petitioned the Interstate Commerce Commission to reorganize, and the I.C.C. had approved the reorganization plans, provided it pass also upon the fees to be paid Kuhn, Loeb & Company for financing the reorganization. On appeal to the Supreme Court a majority of the justices held with the railroad and ruled that the fee charged by the bankers was none of the I.C.C.'s business. Justices Stone, Holmes and Brandeis dissented, Stone writing a powerful opinion in which he laid down the thesis that the I.C.C. was duty-bound to protect the interests of the original St Paul bondholder.

The dissent attracted widespread attention, especially among Stone's former Wall Street associates who had not yet realized that their old friend was deserting them. Stone, all too aware of their reaction, remarked: "The New York lawyers whom I criticized never have forgiven me for that opinion, but not a single one of them ever said that I was not right.'

One of Stone's greatest victories came in the Court's conflict over the American Tobacco Company in 1932 and 1933. Probably it was in this case that he struck the stride which attained such power and brilliance during the battle between the Court and the New Deal.

The American Tobacco case hinged upon the fact that its president, George Washington Hill (who purchased a $2,500,000 life-insurance policy from Jimmy Roosevelt) awarded himself a salary, bonus and "special credits" totaling $1,283,470 in 1930, on top of which the directors voted him stock valued at $1,169,-280; while four vice presidents received an aggregate of $2,077,000 plus generous stock allowances. One of the stockholders, Richard Reid Rogers, claiming this was an unauthorized steal from the stockholders, brought suit in the New York courts; and the question which chiefly concerned the conservative majority on the Supreme Court, to which decision was appealed, was whether the American Tobacco Company, a New Jersey Corporation, could be sued in New York. In the end, Butler, always the champion of the untrammeled rights of big business, wrote a majority opinion denying Rogers the right to sue in New York. Stone wrote a minority dissent in which he emphasized the highwayman methods of George Washington Hill *et al.,* and concluded with: "This is the first time that this Court has held that a federal court should decline to hear a case on the ground that it concerns the internal affairs of a corporation foreign to the state in which it sits."

But the really important part of the American Tobacco case took place in the confidential court discussions before the decision was rendered. There Harlan Stone bared what probably is his fundamental philosophy regarding the present economic system. What he argued was that in the American Tobacco suit his conservative colleagues had an opportunity to police and perfect the capitalistic system which they were so anxious to preserve. Here was a case where the executives of a big corporation quite obviously had enriched themselves at the expense of the minority stockholders. If the profit system is to continue, Stone argued, the Supreme Court must act in cases of this kind or else the entire system eventually must be overturned by the Richard Reid Rogerses and others whom it cheats.

Stone's colleagues took a narrow view of the case, however, and threw it out. Whereupon Stone scored a unique victory. Rogers sued again, again in the New York courts, but this time against Hill and his vice presidents instead of the fiscal agents of the company. And once again, about six months later, the case came before the Nine Old Men. Meanwhile reaction against the Court had been critical, and this time the conservative majority reversed itself, came over to Stone's side, and gave him the pleasure of hearing Justice Butler himself hand down a second opinion holding that "if a bonus payment has no relation to the value of services given, it is in reality a gift in part, and the majority stockholders have no power to give away corporate property against the protest of the minority."

Stone's philosophy in the New Deal cases has been essentially that which he expressed in the American Tobacco suit. If the present capitalistic system is to persist—and he very much hopes that it will—then those who receive its chief benefits must move to share them with those who profit least. And if any group of judges, no matter how erudite and versed in the intricacies of law, seeks to prevent the legislative branch of the government from attaining, by the trial-and-error method, this readjustment, then, in the end, the capitalist system which the Nine Old Men seek to protect may fall.

And almost any evening during the winter, if you knock at Harlan Stone's door, you will probably find him—if he does not come to the door himself to let you in—crouched over his desk or pacing the length of his long study, thinking, poring over the cases before him, the weight, not so much of the world, but of humanity, very much upon his broad shoulders.

CHAPTER VI

The Bruiser

ALL his life Justice Pierce Butler has striven zealously to promote the power and glory of the Holy Roman Church and the power and profits of big business—and for a mediocre man he has done very well both for himself and his spiritual and material masters.

Son of poor Irish parents settling in Minnesota in the days when that state was in the heyday of its expansion, Pierce Butler was raised in a strict religious environment and early in life fixed his eyes on the goal of corporation law. And he arrived. Not only did he spend thirty-five years fighting the battles of the companies to whom he had dedicated his life, but he continues the fight on the Supreme Court of the United States. The only difference judicial robes have meant to Pierce Butler is that as an attorney he pleaded for special privilege and as a judge he creates and sanctifies it.

There is only one other institution which Butler champions as zealously as he does his corporate friends. That is the Roman Catholic Church. Butler's activities on behalf of the Church are carried on in such an energetic manner that the Senate Press Gallery has given him the title of "Papal Delegate to the Supreme Court." He has even given instructions to his secretary to let no divorce cases come near his office, as he considered them "contaminating."

Butler plays a behind-the-scenes part in the life of Catholic institutions which few people realize. He does not hesitate to admonish the Georgetown Law School, a leading Catholic institution, because its law professors are not taken from the ranks of practicing lawyers; and because its law review has the temerity to criticize the Supreme Court. Members of the Catholic hierarchy consult him constantly, and when the Catholic University was selecting a dean for its law school, all candidates had to be interviewed by Justice Butler.

It was Butler, the devout Catholic, who alone dissented from the Court's decision upholding the Virginia statute providing for the sterilization of imbeciles. Justice Holmes, who wrote the majority opinion, sent it around to all his associate justices, as is the usual custom. It was a magnificent document and came back OK'd by all except Butler. From him there was no reply. Finally, as time passed, Holmes remarked to one of his associates:

"I'll bet you Butler is struggling with his conscience as a lawyer on this decision. He knows the law is the way I have written it. But he is afraid of the Church. I'll lay you a bet the Church beats the law."

It did. Justice Holmes, reading the decision, declared:

"Three generations of imbeciles are enough."

To which Professor Powell, reading the opinion to a Harvard law class, added: "Mr Justice Butler dissenting."

Other Catholics have served on the Supreme Court, notably Chief Justice White, and have added distinction to it and to their religion. But they have not brought their religion with them to the bench. Justice White, incidentally, was appointed chiefly as a result of a week-end house party which President Cleveland spent at the home of Senator Bayard of Delaware. Cleveland overheard White, then senator from Louisiana, ask his host if there was a Catholic church in the neighborhood, as he wanted to attend Mass in the morning. Later, Cleveland told Professor Bliss Perry of Harvard that he had "made up his mind that there was a man who was going to do what he thought right; and when a vacancy came, I put him on the Supreme Court."

There was nothing haphazard or accidental, however, about the appointment of Pierce Butler to the Supreme Court.

In 1922 the Minnesota Farmer-Labor movement, rebellious at the highhanded reactionarism of the Hardings, the Daughertys and the Falls, kicked over the traces and elected Henrik Shipstead, an unknown dentist, to the Senate. In doing so, Minnesota ejected from the Senate Frank B. Kellogg, a corporation lawyer who had behind him all the money which big business, jittery over the specter of a radical third party, could pour into his campaign chest. It was a significant victory, and to those in the East who had money invested in the railroads, iron mines and grain elevators of the Northwest, it was not merely significant, but terrifying.

Among those thus afflicted was Thomas Cochran, formerly of St Paul, but now a partner of J. P. Morgan, also chairman of the Bankers Trust Company, director of Braden Copper, Kennecott Copper, General Electric, Copper River and Northwest Railway, the Astor Safe Deposit Company; and, incidentally, a trustee for the New York Association for Improving Conditions for the Poor. Mr Cochran, at that particular moment in 1923, was more interested in projecting his and his partners' interests in the Northwest than in improving the conditions of the poor. The Morgan partners were particularly concerned with the fact that the valuation of the nation's railroads, in which they held large blocks of stock, soon was to come before the Supreme Court, and what could be more appropriate than to have one of the nation's leading railroad attorneys sitting on that Court? In addition to this, Mr Butler was a Catholic and a Democrat— the kind of a Democrat who could be trusted. Mr Cochran, also a Democrat, decided to go down the line for his old friend from St Paul.

Other circumstances were propitious. Chief Justice White had just died, and although President Harding had appointed William Howard Taft in his place, there was considerable agitation for the appointment of a Catholic to fill the vacancy created by the resignation of Justice Day. All of this, plus a push given by George Wickersham, plus another given by Butler's old friend Frank B. Kellogg, contrived to put the appointment across without attracting any public attention to its real sponsors.

Thus, just two weeks after one Minnesota corporation lawyer had been turned out of the nation's highest legislative body after a six-year term, another was elevated to a post where he could lay his reactionary hands on the nation's most vital legislation for the rest of his life.

Before Pierce Butler was confirmed by the Senate, some of the progressives from the Northwest who had helped to eliminate Kellogg challenged the propriety of a prominent railroad attorney sitting on the highest court at a time when important railroad questions were scheduled to come before it. And before confirmation finally was voted, the subcommittee of the Senate Judiciary Committee which considered Butler's qualifications (Cummings of Iowa, Walsh of Montana, and Nelson of Minnesota) all agreed that Butler would be disqualified from sitting in railroad-valuation cases and told their colleagues that he had given a definite pledge to that effect.

The reason for senatorial concern on this point was easy to understand. Pierce Butler was the most famous, most successful and most hard-boiled railroad attorney in the United States. In fact, at the very moment he was appointed to the Supreme Court, he was defending the Minneapolis Street Railway Company, cited for contempt before the Minnesota Supreme Court because it refused to produce certain records showing how it spent a slush fund of $227,000 allegedly used to bribe the state legislature into passing the Brooke-Coleman Act sponsored by the street-car company.

This, however, was one of Butler's relatively unimportant cases. Some of his more worth-while clients included the New York Central; Canadian Northern; St Paul Gas Light Company; Chicago, St Paul, Minneapolis & Omaha Railway; and the Provident Life & Trust Company. He also represented the Chicago & Northwestern Railway in the famous Minnesota rate case in

1907 in which he contended that a state had no power to fix intrastate rates. Butler won in the lower courts but was finally rebuffed by the Supreme Court, though that was in the days before he himself molded Supreme Court opinion on railroad cases. Another case in which the future Justice gave ample warning of his social and economic views came in 1920, when he steered the Minneapolis Gas Light Company into a technical bankruptcy on the plea of one of its own affiliated companies, thus wiping out a favorable contract between the gas company and the city of Minneapolis. It permitted the company to boost rates from eighty cents to $1.31 per unit.

Again, during the World War, Butler, although a militant flag waver, lined himself up with rugged corporate individualism and against the War Labor Board in helping the Minneapolis Steel & Machinery Company, a notorious labor-baiting corporation, to thwart an award of the board.

Most significant of all, however, was Butler's work as attorney for the Great Northern, the Northern Pacific, and the Burlington roads. This was not merely a professional chore for Butler. It was a religion. He came to think of these roads as his roads and their executives as his closest friends. Especially was James J. Hill, foremost railroad pioneer of that day and chief owner of these three roads, his intimate friend. Hill was in the habit of calling Butler at his house at all hours of the day and night. Butler became his closest adviser, and once while attending a dinner at a St Paul club he dropped his soup spoon and rushed to answer a call from Hill. When he returned, one of his dinner companions asked:

"Pierce, what do you think of Hill?"

Butler lost no time in answering.

"Hill," he said, shaking his head reverently, "is one of our greatest men."

One of Butler's chief jobs for the Hill roads and other Western lines was representing them in the long-drawn-out valuation hearing before the Interstate Commerce Commission. These were tremendously important. For this valuation was to form not only the basis for fixing railroad rates under the Esch-Cummins Law, but also it set a figure which no administration could ignore if and when the railroads should be taken over by the government.

And thanks, in large part, to the brilliant, pugnacious tactics of Pierce Butler, that figure was placed at the staggering total of $19,000,000,000.

No wonder that Senator Norris, the elder La Follette, and Norbeck of South Dakota looked a little askance at seating this hatchetman of big business on the Supreme Court. However, Attorney General Daugherty testified: "He is a very high-class man. He is a man of very high character, wonderful experience and good health. His legal learning is complete, and his judicial temperament is one hundred per cent."

So Pierce Butler was confirmed.

Senatorial fears were more than justified.

Butler donned the black robes of judicial omniscience on January 2, 1923. And just six months later, June 11, 1923, he wrote the opinion in the Bluefield Water Works case which was the first milestone in a new method of railroad valuation.

The Bluefield Water Works case, it should be noted, did not directly involve a railroad, and therefore Butler was within the letter of the pledge given by the Senate Judiciary Subcommittee. But it did set a precedent for the valuation of all public utilities, and not even those who belittle Butler's legal intelligence claim that he could have been ignorant of the effect this case would have on his beloved railroad cases which were to come.

At that time the whole question of utility valuation was in a state of flux. Twenty-five years before, William Jennings Bryan stumped the country contending that the value of a particular gas plant or water works or railroad should be measured by the cost of reproducing it at that particular time. Behind his argument was the fact that prices were low around 1896 and the utilities in question could be reproduced for less than the original cost of building them. However, the railroads and utility companies vigorously opposed this. They wanted valuation based upon the original cost of constructing their plants and equipment, which would have been much higher. The issue was all-important because the rates the public was to pay the utilities were based upon a fair return on the value.

Faced with these two arguments, the Supreme Court in 1898 straddled the issue, and in *Smyth* vs. *Ames,* decreed that both factors—cost of reproduction and original cost—should be taken into consideration.

As a result of this decision, many public service commissions took a ten-year average of prices as the basis of fair valuation and fixed their rates accordingly. This usually included prices from both prosperity and depression periods and worked out a fair medium.

But prices had shot up during the days of the World War, so that by 1920, three years before Butler took his seat on the Court, the general price index reached the all-time high of 275, compared with 75 during the days of Bryan's 1896 campaign. And as prices climbed, the railroads and all utilities reversed their earlier argument for valuation based on original cost of construction and came out for cost of reproduction under existing high prices. This meant, of course, that the rates to be charged the public would be proportionately higher.

And the first case in which this new plea of the utilities was tested out came in *Bluefield Water Works* vs. *The Public Service Commission of West Virginia.* Justice Butler had been on the Court only a short time when this was argued. In fact only a few months before he had been urging the Interstate Commerce Commission to base railroad valuation on the present high cost of reproduction. But now he waded into the Bluefield case and handed down an opinion to the effect that the West Virginia Public Service Commission had failed to accord "proper, if any, weight to the greatly enhanced costs of construction in 1920 over those prevailing about 1915."

On the surface this decision did not seem unfair and attracted no particular attention. Mr Butler was not sitting on a railroad case, and no one realized the precedent it was making for railroad valuation. But Butler was driving his nails into the new rate structure for his old railroad clients, one by one. And in the structure of his Bluefield Water Works opinion were tucked away various arguments and phrases which looked harmless enough at the time, and in which all of the Court concurred. They did not know that, three years hence, the new railroad attorney on their bench was to drive his final nail into the valuation structure and justify it by trotting out all of the arguments he had used so innocuously before.

This next case was that of the Indianapolis Water Company, which opposed a valuation of $15,260,400 fixed by the Indiana Public Service Commission by averaging prices during the past ten years—including prewar and postwar—and setting 7 per cent as a reasonable rate of return. The water company, however, opposed this. It wanted its value based upon the cost of reproducing its plant at the much higher postwar prices of 1924, thus permitting it to charge the people of Indianapolis higher rates for their water.

This time Justice Butler drove the final nail into his monument of appreciation to the utilities who made him. He wrote an opinion holding that valuation must be based upon "the cost of reproduction new, less depreciation, estimated on the basis of spot prices as of January 1, 1924." The value of the Indianapolis Water Company was thereby boosted from $15,260,400 to "not less than $19,000,000."

Justices Brandeis and Stone dissented.

In handing down the opinion, Butler gave this particular water company and all other water companies the right to charge into their rate structure the cost of tearing up city-developed land to put in pipes, whereas this land had not been developed when the company first laid these pipes. He gave railroads and power companies the right to charge into their rate structure the cost of getting rights of way over built-up and tremendously expensive property which had not been built up when they first laid their tracks and transmission lines. And he gave them the right to charge for imaginary engineering fees, the hypothetical efficiency of unknown labor, the estimated action of the elements, and the supposed return on supposed investments, all under the guise of ascertaining the highly problematical question of "spot cost of reproduction."

It was the most momentous utilities case since 1890, when Justice Bradley, dissenting in *Chicago, Milwaukee & St Paul* vs. *Minnesota,* declared that the Supreme Court was setting itself up as "final arbiter in the regulation of fares and freights of railroads and the charges of other public accommodations." The majority at that time, spurning Justice Bradley, decreed that the Court would rule on rates. Justice Butler now bent that rule in favor of the utilities.

For some time after that there was not a great deal left for Justice Butler to do. Two years later—1928—the O'Fallon case came along, involving the question of railroad valuation. Butler had represented the Hill roads on this question before the Interstate Commerce Commission, and he now stepped ostentatiously aside. But he had driven his nails carefully. All his colleagues could do was hold with his earlier precedents in the Bluefield and Indianapolis Water Works cases, thereby forcing the Interstate Commerce Commission to base railroad valuation on the cost of reproduction. Thus the value of the nation's railroads was fixed, as Butler in private practice had argued it, at the stupendous sum of $19,000,000,000.

As the years progressed, Justice Butler was not so scrupulous about stepping aside when he found himself occupying a position of obvious prejudice. In 1936 the Great Northern Railroad brought before the Supreme Court a plea to reduce the taxes assessed against it by the state of North Dakota. Mr Butler once had been the attorney for the Great Northern Railroad and all its affiliates. He had been the close friend of James J. Hill. But now he did not step aside. Senators Cummings, Walsh and Nelson—the subcommittee which promised he would not sit in railroad cases—all were dead. So Pierce Butler, completely callous to public opinion, actually wrote the majority opinion.

The power to tax is a right supposedly reserved to the legislative branches of the state and federal governments. But Mr Justice Butler denied this power to the state of North Dakota and scaled $10,000,000 from the tax bill of the Great Northern, his old client.

Joining with him in the majority decision were three other ex-railroad lawyers: Justice Roberts, for nearly thirty years counsel for the Pennsylvania Railroad; Justice Van Devanter, once attorney for the Union Pacific; and Chief Justice Hughes, who had represented many railroads. They all voted with their old clients.

Next day Justice Stone did not sit during arguments made by the Sugar Institute to ease the anti-trust laws. The law firm in New York with which he had been associated twelve years before was representing the Sugar Institute.

In scaling $10,000,000 from the Great Northern Railroad's tax bill, Justice Butler held: "Judicial note must be taken of the fact that late in 1929 there occurred a great collapse of value of all classes of property."

But in 1933—the same year North Dakota made its tax assessment against the Great Northern—the Maryland Public Service Commission also found that there had been a "great collapse of value"; that the value of the Chesapeake & Potomac Telephone Company had come down and therefore the telephone rates necessary to pay a "fair return" on that value also should come down.

But in this case Mr Butler and his colleagues ruled that it "would not only be unfair but impracticable to adjust the value and the consequent rate of return to sudden fluctuations in the price level."[1]

In other words, where big utilities are concerned, the justices once hired by those utilities now decreed from the Olympian heights of the Supreme Court that the 1929 depression must be regarded as "relatively permanent." But where the public is con-

[1] Justice Roberts, who handed down this decision, June 3, 1935, once served as director of the Bell Telephone affiliate of Chesapeake & Potomac and of the American Telephone & Telegraph Company, the parent concern.

cerned, the depression must be judged as merely "sudden fluctuations in the price level."

Thus has Pierce Butler helped to steer his colleagues on the
unswerving path of "Heads, the corporations win; tails, the
public loses."

In the early days of the Northwest, Northfield, Minnesota, was
put on the map by the James boys, who chose it for the scene of
the greatest bank robbery of the generation. More recently
Northfield is known as the early home of the Supreme Court
justice who has done more to enrich the big corporations at the
expense of the public than any other individual in the country.

Pierce Butler was born not far from Northfield on St Patrick's
Day, 1866, just one year after the Civil War. His father, Patrick
Butler, was forced to migrate from Ireland because of the potato
famines, but he came from a well-educated, aristocratic family
which traces its forebears back to 1172, when the LeBoutilliers
first came from France. His ancestors were in as constant conflict with the Fitzgerald clan of that day as Pierce Butler is in
conflict with the Supreme Court liberals today; and one ancestor,
the Marquis d'Ormande, was the most belligerent warrior of his
generation. The name "Pierce" is derived from "Piers," while
"Butler" is derived from LeBoutillier.

The chief thing which distinguished Pierce Butler during his
early days was a tremendous cranium and a hereditary instinct
for fighting. His oversized head was even more noticeable than
it is today and contained considerably more in the way of brains
than those of the other farm boys, although Pierce's five brothers
and two sisters were by no means stupid. Pulling stumps, working in the fields, and milking cows also developed a tremendous
physique, and Pierce became the foremost wrestler and bruiser
of that neighborhood. Pierce's father had graduated from Trinity
College and believed in a college education for his sons. So
Pierce worked his way through Carleton College by washing
milk cans in a dairy, and after a sketchy interval of studying
law was admitted to the bar in St Paul.

Pierce's brothers by that time had gone into the contracting business, which grew by leaps and bounds as the Northwest expanded. Pierce handled their legal work, which became not inconsiderable, and through the influence of his brothers also managed to get a job as assistant attorney of the county. From this he jumped to assistant attorney general of the state, and then into private law practice with Jared How; subsequently with William D. Mitchell, Attorney General under President Hoover.

Butler soon won a reputation as one of the foremost trial lawyers of the Northwest. The secret of his success was a brutal, domineering intimidation of witnesses. There was no charm or intellectual quality about his work, only shrewd, driving energy.

Once, in a bitterly contested divorce case, Butler asked the defendant:

"When you told your wife she must go, did you mean it?"

Defense attorneys were on their feet immediately, objecting: "He didn't tell her she 'must' go, he told her she 'could' go."

But before the judge could rule, Butler sneered at the witness: "Before I am through with you, Mister, you'll tell this court you meant MUST!"

It so unnerved the defendant that Butler had him at his mercy thereafter.

Butler's ruthless and highly successful inquisition of witnesses soon attracted attention, and big cases came his way. Instead of representing plaintiffs in personal-injury cases, he now defended the railroads and the street-car companies against those plaintiffs. In later years Butler once remarked to his friend Seth Richardson, assistant attorney general under Hoover:

"Seth, I don't need to take cases nowadays until I've looked into them to see if they're interesting."

In those early days, however, he took any and all cases, among them some which probably would have sickened his reactionary stomach today. He acted as special attorney for the Justice Department in prosecuting an anti-trust suit against the meat packers in 1910, and also represented the government in a suit against a St Paul milling company for violation of the pure-food law. He lost both cases. He was more successful, however, in representing the Canadian government in fixing the purchase price of the Grand Trunk Railway in 1920. Butler did not believe in government ownership of railways, but a client is a client, and he threw into his argument all the valuation knowledge learned as leading railroad attorney, with the result that he saved the Dominion of Canada $60,000,000. His pugnacious presentation made such an impression on the flabby opposing counsel, ex-President Taft, that when Butler and his railroad friends were angling to secure his appointment to the Supreme Court two years later, Taft, then chief justice, highly recommended him.

By this time Pierce Butler was at the peak of his profession and looking around for bigger and better things. One among thousands of struggling, small-town lawyers, he had become the foremost railroad attorney of the United States. If the land of rugged individualism could do that for the son of a poor immigrant, he told his children, it could do the same for them. Butler's one great break in life, however, was getting the law business of his brothers' contracting firm. Stripping the rich iron ore from the Mesabi and Cuyuna ranges around Lake Superior had netted the Butler family $10,000,000, and in this wealth Pierce Butler shared.

Over his share and other matters, however, there occurred a bitter internecine quarrel which left some of the brothers undying enemies. Not even death reconciled their hatred.

Chief cause of the dispute was the estate of elder brother John Butler, and one of the contributing germs was John's illegitimate daughter. According to an affidavit filed by her in the Ramsey County Probate Court of Minnesota, she was abandoned in a pew of the Church of the Sacred Heart at Duluth in 1890, having been born of John Butler and Mary McGrann, a servant in the Butler home. Shortly thereafter John Butler married Mary McGrann, which under state law would have legitimized the child's birth, but they did not recognize her, and she was adopted by an Andrew and Barbara G. Ruf, who took her at the age of twelve to Hornsilver, Nevada. There she married and was known as Mrs Louise Margaretta Fletcher.

John Butler had no other children. And since his share in the profits of the contracting and iron-mining business was considerable, his will became a matter of considerable interest if not concern to the other brothers. And when he died on September 22, 1926, they discovered that he had made Pierce, Sr, and his two sons, Pierce, Jr, and Frank, executors of his $2,731,733 estate. Out of this they received $700,000. Walter Butler, president of the company, although mentioned in the will, was thoroughly dissatisfied with his portion and from that day was in constant controversy with Pierce, who already had been elevated to the august position of justice of the Supreme Court.

One feature of John Butler's will was that it made no provision whatsoever for his illegitimate daughter, Mrs Fletcher. Walter Butler charged, and there is good evidence to believe this to be a fact, that Justice Butler persuaded his brother specifically to rule his daughter out of his will in order to protect the family name and leave more for the other members of the family. At any rate, the will contained the following codicil: "I intentionally omitted and failed to provide for any child or any issue of any deceased child."

While barring his own daughter, however, the will drawn up by Pierce Butler provided for all of Pierce's children and fourteen other children of his brothers and sisters—a total of twenty-one.

Just as the will was filed, Mrs John Butler, the former Mary McGrann, wrote to her daughter in Nevada on October 26, 1926 as follows:

". . . and Mary, he has left money to take care of you and Barbara [Mrs Fletcher's daughter] all your life, but I want to tell you not to talk to any strangers or tell them anything about yourself. Your father and mother [Mr and Mrs Ruf, foster parents] will also advise you about this. . . . Now if anything should happen to me, Pierce Butler and Frank will take care of you.

. . . And after the estate is settled your income will be regular."

Whether Mrs John Butler knew that the will specifically ruled her daughter out never will be known, for the former Mary McGrann died a few months later, on May 6, 1927.

Meanwhile the feud between Walter and Pierce deepened. And in the winter of 1930 Walter alleged that he took a short trip to Havana, leaving with his brothers full power of attorney over his stock, and that during his absence he was voted out of the presidency of Butler Brothers. How much Justice Butler had to do with this probably never can be ascertained. But certainly the hatred of Walter centered on Pierce, and he became even more bitter and vindictive. Before he died, Walter actually proposed to one or two St Paul newspapermen that they write a book for him in which he would show how Pierce secured his seat on the Supreme Court through a payment of $400,000 to Harding's Attorney General, Harry M. Daugherty, of which $200,000 was put up by the railroads and $200,000 by the Butler family. He planned to send the book to every judge and legislator in the country. Walter, at this point, had become bitter to the point of insanity, and he could get no newspapermen to write such a fanciful treatise. While it is true that the railroads, as previously set forth, pulled many wires to secure Butler's appointment, they operated through such highly effective and respectable channels as George Wickersham, the Morgan partners and Taft.

The climax of Walter's feud against Pierce came when he induced the illegitimate daughter of John Butler to contest her father's will. She charged that the will was procured "by fraud, misrepresentation and conspiracy on the part of the Honorable Pierce Butler and the other two executors, Pierce Butler, Jr., and Frank D. Butler, his sons"; that "undue influence" was brought by Pierce Butler, and that therefore the will is void and she is the sole heir.

A contest of this kind was the last thing a justice of the Supreme Court wanted. Not only might it endanger the fat inheritance he and his children received from John's estate, but it meant washing all the family's dirty linen in public. It would not have been a charming picture. So Justice Butler made an immediate and handsome settlement upon Mrs Fletcher and the suit was dropped.

The aura of respect which must surround a Supreme Court justice, no matter what his past, was preserved.

In Washington, Pierce Butler leads a quiet and highly respectable life, surrounded by his law books, his prolific family and a few intimate cronies. And in his own routine way the Justice seems to get quite a kick out of life. His closest friend is seventy-eight-year-old, hidebound Justice Van Devanter, whom he got to know when the latter was a judge on the Eighth Circuit Court of Appeals. Now they vote together in the secret discussions of the Court and golf together every Sunday morning at Burning Tree. It is the chief recreation of both, and they would not let anything interfere with it, even transferring from Chevy Chase because their associate, Justice McReynolds, got disagreeable even beyond their endurance.

Butler plays a good game of golf for his age—between 105 and 110. Van Devanter is just behind, with scores around 108 and 112. Butler can outdrive Van, but Van is a better putter. Justice Roberts used to play with them occasionally, but finds it painful to play golf since he injured his shoulder in a spill from his horse several years ago.

Butler loves to tell how he was riding to work in a street car one morning in St Paul when he saw a Jewish tradesman acquaintance in the car and remarked:

"Abie, you don't look well, this morning. What's the matter?"

"Pierce, I vus all night playing poker—and—almost I lost!"

This remains Butler's favorite story, and one Sunday morning while Butler was playing with Justice Van Devanter, Seth Richardson spotted them and called across the fairway:

"Hey—you—which of you won that first hole?"

Butler cackled back:

"Seth—almost I lost!"

Except for Seth Richardson, the two old men usually play alone. Burning Tree has a system of matching blind foursomes —that is, all breakfast together Sunday morning, and then names are drawn out of a hat, and whichever four come out together play together that morning. Richardson does the pulling and once invited Butler and Van Devanter to join them. But they declined, explaining that they didn't like to get up too early on Sunday. Richardson asked if they were declining because they didn't want to mingle with pick-up matches, to which Van Devanter replied:

"Oh no, not at all. We like to meet people. It's just that we're tired after Saturday conferences and would rather play later Sunday morning." To which Butler nodded agreement.

So they appear on the course about eleven-thirty, when the links are comparatively deserted, and spend the morning ambling about the links, talking about fishing or duck hunting or, almost more than anything else, the New Deal.

However, at the nineteenth hole in the clubhouse locker room, they don't seem to mind fraternizing with the large number of fellow golfers sitting around naked or in their underwear drinking highballs. Butler has a highball, or in hot weather they both take iced tea. Butler seems to get quite a kick out of getting out from under his black nightgown and always contributes a story or two, or reminisces about the early days in the Northwest. The crowd which frequents the Burning Tree Club, incidentally, is made up chiefly of those who would believe in the second coming of Christ only if He bore the seal of approval of the Republican National Committee.

Butler is a consistent diner-out and lives in a plain house on 19th Street, where he puts on no especial airs. To look at his furnishings no one would guess that he is the wealthiest member of the Supreme Court, any more than one would guess from looking at his stolid Irish face that he was the chief brain and mainspring of the court reactionaries.

Butler also has a summer place at Blue Ridge Summit in

southern Pennsylvania, not far from Washington, where his children and his grandchildren visit him. He has developed a strong vein of domesticity, doubtless inherited from the family-consciousness of Patrick and Mary, and has equaled their brood of eight children. He is just as devoted to them as he appeared to be the opposite in the case of his brother John's illegitimate child.

The Butler children tell a story on their father to the effect that, in the days when he was a young and hard-working attorney with scarcely any time to see them, their mother rebelled at taking care of the brood and went out one night, leaving him to put them to bed. Returning later, she asked her husband whether he had had any trouble and got the reply: "Only with that one who said he wanted to go to bed over at the neighbor's house." According to the Butler children, their father had put a neighbor's child to bed.

Whether or not there is any germ of truth in this, Butler has been a most devoted father in his latter years. One of his daughters, Mary, died while a Red Cross nurse during the war, and the other daughter, Margaret, is afflicted with an incurable malady which makes her an invalid for life. Intellectually brilliant, she has great difficulty in talking or even holding up her head. Her father is her constant and devoted servant, taking her to early Mass every Sunday and having her sit with guests at dinner even on formal occasions.

At a recent family reunion, the Justice called all his numerous grandchildren to his knee, and one by one each told his story, his troubles, his desires, his hopes, before the old judge would consent to mingle with the grown-ups. He would rather visit with them, for in the children he sees the hope of a greater and even more illustrious Butler name, a name which he is conscious of having elevated from the obscurity of a Minnesota farm to the glamour and glory of the United States Supreme Court.

There are certain inconsistencies in the life of Pierce Butler which clash with head-on momentum. While he is the benign and lovable parent in his own home he can be, and has been, utterly thoughtless of millions of children whose lives are short-ened through premature labor, or of their mothers, forced to neglect them because of long working hours. With his own children protected by a millionaire's inheritance, Butler took a leading part in killing the Child Labor and Minimum Wage laws. Again, while Butler is the acme of pleasantness and jovial charm among his dinner guests and golfing companions, he can be and is the most bare-fisted bully on the Supreme bench in the cross-examination of counsel or in attaining any objective which he sets for himself. A slow and ponderous thinker, his decisions are dull, uninspiring and written in a slovenly man-ner. He is inclined to be sullen and, when a case goes against him, takes no pains to conceal his resentment against the other justices. No other man on the Court, not even McReynolds, displays the same intellectual brutality.

It was during his early days in St Paul that Butler got the reputation of being vindictive and unscrupulous toward anyone who opposed him. For eighteen years he served as regent of the University of Minnesota—eighteen years of hell for any pro-fessor who dared express a liberal viewpoint or teach anything save old-fashioned fundamentalism. The University of Minne-sota became his university, just as the Supreme Court has become his court. With usual bulldozing tenacity, he wanted to monopolize it. Officials of the university he treated as office boys. No instructor was too insignificant for Butler to pry into his social and economic views. Ex-President Tolwell, who got out about the time Butler became a regent, referred to him as "a huge bully," while President Coffman, for a brief interval, resigned.

Several professors lost their jobs as a result of Butler's jesuiti-cal intolerance. One was Professor William A. Schaper, well-known authority on political science, who had drafted a liberal franchise clause in a proposed home-rule charter for Minneapo-lis. Naturally the franchise clause affected the big utilities which served the city, and Butler was attorney for the Minneapolis

Street Railways, the Minneapolis Gas Light Company and other companies. He called Professor Schaper on the telephone personally, notified him to appear before the Board of Regents and, after a half-hour of heckling, ordered his dismissal on the grounds of pro-German activities, refusing, however, to prefer any written charges against him. Later the Labor Conciliation Board investigated the case and recommended that the Board of Regents reconsider it. But Pierce Butler had spoken, and his word, even then, was as omnipotent as it is today on the Supreme Court.

In another instance, Dr John H. Gray, professor of economics, secured leave of absence to serve as adviser to the Interstate Commerce Commission on railroad valuation, where he opposed the principle of valuation which Butler was arguing before the same commission on behalf of the Great Northern. When Gray came back to Minneapolis he found himself summarily dismissed. Other teachers whom Butler forced out of the university were Gerhard Dietrichson, professor of chemistry, and Dr Stanley Rypins, a professor of English, who had the temerity to join the progressive Committee of Forty-Eight. So highhanded a heresy hunter had Butler become immediately before his appointment to the Supreme Court that the Minnesota legislature had before it a resolution refusing his reappointment as regent, while the city council of Minneapolis sent a resolution to the Senate opposing his confirmation as justice.

It was during these same years in St Paul that Butler aligned himself with one of the worst Red-baiting incidents of the World War. A group of small-town businessmen in Luverne, Minnesota, had taken a farmer named John Meintz from his home, carried him across the state line, and delivered him to another gang which tarred and feathered him. Meintz's sole crime was that of helping finance the weekly newspaper of the Non-Partisan League. Later he brought suit against the thirty businessmen, and Butler, outstanding Red-baiting attorney of the Northwest, came to their defense, concocting the highly imaginary plea that the defendants were friends of Meintz and had kidnaped him to protect him from bodily injury. When the case got to the higher courts not even the bruiser tactics of Pierce Butler could save it, and the thirty businessmen agreed to pay Meintz $8,000.

As a Red-baiter, Justice Butler has been superbly consistent. In the cases of Bland and MacIntosh, of Rosika Schwimmer, of Benjamin Gitlow, of Abrams, Pierce, the Philadelphia *Tageblatt* and all the espionage and naturalization cases arising since the war, Pierce Butler has consistently and without a moment's hesitation voted for government intolerance.

He takes only slight pains to conceal much the same intolerance toward his liberal colleagues of the Court. He is not surly or rude as is McReynolds. But he has no respect for the liberals' views and does not hang photographs of Brandeis and Holmes with the collection of other justices on his study wall.

One reason for Butler's scorn for his liberal colleagues is that they stepped out of the cloistered atmosphere of the college or of remote-control law practice onto the bench without first making their mark fighting at the lower bar. Both he and Roberts spent the early years of their life as jury pleaders. Van Devanter, Sutherland and McReynolds also came to the Court as practicing attorneys, although their rough-and-tumble pleading was not so extensive. But all of them look down upon the qualifications of Cardozo, who they consider jumped from college to a very select law practice and then to the bench; and upon those of Stone, who jumped from the deanship of Columbia Law School almost immediately to the bench; and upon those of Brandeis, who, although a practicing lawyer, had spent years in liberal crusades before he came to the Court. Hughes they consider a middle-of-the-road Y.M.C.A. Baptist with an evangelical outlook who entered the legal profession at the top, handling only the great cases and keeping carefully aloof from the school of hard knocks in the police and common-pleas courts.

None of this, in the opinion of Butler, is the experience that qualifies a man to pass on acts of Congress and the legislation of states as a member of the highest court of the land. Arguing in the reverse, presumably he believes that what a capable Supreme Court justice requires is long experience in championing big corporations, in bulldozing liberal professors, and in defending mobs which tar-and-feather farmers. At any rate, that is the seasoning which graduated Butler to the balance and judicial calm of our highest bench.

So Pierce Butler has set himself the task of keeping the conservative wing of the Court intact, keeping it always one vote ahead of the distrusted and unqualified liberals. He has become the greatest proselyter, the most effective lobbyist, on the Court. He does not make a public spectacle of his bitterness as does McReynolds. He does not hesitate as does Hughes. He is subtle but undeviating. Only a sledge hammer could change Butler. He knows what he wants. He knows where his colleagues are weak. He has the Irishman's instinct for politics, and he plays it within the Court. He is effective because he works so quietly.

Just before Justice Cardozo was appointed, when there was considerable discussion in the press about the necessity of appointing a liberal justice, Butler remarked to a friend:

"They seem to be worried about appointing a liberal to the Court. But they shouldn't worry. I'll take care of that."

And he let out one of his deep belly laughs. But he was not joking. He did take care of that. He not only weaned Owen Roberts over from the liberal wing, but made him chief spokesman for the conservatives.

Butler is a millionaire now—the only millionaire on the Court—risen from the farm of an Irish immigrant. And Pierce is not ungrateful. He would no more think of deserting the side which gave him his place in the sun than he would think of deserting his large brood of children. Long ago—January 1915—before Pierce Butler even thought of donning the black robes of judicial omnipotence, he wrote in the *Journal of Political Economy:*

"Should all the rewards which are due to the foresight, wisdom, and enterprise of the men who conceived and constructed wisely be transferred by legislative authority to others?"

That has been the guiding star of Pierce Butler's life. He has never deviated from it.

He had his eyes glued on it when he wrote the opinion in the Nebraska bread-weight case, setting aside a law enacted by the legislature to protect consumers from dishonest bakers. He had his eyes on it when he struck down the Pennsylvania state law seeking to protect immigrants from being cheated by crooked steamship companies—despite the fact that his father was an immigrant. He had his eyes on that star also when, in the Panhandle Oil Company case, he established the farthest legal outpost ever attained by corporations in governmental immunity, namely, exemption for the company in paying taxes to the state of Mississippi on gasoline sales to the United States Coast Guard located there, because such sales made it a *federal instrumentality*.

He has never taken his eyes from that star, and they are more closely glued to it today than ever.

All his life Pierce Butler has been a Democrat—an Al Smith Democrat. And as Al's hatred for Roosevelt has deepened, so also has Butler's, a hatred not merely against the President, as is Al's, but against all things for which the President stands.

Once Butler was called upon to judge a debate at a St Paul high school. The question was: "Resolved, that compulsory military education should be abolished."

There were three judges, Butler presiding. One judge held for the affirmative, the other for the negative. Faced with casting the deciding ballot, Justice Butler did not hesitate.

"The debate has been well argued," he decreed. "In the clearness of its presentation and weight of argument, the affirmative has been superior. But no good American citizen should oppose compulsory military education, and therefore I cast my vote for the negative."

For sixteen years Pierce Butler has been casting his vote from the Supreme bench with similar evenhanded impartiality.

CHAPTER VII

The Philadelphia Lawyer

Owen Josephus Roberts is the biggest joke ever played upon the fighting liberals of the United States Senate.

He was confirmed by them as one of their number. He has turned out to be the foremost meat-axer of their cause.

And the joke is entirely their own fault. Roberts did not deceive them. They deceived themselves.

Had they taken the slightest trouble to dig into his past, to consult the files of the Library of Congress, they would have found that Owen J. Roberts all his life had been nothing more than what he is today—a hard-working, extremely able, highly successful corporation lawyer, recommended to Mr Hoover by another corporation lawyer, George Wharton Pepper, who later was to win from him one of the most important cases in Supreme Court history, the invalidation of the AAA.

But they were too tired after waging their unsuccessful fight to defeat the confirmation of Hughes as chief justice and after their successful fight against the confirmation of John J. Parker of North Carolina. Parker, a judge of the Circuit Court of Appeals, was appointed associate justice in the spring of 1930 to replace the late Justice Sanford. Whereupon Walter White of the National Association for the Advancement of Colored People dug up the fact that Parker had been guilty of anti-Negro prejudice, and together with the A. F. of L., which disclosed that he had been unfair to organized labor, started a barrage against Parker which resulted in the Senate's defeat of his confirmation. Roberts was selected by Hoover immediately afterward as the hero of the Teapot Dome oil-scandal prosecutions, sure to be confirmed. And he was.

Meanwhile the Senate liberals have watched Judge Parker, whom they defeated, strike two notable blows for liberalism: a decision upholding the right of the government to finance municipal power plants; and a decision sustaining the Railroad Labor Board that a majority in a labor election, even though not a majority of the eligible voters, is entitled to represent all the workers.

Meanwhile, also, they have watched Owen J. Roberts, elevated to the Supreme Court because of Parker's anti-Negro prejudice, hand down a host of decisions calculated to produce economic slavery for the white and black races alike.

It was not merely a joke on the liberals of the Senate. It was gall and wormwood.

Unwittingly Owen J. Roberts also has played something of a joke on himself. Had he played the game in a more farsighted manner he had an excellent chance of becoming chief justice, or President of the United States. He has youth, health, great ability, rare charm and a convincing, powerful personality. But his eye was glued too closely to the main chance. He could not focus upon the more distant horizon.

When Roberts graduated from the University of Pennsylvania, the college yearbook placed this quotation under his picture: "Fain Would I Climb." Youth has an uncanny way of judging its own kind, and that evaluation of Roberts in 1895 is as true of him today as it was then.

Like all good corporation lawyers, Roberts has leaned toward the prosperous side. The case that paid the fees is the one that he has championed. On the Supreme Court he has not changed. The only difference is that now he does not argue the case; he decides it. More than any other member of the Court, he has the key vote. And more than any other member save the Chief Justice, he has backed and filled as the tide of public opinion has ebbed and flowed. During his first term in this position, and while still basking in the confirmation tribute of the Senate liberals, Owen Roberts chalked up a hundred-per-cent liberal record. But during the height of the depression two years later, with Hoover and the Republican party beating the drums of class hatred in a desperate attempt to win an election, Roberts eased back toward the reactionary fold.

Eighteen months later, with the New Deal triumphant and all-powerful, Roberts handed down a ringing decision in the major court test of that period upholding the right of New York State to regulate milk prices. But in 1935, with the forces of reaction beleaguering the New Deal from all directions, once more Roberts flopped back to the winning side, where he became its lustiest swinger of the meat axe against any act of Congress savoring of liberalism.

Being thus preoccupied, it is no wonder his eye has strayed from the long-range objective.

There have been two great factors in the life of Owen Josephus Roberts: his wife; and the complacent, mid-Victorian atmosphere of the City of Brotherly Love and Big Incomes—for those who stand in with the city rulers.

The first is a charming, sometimes bullying little lady who has been Roberts' pal, inspiration and goad for thirty-two years, who reads his opinions, listens to him rehearse them, and on many important occasions has worn the pants in the Roberts family. Mrs Roberts is ardently reactionary and doesn't care who knows it.

Regarding the second, Owen Josephus did not originally stand in with the city masters, but, through studious application of the motto won in college, he got there in short order.

Owen Josephus was born in 1875 in lower Germantown, a very respectable neighborhood, despite the name "Smeartown," applied to it by less delicate Philadelphians. His father's house stood on Fisher's Lane—a celebrated stretch of roadway, which less than a year before had been used by the kidnapers of the never-found Charley Ross. Josephus Roberts, the father of the Justice, was a well-to-do hardware merchant and wagon dealer who, after his retirement from business, served two terms as a Republican member of the Philadelphia Common Council, thus planting the seeds of Owen's political heritage at an early age. Josephus was the son of William Roberts, a Welshman, who migrated to the United States and prospered as a miller in Montgomery County north of Philadelphia. The mother of the Justice was of Pennsylvania Dutch stock. Owen received his preparatory education at the Germantown Academy, a private school, and then went to the University of Pennsylvania. He graduated in 1895, when he was only twenty, and three years later received his degree in law.

Roberts was the plugging type to be found in every college class. He was not an athlete, nor a natural-born leader with a magnetic personality. He did not rate Delta Psi or Delta Phi, the two foremost fraternities on the campus, though he did join Psi Upsilon, then forging to the front. Nor did he belong to any of the ritzy and secret "honorary" societies, but helped to organize instead "The Six Footers' Club," all of them proud of their height and size of foot. Roberts was six feet one-half inch; shoe, 12-D.

But while he wasn't the biggest shot in his class, everybody knew Roberts was there.

He worked hard and deliberately to be a leader in all nonathletic extracurricular activities. He was a perennial and persistent candidate for the chairmanship of this committee or that, and upon graduation was able to list in the college yearbook the following array of achievements: chairman of the freshman-sophomore supper committees; member of the board of governors of the Y.M.C.A.; judge of elections of the Athletic Association; member of the University Republican Club; treasurer of the Franklin Debating Union; assistant marshal of the Washington's Birthday Celebration; class historian; chairman of the board of editors of the yearbook; editor of the *Pennsylvanian*—

a tabulation which was longer than that of any other student, except David Halsted, Jr, the class president, who slipped one over on Roberts by recording all his ex-officio titles, thus getting one line of type more than Owen Josephus.

Owen's indefatigable industry, plus a retentive memory and a ready aptitude for "horsing the profs," kept him constantly near the top of his class and won him special honors in mathematics and Latin, together with Phi Beta Kappa. His graduation thesis was an airy bit entitled "The Agamemnon Myth As Treated By the Attic Dramatists."

Even at that early age, Roberts' fellow students slyly satirized his knack of keeping the eye on the main chance by portraying him in the class yearbook as a professor telling his class: "There is one practice of which, at the beginning of my college course, I resolved never to be guilty—the practice of gaining the good will of a professor by simulated interest in his words, by feigned zeal for his subject, by hypocritical amusement at his pleasantries. I refer to what is known in vulgar parlance as 'leg pulling.' As I said, I resolved never to be guilty of this."

In Law School, Roberts concentrated on two things, scholarship and making valuable contacts, in both of which he was most successful.

He won the Law School essay prize with a sonorous dissertation on "The Rights of Minority Stockholders in the Management of a Corporation"; and a fellowship for combined graduate study and teaching as an instructor. Also, and far more important to his future, he attracted favorable attention among the University Crowd.

It is necessary to know Philadelphia to appreciate the full flavor of this last achievement. Up until the World War what was known as the "University Crowd" dominated the professions, finance, society and politics of the City of Brotherly Love. University of Pennsylvania bankers sent business to University of Pennsylvania lawyers. Penn lawyers extended a helping hand to other Penn lawyers. Even graduates of the university's Medical School did what they could to boost other Penn doctors up the ladder. If a Penn man stood in with the "crowd" he had a Pullman ticket to favor and preference.

"Playing the University game" it was called in that day, and Roberts played it to the limit and with great success.

Classmates of the Justice say that upon graduation from Law School he was a little dubious about his future as a lawyer and talked of teaching as a more secure berth. In the end, however, he played safe. He opened a law office with a classmate and simultaneously accepted an instructorship in law at the university. The latter provided an income, and the former gave him an entering wedge into an active practice of law. Roberts continued a member of the Pennsylvania law faculty, rising to the status of full professor, until 1918, when he resigned to become a special deputy attorney general to prosecute wartime sedition and "spy" cases.

One of the university crowd whom Roberts played early in the game was John C. Bell, once a famous Penn football star, later a university trustee and an influential political figure. Bell was appointed district attorney of Philadelphia in April 1903 to fill a vacancy and decided to make his promising young friend from the university his first assistant at $5,000 a year. But the hard-boiled politicos of the city machine hit the ceiling.

"Say, where do you get that stuff?" demanded Iz Durham, Republican boss. "A $5,000 job is a $5,000 job, and we're not going to stand for its going to some student still wet around the ears who never pulled a doorbell in his life and probably hasn't even voted. The appointment is out."

Bell had to back down. But he did not desert his young protégé. Quietly he put him on as "special assistant" for a month without pay. Then he slipped him on the regular payroll as second assistant, and before the year was out he had promoted Roberts to first assistant. And to complete the job, Bell had an ordinance eased through the city council providing pay for Roberts during the month he served as special assistant "without pay."

Besides supplying a handsome income for a young attorney,

Roberts' job in the district attorney's office was an invaluable training ground. Hard-working and ambitious, he made the most of it and soon gained a reputation for his persuasive performances in front of the jury box. Big, impressive, fast-thinking on his feet and an effective pleader, he scored a large percentage of victories in the criminal courts. Roberts remained in the district attorney's office until the end of 1904, resigning to accept a still better position offered by another university friend.

Those were the golden days when the popular sport of Philadelphia lawyers was "suing the P.R.T." The Philadelphia Rapid Transit Company is one of the country's most fantastic corporate monstrosities. The Wideners, the Elkinses and other socially prominent financial operators had finagled scores of so-called "underlier" franchises from the state legislature, some running for 999 years. On the strength of these grants they had organized transit companies, watered their stock up to the gunwales, then sold or leased the companies. This weird pyramid was finally combined into one system and leased to the Philadelphia Rapid Transit Company.

P.R.T. was organized in 1902 and soon proved a happy hunting ground for Philadelphia lawyers. By 1905 a not insignificant number of the city's population was engaged either in suing or defending the P.R.T. One set of lawyers did a land-office business prosecuting damage suits on a fifty-fifty basis, and another set pulled down lush fees defending them. In fact many of Philadelphia's most distinguished legal lights today got their start to fame and fortune doing "negligence work" for P.R.T.

Outstanding among them is Owen Josephus Roberts.

Chief counsel for P.R.T. at that time was Charles Leaming, of a wealthy, socially prominent family—and, of course, a Penn man. Roberts had not overlooked cultivating Leaming, and Leaming in turn was much impressed with Roberts' hypnotic power over juries, with the result that Penn-man Leaming offered Penn-brother Roberts a job on the P.R.T. legal staff.

This was a real feather in the cap of a thirty-year-old lawyer and meant that Roberts now had both feet on the escalator to success. Being a P.R.T. attorney brought not only a handsome yearly retainer but opened new fields for profitable social and business contacts. Furthermore it afforded an unusually wide experience in civil law, and Roberts soon became one of Leaming's ablest assistants in fighting damage actions.

He was worth every cent that P.R.T. paid him. Illustrative of how well Roberts served his clients and also of his remarkable memory was the case of a woman who sued for damages for a leg she claimed was injured when she fell from a street car which started suddenly. But she refused to show her leg. Several years before this, Roberts had defended the P.R.T. against a German baker, whose wagon was smashed by a street car and who claimed an injured leg. But he also had refused to show the leg in court. And despite the contention of the P.R.T. doctors that the injury was a fake, the jury awarded him $3,500. The day the case of the injured woman came to trial, Roberts, looking over the strike list of jurors, noticed that five of them had crosses beside their names, denoting that they had sat in similar accident cases. Roberts, however, had only four strikes at his disposal. Examining the jury closely, he recognized the baker who, long before, also had declined to show his injured limb. So, working on the theory that jurors will never let others get away with practices which they themselves got away with, Roberts let the old German remain on the jury. He won the case.

Roberts' legal work for the P.R.T. took only part of his time, and he was free to devote the remainder to building up his own practice and promoting contacts with the university crowd. Three of these were to make highly important contributions to his business and political advancement. They were:

Sydney Emlen Hutchinson—son-in-law of E. T. Stotesbury, the latter being a partner in J. P. Morgan & Company.

George Wharton Pepper—former United States senator, eight years Roberts' senior at the university and one of his law teachers.

Thomas Sovereign Gates—now president of the University of Pennsylvania and a former partner of both Drexel & Company and J. P. Morgan & Company.

The ties between Roberts and Gates became especially close when the two men married sisters, the Rogers girls of Fairfield, Connecticut. Tommy Gates was two years ahead of Roberts at Penn, entered the law office of John G. Johnson, then became trust officer of a Philadelphia bank, a job that paid $6,000 a year and required little work. Tommy thought he was fixed for life. But he was just beginning. After the death of the first Mrs Gates, he married Mary Emma Gibson, a whisky heiress, and shortly thereafter was elevated to a vice presidency in the Pennsylvania Company—an insurance and banking concern. From this post it was only a short step, through the kindly offices of Penn-man Hutchinson, to an important position and eventual partnership in both Drexel & Company and J. P. Morgan & Company. Tommy Gates remained with the Drexels and the Morgans until 1930, by which time he had accumulated a fortune and retired to become president of his old alma mater.

As he moved steadily upward in finance and society, Gates did not forget his friend and ex-brother-in-law, Owen Roberts. Many important big-fee clients found their way to Roberts' office at the suggestion of Tommy Gates.

With his university teaching position, his P.R.T. jury work and his own growing private law practice, Roberts was doing very nicely. But still something was missing. He was popular, able, had the right contacts, but professionally he had not yet arrived. He lacked a "firm." The year 1912 supplied that deficiency.

At that time William W. Montgomery, Jr, who inherited much of Charles Leaming's non-P.R.T. practice, together with Charles L. McKeehan, who handled the lucrative law business of the banking house of E. W. Clark & Sons, decided to form a partnership. To round out the firm they needed a top-notch trial lawyer with the right connections, and Roberts was the perfect choice. He also was looking for exactly what they could give him—a substantial front for his rising reputation, and the firm became Roberts, Montgomery & McKeehan. It lasted until McKeehan was appointed to the federal bench, after which Roberts and

Montgomery continued partners until the former was appointed to the Supreme Court.

The new law firm boomed from the start. It got the cream of big-business clients, among them the Pennsylvania Railroad, the Pennsylvania Company, Bell Telephone, the P.R.T., Equitable Life Assurance, E. W. Clark & Sons, and Drexel & Company. As the partnership prospered, so Roberts' personal fortunes prospered. He was made director of the Equitable Life Assurance Society, Franklin Fire Insurance Company, the Real Estate, Land Title & Trust Company, the American Telephone & Telegraph Company and Bell Telephone. In later years, incidentally, Roberts did not step aside when the Supreme Court considered the rate case of *Maryland* vs. *The Chesapeake & Potomac Telephone Company,* an affiliate of these two firms. Instead he wrote the opinion giving the telephone company an increase in rates.

Roberts' most important contribution to the cause of big corporations was the organization of Pennroad. This was a deliberate and successful dodge to get around the decree of Congress that one railroad cannot acquire another without Interstate Commerce Commission consent. Therefore Roberts set up a holding company called Pennroad, which purchased not only the Pennsylvania Railroad but also the smaller lines which the Pennsylvania wanted to acquire. In Wall Street it was hailed as one of the smartest tricks evolved to evade Congress. No wonder that when the Pecora Banking Investigation Committee of the Senate delved into the finances of J. P. Morgan & Company, it found that the name of Owen J. Roberts had been on the preferred list to which the Morgans sold special stock issues well below the market quotation.

Through the influence of his university friends in 1920 Roberts was made a member of the very exclusive and very powerful Board of City Trusts. This body handles the trust funds left to Philadelphia, chief among them being the immense Stephen Girard estate. Another member of the board was Roberts' old friend, Sydney Emlen Hutchinson, whose insurance company writes most of the business for the board and its properties.

With this boost up the ladder, Roberts attained full standing in the inner hierarchy of Philadelphia bourbonism. He had arrived. From that point on, he acted and talked like all votaries of big business.

Addressing the Trust Company Division of the American Bankers' Association, Roberts bitterly denounced the Senate Judiciary Committee, then engaged in investigating the oil industry and in bringing to light the fact that Walter C. Teagle, president of the Standard Oil Company of New Jersey, received a salary of $125,000 a year—$50,000 more than the President of the United States. Upon the disclosure of Teagle's salary, Roberts frowned. He told his applauding listeners it was part of a secret plot to arouse public sentiment in favor of the nationalization of oil.

"Everywhere you turn," he cried, "judicial and semijudicial administrative commissions, investigating bodies, inspectors of every known variety are found. The result is that the business man in America today feels that he is doing business with a minion of government looking over his shoulder with an upraised arm and a threatening scowl.

"Are we prepared to revise our ideas of government? Are we prepared to go into a frank state of socialism in this country with all that it means in the suppression of ambition, in the deterrence of industry, in the holding back of men who want to arrange their affairs for their good and . . . for the good of us all . . . Are we to go into a state of socialism, or are you men, and men like you, prepared to get out, take off your coats and root for good old-fashioned Anglo-Saxon individualism?"

These words were spoken in February 1923. The fighting liberals of the Senate could have looked them up very easily had they been interested. But they did not. In retrospect those words are now a key to Roberts' savage championship of reaction. Except for one or two brief interludes, he has been quite consistent. He has only practiced what he preached.

There were other telltale clues to Roberts' economic and political philosophy, among them his fight to seat Philadelphia's malodorous Republican boss, William S. Vare, as United States senator. Roberts was then a director and counsel for the Philadelphia Chamber of Commerce, and despite the fact that a Senate investigating committee had revealed widespread corruption and the expenditure of huge slush funds in Vare's election, Roberts spurred to the defense of the South Philadelphia garbage collector with this legal opinion: "The Senate has no right or power to exclude or question the fitness of a senator selected by a state as its representative if he has been duly appointed or elected." Apparently, he did not take the trouble to consult the Constitution of the United States which he was to quote so often in the future. Had he done so he would have found that under Section 5 of Article 1: "Each House shall be the judge of the elections, returns, and qualifications of its own members. . . ."

The Senate which he criticized so vigorously was to provide the chief means of sending one of the Teapot Dome defendants, Harry F. Sinclair, to jail.

Roberts' debut to the national arena in 1924 was due chiefly to his old University of Pennsylvania friend, George Wharton Pepper, then a United States senator. Coolidge had been forced by senatorial clamor to prosecute the Teapot Dome cases and was having difficulty finding a Republican lawyer whom the Senate would accept. Tom Walsh of Montana, whose senatorial investigation had exposed the smelly mess, was the logical man, but Coolidge secretly feared him. In this dilemma, Pepper quietly summoned Roberts to Washington, introduced him to Coolidge and recommended him as the answer to the latter's worries. Coolidge promptly sent his name to the Senate.

Despite Pepper's urging, Roberts hesitated before going to see Coolidge. He was making big money at the time—$150,000 a year —and the law (although changed later) did not permit him to continue his private practice. However, it was a propitious movement in other respects. Roberts was forty-nine years old, in perfect health, wealthy, and at the top of the Philadelphia bar.

Prosecution of the oil cases would enable him to branch out into new and spectacular fields. So he took the plunge.

It is characteristic of Roberts that, whatever he does, he does with all the energy and ability at his command. As a student at Pennsylvania, as a jury pleader for the P.R.T., as a big corporation counsel and as writer of reactionary opinions for the Supreme Court, Roberts has given his client or his colleagues the benefit of every ounce of his powerful, fast-thinking personality.

His work in prosecuting the Teapot Dome oil scandals was no exception. It was a superb performance and made his Democratic colleague, Atlee W. Pomerene, appear as useful as a one-armed straphanger in a New York subway. Roberts not only did all the work but even advanced money from his own pocket to pay the running expenses of the prosecution. In the civil suits he won a sweeping victory, recovering all the property stolen from the government. In the criminal trials, District of Columbia juries, notorious for their spineless mediocrity, proved too much even for Roberts' brilliant courtroom strategy. He was able to convince one jury that Secretary of the Interior Albert B. Fall was guilty of accepting a $100,000 bribe, but another jury acquitted the oil millionaire, Edward L. Doheny, of giving it. Harry F. Sinclair, the other oil tycoon, also escaped conviction of conspiring to defraud the government, but fell afoul of the Senate and the District of Columbia court on charges of contempt and jury shadowing. He served a short term in jail.

It was not an overwhelming victory, but probably it was better than anyone else could have accomplished. And it was enough to stamp Roberts in the eyes of the Senate and of the press as the foremost prosecutor of his day.

During the relatively short time they have been in Washington, Justice and Mrs Roberts have carved out an important social niche for themselves, and as charming a one as is possible among the stuffy people who consider themselves the elite of the Capital. The Justice is one of the hardest-working members of the Court and lets nothing interfere with the opinions which roll from his agile and sometimes verbose pen. But, probably more than any other justice, he finds time to attend Washington's most exclusive dinner parties. Part of his social activity undoubtedly is the result of Mrs Roberts' bustling yen to be seen among the right people. Mrs Roberts has a sparkling wit, and a sense of discretion which gives her husband agonies, but the combination makes her a delightful dinner companion, and the Robertses are in demand.

The Justice himself is not without a sense of humor. One evening, at one of Mrs Borden Harriman's famous supper parties, the discussion swung round to the Supreme Court, and Heywood Broun suggested to Roberts that all the justices take regular sabbatical leave just as do university professors.

"Every seven years, Mr Justice, you ought to go out and get acquainted with the people," Broun proposed. "You ought to go out and ride in day coaches and in the smoking cars. You ought to talk with farmers and filling-station operators. Then perhaps the Court would get some real economic and social philosophy."

To which Justice Roberts shot back: "But I haven't been on the Court seven years."

Mrs Roberts is more than a wife to her husband. She is a real companion and pal, and frequently the two can be seen hiking through the streets of Georgetown enjoying their exercise and each other's company as if they were married yesterday. Mrs Roberts is also something of a manager. In a firm and sometimes joshing manner she leads her husband in the paths which she has picked. And if he rebels, she has a stock method of kidding him into obedience.

"Owen," she says, "remember! You're just an old man! One of the Nine Old Men!"

While she would not for a moment intrude her ideas on the legal details by which her husband arrives at his opinions, nevertheless her own opinions on such things as the New Deal, crop control, labor legislation and class consciousness, expressed freely and with pithy vigor over the breakfast table during recent years, undoubtedly have played a more decisive part in some of the recent decisions of the Supreme Court than some of the lawyers who argued them. Mrs Roberts usually goes up to the Court to hear them argued. And she always goes up when her husband is to recite from memory one of his dramatic opinions in the graphic, forceful manner of his old jury-pleading days with the P.R.T.

Mrs Roberts is frankly and avidly against the New Deal and, much to her husband's distress, has no hesitancy in announcing it at every dinner party she attends.

"I don't see why the Republicans didn't nominate someone like Senator Hastings for President," she once said, referring to the Delaware representative of the Du Pont dynasty.

The Justice himself is more tolerant. He himself admits that he has been a Republican all his life, but adds a little naïvely, "Of course, I can't vote now," forgetting that his one vote on the Supreme Court sometimes has wielded more power than both houses of Congress and the entire farm vote of the country. The Justice has occasional words of praise for Roosevelt, and after the latter vetoed the bonus bill, Roberts remarked:

"That veto will not lose the President a single vote. Everyone respects a man who has the courage to say no."

Perhaps because he is young and has been on the Court relatively a short time, Roberts, although discreet, is franker than any of his colleagues save Justice Stone. Once at the annual White House reception to the judiciary he was discussing his AAA decision with Joseph B. Keenan, Assistant Attorney General.

"I thought the arguments of the government," Roberts volunteered, "were excellent. Especially those of the Solicitor General."

Only three days before, he had rendered his opinion knocking those arguments into a cocked hat.

In Philadelphia, Roberts owned a large town house on Delancey Street near elite Rittenhouse Square. Since coming to Washington, however, he has sold this house and acquired a modest but very comfortable home in historic Georgetown. It is surrounded by a garden in which Mrs Roberts putters every spring; and with a sweeping veranda, upon which, during a sunshiny afternoon, the Justice relaxes in an easy chair, a stack of books by his side, while his daughter, Elizabeth, works at a large easel. They are devoted companions, and just after her father handed down his famous AAA opinion, Elizabeth won an art prize with a painting entitled "Vegetables."

Although they enjoy Washington, the entire Roberts family can hardly wait until spring to get up to their farm in Chester County, Pennsylvania. Here, just outside Phoenixville and about twenty miles from Philadelphia, Roberts has combined six small farms into one estate of 650 acres. He calls it "Bryn-Coed" which is Welsh for "Wooded Top of the Hill," and it is his pride and joy.

Most of the farm Roberts leases to a regular farming corporation, but one section he operates himself as a dairy farm and takes great pleasure in doing it. He has a large, rambling two-story house, half of it dating back to the early eighteen-hundreds and the other portion being a brownstone addition which he built. It is screened by a row of tall firs and sits at the head of a lane of apple trees. There is also a small modern greenhouse, where the Roberts gardener specializes in Mrs Roberts' favorite flowers, lilies and carnations. During the winter, shipments of the blooms are sent regularly to the Georgetown house, causing Mrs Roberts' stunning pink, red and white carnation centerpieces to be the envy of her friends.

Roberts operates his large estate on a strictly business basis. He makes daily milk deliveries to a dairy, raises all his own feed, vegetables and fruit, including apricots, and two years ago when he had some extra bales of alfalfa, sold them when the price was up. The Justice is proud of his produce, and all weekend visitors are sure to go away with their car overflowing with vegetables. Roberts also is proud of his dairy herd and its equipment, which is the best in the neighborhood. He has thirty registered Guernseys, housed in a new $35,000 barn. He used to sell his milk in Phoenixville but, learning that a company in Montclaire, across the Schuylkill River, was paying better prices, he transferred to it. Roberts used to raise pigs, but gave it up in 1934, though not because of the AAA baby-pig program. He has never subscribed to the AAA crop-curtailment thesis.

When he was younger, Roberts did considerable canoeing and fishing, but since going on the bench has done little of either, even selling a Pocono Mountain camp he once owned. Once an enthusiastic horseman, Roberts has enjoyed little of that form of exercise since "Snooks," his favorite nine-year-old single-footer, fell with him several years ago and broke his arm. Roberts still has "Snooks" but rides infrequently. His chief exercise now comes in the summer, during which the Justice, clad in khaki breeches and old shoes, helps with the lighter work of his farm. He used to rise at an hour rivaling that of any farmer, but in recent years has grown more conservative.

The Justice affects no squirely airs and is popular with his neighbors, frequently driving his own battered station wagon to Phoenixville, where he attracts no special attention. In fact, many of the townspeople don't know who he is. That included James Quinn, circulation manager of the Phoenixville *Republican,* who got off a train one afternoon and, noticing a tall man in worn workclothes climbing into a car, asked for a lift. His request was granted, and on the way Quinn quizzed his driver about crops and farming conditions and got all the answers. At his office, Quinn thanked the farmer, and it was not until he got inside, and was asked by members of his staff how long he had known Roberts, that he learned who he was.

The Robertses patronize a chain-store grocery on Bridge Street, the "main street" of Phoenixville. It operates on a strictly cash-and-carry basis, but through special arrangement with the New York office, the Justice has a charge account—the only one in the place. Once or twice a summer he drops in at Martin & Martin's, leading men's clothing store, and stocks up on personal necessities. He never asks the price of an article, merely orders it. Mrs Roberts is a much more exacting shopper. Not long ago she ordered some deck chairs to give to a near-by summer camp of the Pennsylvania Academy of Art. The local hardware merchant thought they were for her personally and sent "Gold Seal" chairs. When Mrs Roberts got the bill and discovered they cost $4.25 each she scolded him vigorously.

Although Roberts has withdrawn from most of his once-varied activities, he still continues to be chairman of the Chester County Council of the Boy Scouts of America and every year contributes $750 toward a $20,000 fund which the council raises to send its troops to a summer camp in Maryland. Roberts visits the camp every summer, and one year gave a party on his farm for the forty scoutmasters of the county.

Perhaps because Roberts has no sons of his own, he has always taken a great interest in boys, and one thing which he liked most about being on the Board of City Trusts in Philadelphia was his contact with Girard College, an excellent school for orphan boys founded by Stephen Girard and administered by the board. Most of the boys at Girard regard the members of the board as mossbacked old fogies, but Roberts they always liked. He established his popularity as a speaker at the Sunday chapel exercises, where he gave such excellent straight-from-the-shoulder talks that he has been a regular speaker at the Girard commencement exercises almost ever since. On one occasion Roberts shared the honors with Joseph P. McLaughlin, the orator of the senior class, who was warmly congratulated by Roberts.

"I enjoyed your speech very much," said the Justice. "You were very good indeed."

"Thanks," replied the youngster, unabashed. "I thought you were all right, too."

On his trips to Phoenixville, Roberts frequently drops in at the principal drugstore to buy tobacco. Usually he smokes a pipe, but one of the clerks once persuaded him to buy some cigars—ten-centers called "Walnuts."

"That was the line we were pushing," the clerk explained. "I asked Mr Roberts how about some cigars. He just says 'Give me a cigar,' and as we're trying to sell this kind, that's what he got. He's a push-over, really, for a salesman who is trying."

When Roberts comes to town alone he often drapes himself

against a mailbox and chats about crops and prices with passers-by who know him. Occasionally, on these trips he remains over for supper at the Bridge Street Eating House, a Greek restaurant run by John Sotier. It isn't the best place in town, but it is quiet and clean, with a white-tile counter down one side and booths on the other. Roberts invariably has a tenderloin steak, with mashed or boiled potatoes and fresh vegetables. He will not eat canned vegetables, nor does he take dessert. Sotier has a liquor license, but Roberts drinks milk with his meal.

The dinner costs seventy-five cents and Roberts leaves a fifteen-cent tip—which rates him high in Sotier's.

After supper the Justice wanders two blocks up Bridge Street and takes in the early show at the Colonial Theater; admission price, twenty-five cents, plus two cents Pennsylvania state tax. The pictures are about three weeks behind first-run city houses.

Thus flows the pastoral life of the dynamic gentleman who has become such a storm center of the Supreme Court.

Justice Roberts became the storm center of the Court after he wrote the opinion by which the Nine Old Men, 6 to 3, declared unconstitutional the Agricultural Adjustment Act. The steps by which Roberts arrived at that opinion and the bitter intercourt discussion it aroused are discussed elsewhere in this book. It is sufficient to state here only that it was a distinct surprise that Roberts should have written the opinion, and that it continues to be one of the most criticized decisions ever handed down by the Supreme Court.

Roberts' authorship of the opinion was a surprise chiefly because he had handed down a ringing decision in the Nebbia milk case only eighteen months before, upholding one of the most moot and vital principles of the New Deal, the right of the government to fix prices and to regulate industry. In this case it was the right of New York State to regulate milk prices.

"A state," Justice Roberts had decreed, at a time when the Roosevelt administration was at the peak of its popularity, "is free to adopt whatever economic policy may be reasonably deemed to promote public welfare and to enforce that policy by legislation adapted to its purpose. The courts are without authority either to declare such policy, or, when it is declared by the legislative arm, to override it. . . . This Court has from the early days affirmed that the power to promote the general welfare is inherent in government. . . . The Constitution does not secure to anyone the liberty to conduct his business in such fashion as to inflict injury upon the public at large, or upon any substantial group of the people."

These words had a ring almost identical with that of Justice Stone in the AAA case when he said: "For the removal of unwise laws from the statute books, appeal lies not to the courts but to the ballot and to the processes of democratic government."

They did not sound like the words of the same Roberts, uttered eighteen changing months later, from which Stone dissented.

"Powers not granted [to the federal government] are prohibited," Roberts decreed in the AAA case. "None to regulate agricultural production is given, and therefore legislation by Congress for that purpose is forbidden. . . . It does not help to declare that local conditions throughout the nation have created a situation of national concern. . . . We are not now required to ascertain the scope of the phrase 'general welfare of the United States' or to determine whether an appropriation in aid of agriculture falls within it. . . . If the act before us is a proper exercise of the federal taxing power, evidently the regulation of all industry throughout the United States may be accomplished by similar exercise of the same power."

The ridicule which legal authorities heaped upon Roberts' reasoning was the most caustic in years. Professor Henry M. Hart, Jr, of the Harvard Law School, published a review showing that Roberts' arguments would make the protective tariff unconstitutional. Dr Howard Lee McBain, professor of constitutional law at Columbia, declared: "One can hardly escape the conclusion that the Court was determined to kill this law no matter what sacrifice of logic and reasoning was necessary in the process of torturing the Constitution to that end." John T. Flynn, after showing how Roberts had contradicted himself in successive paragraphs of his opinion, concluded: "The result of Justice Roberts' decision is that the American people are the only people in the world who cannot deal with their economic problems."

But the most penetrating observation came from that uncompromising representative of wealth and reaction, ex-Senator David Aiken Reed, who said:

"I agree with Mr Roberts' conclusions, but I wish to God he'd written a better opinion."

What all of these gentlemen failed to appreciate, however, was a condition which best can be expressed in Justice Roberts' own words: "I wrote the opinion for the majority. It was a great responsibility, since usually this is the task of the Chief Justice. The views were not mine alone, but those of my colleagues."

This was true. The fact is that Owen J. Roberts has now become the spokesman for the reactionary wing of the Court. He has now stepped into the place once occupied by the aged and failing Sutherland, and is now put forward by his die-hard colleagues to weave into circuitous opinions all of their diverse legal verbiage. Sutherland, they had selected as spokesman because he was suave, gentle, too dumb to realize that he was being made the goat, and loved to bask in the limelight. His gracious, soft-spoken manner was an excellent megaphone for the economic dynamite which fell from his lips. He had the knack to camouflage the main points of his opinions with high-sounding constitutional law, and Roberts, his successor, is equally, if not better, adapted for this role. He is young, has a magnetic personality and the best delivery of any member of the Court. He is a good legal technician and can write opinions as clear and concise as his AAA opinion was purposefully ambiguous. Even more important, his early record of liberalism on the Supreme Court divorces him in the public mind from the extreme reactionaries, makes him appear to occupy a position of careful judicial balance. And finally, Roberts has thrown himself with a willful religious fervor into the work of holding fast the type of rugged individualism which he learned as a struggling lawyer in the mid-Victorian city of Philadelphia.

The manner in which Roberts came to assume this role is an interesting study of human psychology.

When he first came to the Supreme Court, he expressed to friends, with characteristic candor, some doubt as to whether or not he could become a judge. All his life, he pointed out, had been spent as an advocate. He was at his best in taking the position in which his client found himself, whether right or wrong, and working out a plausible defense or attack to suit the immediate requirements. His mind was not accustomed to the judicial approach, to weighing the right or wrong of a question or its conformity to the law. Instead he was accustomed to building up the law around the particular side of the case on which he found himself—as, undoubtedly, he did in the AAA decision.

So Owen Roberts, full of cross-currents and doubts within himself, came to the highest bench of the land just after a brief but impressionistic immersion in a bath of liberalism during the Teapot Dome prosecution. And as a result, his first two years on the Court reflected that immersion. He voted with the liberals in every important case.

Then the gold plate of the Teapot Dome experience began to tarnish, and the dross of the old Philadelphia amalgam showed up in spots underneath. Roberts, however, still sat at the crossroads, still uncertain regarding the conflicting currents within himself. Also, he sat beside one of the most irreconcilable, scheming and effective Irishmen ever to occupy a place on the Supreme bench. Pierce Butler not only sat on Roberts' left but was a frequent visitor at the Roberts home. In Butler there are no cross-currents. He has an undeviating, single-track mind. He knew exactly what he wanted, and that was to win the newest member of the Court over to the reactionaries. He knew how apt a substitute he would be for the failing Sutherland. And he knew that if he did not win Roberts, Butler's cause was lost, for the new Chief Justice showed skittish indications of hovering round the liberals. So, by a wisecrack here and a subtle argument there, he went about the task of wooing Roberts. Despite his boorish manners on the bench, Butler can be an extremely attractive person when he wants to. In fact, he is the best personal lobbyist on the Court.

Eventually he got Roberts. He got him chiefly through Roberts' desire to get away from the conflict within himself, and his desire to settle down to one easily acceptable, never-deviating dogma.

But Butler was aided by other factors.

Roberts found that dogma in the winter of 1935–36—just before his AAA decision. And before he discovered it, he went through one of the most troubled and crisscrossed periods of his life. His trouble was that disease which affects many prominent men in election year—*presidentitis*.

At that time, Landon still was a typically unknown governor of a typical prairie state, and the Republican party was casting about for a candidate with prestige and popularity to defeat Roosevelt. Roberts' name figured prominently in the speculation. His handsome, virile appearance, his impressive record as Teapot Dome prosecutor, the aura of liberalism surrounding his early decisions, and the favorable geographic position of his state, which commands the second largest vote in the electoral college, all gave powerful momentum to his stock as nominee of the Republican party.

Roberts considered the possibilities most seriously. So also did Mrs Roberts. He was torn between risking his fate to ballots or keeping his key position on the Court. And he was very much aware of the fact that he could tip the scales either way among the Nine Old Men.

Finally Mrs Roberts decided it for him. There was no use risking Owen's future, she felt, on such an uncertain thing as politics, especially when the position which Owen now held really was more powerful than that of the President.

"Owen's duty," she told other members of the family, "is to use his position to stabilize the country."

After Roberts concurred in decapitating the Railroad Retirement Act, a newspaper friend remarked to the Justice that that decision was not likely to win many labor votes for his candidacy.

"No," replied Roberts, "I figure that cost about three million votes."

But by that time Roberts had made up his mind. "Everyone respects a man who has the courage to say no," Roberts said of Roosevelt after his bonus veto. And to the New Deal legislation which comes before him, he has determined to keep on saying NO.

Reactionary consistency has now become his god. It is not altogether a happy worship. For the god is an uncompromising, jealous god, permitting no questioning of legal precedents or constitutional rights, insisting only upon a dull, unceasing marking-of-time before the twin altars of the social and economic status quo.

But Roberts has seen his bearded friend, the Chief Justice, making agonized salaams before the God of Uncertainty, and while he is not happy where he is, he fears to move. He has embraced the safe legal catholicism of Pierce Butler and is determined not to let it go.

He has set his face in one direction and wants never to turn back. Owen Roberts is out to stabilize the country.

CHAPTER VIII

The Crusader

Between Justice Louis Dembitz Brandeis and the other enlightened jurists who have made Supreme Court history exists a fundamental distinction.

The latter primarily have been philosophers, enunciating stirring canons of liberty and justice. Beyond that they have not gone. Having laid down their lofty precepts, they entered no camp; kept aloof from the din and clash of the fray.

Not so Brandeis. He has not been content to remain on the side lines.

To him the passive role of proclaiming doctrine is not enough. First and foremost he has been a crusader.

This is the historic role which Brandeis fills in the life of the nation. It was as a crusader that he came to the Supreme Court over the desperate opposition of entrenched wealth, and it is as a crusader that for twenty years he has carved his epochal place as a jurist.

Brandeis frequently has been denounced by apostles of vested interests as a revolutionary who wished to destroy capitalism. And he has been just as bitterly denounced by radicals as a protector of capitalism. The truth is that he is neither. He is a crusader chiefly for human rights. His economic philosophy is rooted deep in American history. Thomas Jefferson was its founding father; Andrew Jackson, Abraham Lincoln, the elder Robert M. La Follette and Senator George Norris its greatest political exponents.

The essence of his theory is economic democracy, a social order in which the great mass of men, the little men, are assured of economic security and a share of the wealth they produce. Brandeis does not believe in collectivism. He is friendly but not an ardent champion of unionized labor or of Soviet Russia. He is as uncompromisingly opposed to this type of economic control as he is to that by capital. He fears the concentration of power in any form—whether in the hands of a President, an international banker or the NRA.

"Look at ancient Athens," he says. "It was no bigger than a county in Texas. Yet how important to the world."

The key to this famous antipathy to bigness is his hostility to any infringement of personal or economic liberty. Giant economic units, whether capitalist or collectivist, he holds, are menaces to individual security. The happiness and well-being of great masses of men become dependent on the will and self-interest of one individual or of one small class. If a large corporation shuts down operations, the economic structure of thousands is instantly destroyed; whereas, if these workers were employed in small shops, the suspension of a plant would affect only a few, and these could be quickly absorbed. Thus Brandeis reasons.

Also he reasons that there are not enough exceptional men in the world to direct wisely and efficiently any great concentration of corporate or social power.

"How can you know all of the things which take place in your vast organization?" he once asked the head of a great store system.

Brandeis is a great lover of mankind, yet at heart he is profoundly skeptical regarding man as an individual.

He distrusts man's ability to cope with the intricate economic complexities of the age, with the stupendous concentration of power put into his hands by modern machinery.

"Size brings monopoly instead of competition," says Brandeis. "Size submerges the talents of millions of people, and the wealth of the nation is gauged by the capacities of great numbers and not by the few. There is only a little difference between the capacity of the big men who dominate these empires and the rest of us lowly folk"—and he points to himself.

This is the explanation of why he struck down the NRA, yet at the same time has blasted his reactionary colleagues for denying to states and the federal government the right to experiment with social and economic regulation. To Brandeis, the dictatorship of the Blue Eagle was as sinister as the obstructionism of his Tory colleagues.

Brandeis has watched the development of the New Deal with intense interest and sympathy, though sometimes strong disapproval. And more than any other justice he has dropped a quiet and occasional hint to the official involved when a certain policy seemed to be heading toward disaster. General Johnson once came to see the Justice, quite by surprise, during the early days of the Blue Eagle. Brandeis never had met him, and did not know he was coming, but in his mild-mannered way he warned the NRA administrator that the tremendous concentration of power in the hands of one agency and the code domination by larger and better organized firms were bound to cause him trouble. No clearer warning could have been given that when the National Industrial Recovery Act came before the Supreme Court, whether in the Schechter case or any other, it would be vetoed, at least as far as one justice was concerned.

Brandeis went even further with Secretary of Agriculture Wallace in regard to his crop-curtailment program, calling in Gardner Jackson, one of Wallace's former assistants, to say that he was much worried over the fact that the program was causing the United States to lose its world cotton markets. If cotton continued at such high prices, he predicted, Russia and Brazil would soon edge American cotton completely out of the market, leaving the South bankrupt. And he was especially concerned with the plight of the Southern tenant farmer or share cropper, forced to move from his pitifully small farm because of the reduction of cotton acreage. Brandeis specifically asked that this message be taken to Henry Wallace and to Chester Davis, the latter then administrator of the Agricultural Adjustment Administration. He also urged Jackson to organize the small Southern share croppers into some form of co-operative or union capable of demanding better economic treatment.

Thus, on and off the bench, Brandeis carries on his crusade. No other member of the Supreme Court has sent forth so many of his young friends and disciples to play important roles in the Roosevelt and other administrations. He taught them his philosophy, his spirit of crusade, and has watched them as they went out to carry his banner. Sometimes he has watched them with approval, sometimes he has not. James M. Landis, his one-time secretary, he has watched in the important post of chairman of the Securities and Exchange Commission, an able regulator of the bears and the bulls of Wall Street. Dean Acheson, another secretary, he has watched first as Under Secretary of the Treasury, later as a utilities attorney in testing out the constitutionality of New Deal laws before the Supreme Court. And Louis R. Glavis, whom he once defended in the Pinchot-Ballinger fight, he has watched as head of the greatest secret-service agency in the government.

Brandeis had acted as counsel for Glavis in 1910 when, as investigator for the Interior Department, he was dismissed for exposing an Indian land-grab scandal which reflected upon his chief, Richard A. Ballinger, Secretary of the Interior. Brandeis' annihilating cross-examination caused the resignation of Ballinger and exposed the fact that Taft had lied deliberately to shield his cabinet officer.

Twenty-three years later, Brandeis saw the man he had defended reinstated in the Interior Department as chief of the Bureau of Investigation, watched him assemble a force of a thousand supersleuths in an imitation of the Soviet OGPU, and heard reports of the greatest activity in wire-tapping, shadowing and infringement upon the personal privacy of American citizens since the World War. It was the activity of "Glavis's men" in the Texas oil fields which helped to prejudice Brandeis against the attempt of the Roosevelt administration to regulate the production of oil—a theory of regulation which coincided with Brandeis' own ideas of economic control except on one point: it favored the big oil operators. On top of this, Glavis created a corps of secret police to aid those big operators. So Brandeis cast his vote against the regulation of this vital national resource, even joining with his conservative colleagues in trumping up the excuse of unconstitutional delegation of power in order to do so.

Afterward he dropped a quiet hint regarding the OGPU activities of his former disciple, in a place where he knew it would do the most good.

"All this tapping of telephone wires," he said in his usual mild way, to Harry Slattery, personal assistant to Secretary of Interior Ickes, "all this—I hate to use a nasty word for it—but all this espionage. We had it during the war. But in ordinary times, it's not compatible with our American system."

Glavis' espionage activities were curtailed, and shortly thereafter he was dropped.

The crusader on the Supreme Court was keeping a watchful eye on the men and movements he has molded.

Louis Dembitz Brandeis was born in Louisville, Kentucky, in 1856, of parents from whom he inherited his devotion to democracy and his crusading fervor. His father and mother were German Jews who had fled to the United States after the failure of the German revolution in 1848. His maternal grandfather had led a revolution in Poland as early as 1830. His uncle, Louis Dembitz, was a delegate to the Republican convention in 1860, where he helped to nominate Lincoln, while Brandeis' father was an outspoken Union supporter, despite his residence in a Southern community. The Justice can still remember how, as a child, he accompanied his mother while carrying food and medicine to Northern soldiers under the cover of darkness.

Brandeis' father was a grain merchant who made a substantial income but never permitted the subject of money to be discussed in his home. His two boys, Alfred and Louis, had all the advantages of the material things in life, coupled with a common-sense upbringing which avoided the usual disadvantages. Louis's youth was that of any normal youngster, and except for a little excess of belligerency, which might have been equally evident in an embryo gangster, there was nothing in those early years to indicate the crusading career in store for the son of the Louis-ville grain dealer.

Perhaps because he was four years younger than his brother Alfred, and also because of his natural precociousness, Louis usually was put forward by his playmates as their juvenile trigger man. Whenever a newcomer appeared in the neighborhood, es-pecially if he was what they called a "Lord Fauntleroy"—chief qualification for which was wearing shoes in the summer—Louis was egged on to do battle. Thus began his attacks upon plu-tocracy.

There was one fight in which he participated, however, in which he needed no goading. Cause of the altercation was a fair-haired and pigtailed young lady who loomed large in the life of the youthful jurist, but now—O Fate—is remembered by him only as Emma. At a dance one night, another boy, Julius von Borries, also imbued with the conviction that Emma was essential to his future happiness, asserted that conviction, and next day he and Brandeis fought it out for the hand of the lady. History does not record who won the fight, but in later and much more mature years Brandeis married Alice Goldmark of New York, whose parents, like his, fled Germany in 1848, and who has been to the Justice as understanding and devoted a wife as Emma was glamorous in those romantic, turbulent days just after the Civil War.

Miss Alice Grady, secretary to Brandeis for twenty-two years before he was elevated to the Supreme Court, tells many stories of his boyhood, all bearing out the fact that he was anything but the aesthetic, sensitive person he is today. On one Fourth of July, while the Civil War was still raging, Louis and his brother were celebrating the independence of their country by dampen-ing small quantities of black powder, then setting fire to it with a match. Suddenly a spark touched off the entire powder flask, frightfully burning the boys' faces. They washed the powder off in order to conceal the accident from their mother, but soon their faces had swollen pitifully. It was several weeks before they fully recovered.

On another occasion the Brandeis boys were engaged in the pastime of propping a straw man in a doorway, then ringing the bell. But this time, the precipitate toppling forward of the straw man caused the maid to faint, and the owner of the house came to the door with a shotgun. Fortunately, the Brandeis boys were well hidden.

Underneath this youthful impishness there must have been much of the kindly sympathy which has been one of the Brandeis' chief qualities in later life. It gleamed forth even then as Lizzie, the old family cook, testified:

"Mr Louis was the thoughtfules' boy in this world. I remember very well when I went to Mattapoisett. I didn't know how white folks went in bathin'. I got a bathin' suit, but there wa'n't nothing to it below the knees. I jus' thought I couldn't do it.

"So I walked down on the beach to watch the others swim, and there was Mr Louis lying flat on his back in the sand. I said: 'Why ain't you in bathin', honey?' And he said: 'I'm waiting for you, Lizzie.'

" 'Go on,' I said, 'I ain't goin' in. I'm afraid of the salt water.'

" 'That's all right, Lizzie,' he said, 'I won't let it hurt you. And I ain't goin' in one step until you come along.'

"So rather than have him lose the nice swim, I jes' had to go and put on that bathin' suit, and he led me in just like I was a fine lady."

The Brandeises were a wealthy, aristocratic family, some of them marrying gentiles, the St Louis Taussigs. Young Brandeis saw little of his people. He studied at the University of Louisville, at Dresden, Germany, and took his law degree at Harvard in 1877. He was then twenty-one, a brilliant, well-educated youth, but one who enjoyed the lighter things of life as much as the deeper, and who got bored, after one year of law practice, in the provincial city of St Louis and returned to Boston and the more enjoyable haunts of his law-school days. At Boston he mingled with his old friends among the blue-bloods of Back Bay and found himself building up a corporation law practice not greatly dissimilar from that of Hughes or Butler or Roberts in their youth. The only philosophy which appeared to motivate his practice in those very early days was how best to steer his clients toward their chief goal, that of increasing dividends.

To that end he served as counsel and director of the United Shoe Machinery Company, beginning in 1899, and drew up for it a leasing system which later he repudiated and which was the subject of bitter attack at the time of his Senate confirmation. The leases contained a "tying in" clause whereby the shoe factory that rented one type of machine from the United Shoe Machinery Company also had to take all of its machines. The machines continued to be the property of United and could be recalled at any time on only thirty days' notice, meaning possible bankruptcy to the renting manufacturers. Brandeis not only helped organize the company but defended the system as legal, appearing before a committee of the Massachusetts state legislature, where he said that it had the advantage of renting machinery to the small manufacturer at exactly the same price as to the big, whereas the big manufacturer had the advantage of discounts in purchasing larger quantities of leather and raw materials. He also defended the leases as legal monopolies similar to patents.

In 1936, when the Rust Brothers of Memphis, Tennessee, were perfecting their revolutionary cotton-picking machine, Brandeis was consulted regarding a leasing plan whereby they would sell no machines, but lease them only to growers who guaranteed not to throw field hands out of work. But the Justice was skeptical.

"My own experience," he said a little ruefully, "is that it is impossible to control machinery for social ends without tremendous financial backing. We had hoped to do that with the

United Shoe Machinery Company, but it turned out the reverse."

Years before this, however, he had discovered his mistake with the United Shoe Machinery Company and in 1906, after urging certain policy changes on S. M. Winslow, its president, Brandeis resigned as counsel. The next year the Massachusetts legislature passed an act outlawing the "tying in" clause. For several years thereafter Brandeis turned down retainers from competitors of the United Shoe Machinery Company, but five years later—in 1911—he acted as counsel for the Shoe Manufacturers' Alliance, a group of smaller manufacturers fighting United's monopoly, and appeared before the Massachusetts legislature to denounce as unlawful restraint of trade the leasing system he once had defended.

Brandeis returned its $2,500 fee to the Shoe Manufacturers' Alliance, but paid that amount from his own pocket into the receipts of his law firm. He felt that while he could afford to give his own time to public causes, he could not rob his law partners of legitimate fees. The blue-blood leaders of Boston business with whom Brandeis once associated never forgave him for turning against his old client.

But something had begun to ferment in the breast of Louis Brandeis several years before this—something planted there by his father who fought for freedom in Germany and by his grandfather who fought for freedom in Poland and by his uncle who fought for freedom in the United States.

Trying to diagnose that fermentation in later years, Brandeis said: "I think the steel strike at Homestead first set me thinking about the labor problem. I had been asked to deliver a series of lectures on common law at the Massachusetts Institute of Technology, but after the Homestead riots I saw that our common law was inadequate and I threw the lectures away."

So, one by one, Louis Brandeis discarded the conventional ideas he had learned at Louisville and Harvard and molded his character as the "People's Crusader" he is today.

At that time he had one of the most lucrative law practices in

Boston, but he began deliberately to set aside part of his time for public welfare work. His start was a very modest one. "I first went through the stage of charitable work," he said later. One of his first "causes" was that of the consumer. The famous Dingley Tariff Act was being written in 1897, the beginning of the high-tariff policy which the rest of the world has so aptly emulated. Almost every industry in the country had sent representatives to Washington to demand protection, and during the height of their clamor a young man with a quiet manner and a cultured accent rose before the House Ways and Means Committee and said:

"I desire to speak in behalf of those who form a far larger part of the people of this country than any who have found representation here."

Chairman Dingley looked peeved. He remarked that this was not the proper place for a free-trade speech. But finally, after much laughter and jeering, the young man was given five minutes.

That marked the beginning of Brandeis' crusade for the public. He next attracted national attention in opposing a fifty-year lease of the Boston subway, forcing the traction company to take a twenty-year lease on terms favorable to the city. After that fight, the head of the citizens' committee which worked with Brandeis asked him for his bill.

"There is no fee," Brandeis replied. "This is part of a plan of mine. As soon as I can do so I hope to give the larger part of my time to public work."

After that he waged a similar fight against the Boston Elevated Company and against the Boston gas company, forcing it to adopt a sliding rate scale by which dividends increased as rates decreased. Brandeis also waged a terrific battle against the efforts of the New York, New Haven & Hartford Railroad to secure the Boston & Maine and monopolize the transportation of all New England. He exposed the manner in which the Equitable Life Assurance Society was wasting the resources of its policyholders, and organized a plan of state insurance which still stands as a model for the nation. He championed the constitutionality of the Oregon minimum-wage law for women and successfully fought it through half a dozen courts. And in 1910 he was drafted by both sides as arbitrator in the bitter strike of the New York garmentworkers, succeeding not only in bringing about peace, but in establishing a relationship between workers and employers which has served as a model to this day.

Up until this time, Brandeis had not come into contact with any except the highest type of Jew, and his experience with the Jew of the ghetto during the garmentworkers' strike marked the beginning of his active interest in the Zionist movement. A few years later he became head of the Zionist organization in this country, continuing until he was appointed to the Supreme Court in 1916. In 1930 he was offered the presidency of the World Zionist movement, but acceptance would have necessitated his resignation from the Court, and he declined.

Long before this, the name Brandeis had become anathema to his old friends in Boston and to representatives of vested interest throughout the land. He was declared a traitor to his class, and no one, save possibly Franklin D. Roosevelt in recent years, was so hated. This hatred reached its high point during the railroad-rate hearings in 1910, when Brandeis represented all the trade organizations along the Atlantic seaboard before the Interstate Commerce Commission in fighting the proposed rate increases. The railroads, he claimed, could save a million dollars a day—a statement which subsequent years have proven to be correct.

In these hearings, as in all his fights, he was superbly ruthless. He never gave quarter or asked for it. He had a passion for facts, more and more facts, always at his fingertips. And he hurled them at the big railroad executives in the most inexorable cross-examination of that era. When he finished with Sam Rea of the Pennsylvania Railroad and Alfred H. Smith of the New York Central, they left the stand hardly knowing their own names.

Imagine therefore the consternation of big business when Woodrow Wilson sent the name of Louis Dembitz Brandeis to the Senate as associate justice of the Supreme Court!

Once before, just after his election in 1912, Wilson had selected Brandeis for high office, planning to make him Attorney General. Immediately the Elihu Roots, the Tafts, the Lodges and the Lowells held up their hands in righteous horror and warned: "Dangerous Radical!" And Wilson had withdrawn his appointment. But in 1916 Wilson faced a difficult campaign for re-election. He had already lost the big-business vote, especially that of New England, and he needed the Jewish vote. To get it he promised Louis Marshall, Samuel Untermeyer and Charles R. Crane to appoint Brandeis to the Supreme Court. From this he could not recede.

The fury of the reactionaries was boundless. Every former president of the American Bar Association joined in the howls of rage. Taft, still nursing a grudge from the Ballinger investigation, led the attack. S. M. Winslow, head of the United Shoe Machinery Company, rushed to Washington to testify before the Senate Judiciary Committee. Here, claimed the Boston bar, was tangible evidence of dishonesty against a former client. And although Winslow admitted that Brandeis, in fighting United, used no information he got as attorney for United, they used the shoe-machinery case as their main gun in the Senate fight against confirmation.

The fight became a titanic struggle which dragged out from January until June. As the chamber approached the deciding vote the outcome was in doubt. It was at this point that the Chicago *Tribune,* now one of the most reactionary newspapers in the country, carried a front-page story drawing a deadly parallel between Brandeis' legal career and that of the leaders of the bar who were fighting him. The article charged that every one of these men was motivated by a personal grievance. It showed that they had been arrayed against Brandeis in important cases and had gone down to defeat before him.

The late Oscar Underwood, Democrat from Alabama, only

recently had come to the Senate from the House. He was a conservative, but of rigid impartiality, and because of this carried great weight with his colleagues. Underwood was still uncertain in his own mind about the appointment when Elisha Hanson, then a member of the Washington staff of the *Tribune,* came to him with his paper's article.

Underwood was deeply impressed with the facts it presented, asked Hanson to get him ninety-six copies of the issue, and placed one on the desk of every member of the Senate. The article proved effective. A number of senators, who, like Underwood, were still uncertain, became convinced that the outcry against Brandeis was tainted. In the final showdown they voted for him. He won by a creditable margin.

But there was one vote in the roll call which aroused widespread surprise. This was the unexpected "No" of Senator William S. Kenyon of Iowa. A militant progressive and staunch ally of the elder Senator La Follette, Kenyon was one of the first to acclaim Brandeis' appointment. But in those days the dry forces were omnipotent in some states and the Anti-Saloon League was one of the organizations which turned thumbs down on Brandeis. It accused him of being a "tool of the liquor interests," as a result of having been employed as attorney for Massachusetts brewers to put an end to a blackmailing racket which was flourishing in the legislature. It had become the practice of grafting lawmakers to introduce drastic dry measures and to threaten to press them unless bought off. These demands finally became so heavy that the brewers refused to be shaken down any longer and employed Brandeis to break up the system. He exposed it, drove the guilty legislators to cover and put an end to their exactions.

Because of this professional connection, the prohibitionists, led by the Anti-Saloon League, opposed Brandeis; and Kenyon, a fanatical dry, was persuaded to disregard his original endorsement and vote shoulder to shoulder with the reactionaries against confirmation.

Senator Borah, who also voted against confirmation, since has apologized, but President Lowell of Harvard, who took the lead in the Boston opposition, remained silent.

Five years later when President Harding appointed Taft chief justice, many were surprised to discover that a warm friendship existed between Taft and Brandeis. Because of the bitter Ballinger episode and Taft's subsequent display of vindictiveness, it was generally believed that the two men were not on speaking terms. But one day, several years after his appointment, Brandeis was out taking his regular evening stroll just before dinner, which is served punctually at seven. It was a rainy, misty evening, and he was hurrying back to his home when, in turning a corner, he bumped into a large, portly gentleman also walking rapidly.

Brandeis looked up, but before he could say anything the other man held out his hand and said:

"Isn't this Mr Brandeis? I am Mr Taft. I once did you a great injustice, Mr Brandeis. I am sorry."

"Thank you, Mr Taft."

"Good night, Mr Brandeis."

"Good night, Mr Taft."

Justice and Mrs Brandeis live very simply in an old-fashioned apartment house which still survives the inroads of the more modern palaces built by ex-President Hoover, ex-President Wilson, ex-Senator Reed and ex-Under Secretary of State Castle just two blocks away. The Negro elevator boy takes visitors up in a lift reminiscent of the horse-and-buggy days, and it is not necessary to be announced in advance. The Brandeis apartment is simple almost to the point of austerity. The furniture is old fashioned and none too comfortable. The food, served by an aged Negro, is equally plain. Usually there is no cloth on the table.

"Man," the Justice once told a young friend, "should live austerely. The greatest menace to freedom is an inert people. And, son," he added, "there are no degrees of austerity. Either you are austere or you are not austere."

The Justice dines out almost never, not even accepting invitations to the White House. But the Brandeis home is the focal point of leaders from many walks of life who come for advice, companionship and inspiration.

In his quiet, unobtrusive way, Brandeis wields a wider influence than any other justice on the Court. Lawyers, business executives, social workers come from New York and other cities when he is able to see them, as he nearly always is. The Justice is consciously and deliberately a teacher, particularly with young people. Sympathetic and patient, he definitely seeks to pass on to the younger generation a point of view, a courageous philosophy of life that may help the next generation to face its problems.

Recently he suggested to three young lawyers in the Roosevelt administration—among them Alger Hiss and Tom Blaisdell— that they give up the task of making a living and dedicate the next few years to mingling among farmers and workers in order to study their problems and appreciate their point of view.

"We are sure to have for the next generation," he told them, "an ever-increasing contest between those who have and those who have not. There are vital economic, social and industrial problems to be solved. And for these we need our ablest men. The reason why we have not made more progress in social matters is that these problems have not been tackled by the practical men of high ability, like those who have worked on industrial inventions and enterprises. We need *social inventions,* each of many able men adding his work until the invention is perfected."

At one time before he went on the bench, Brandeis was worth $2,000,000, but he has given most of it away. It costs little for him and Mrs Brandeis to live, so that they also give away a large part of his $20,000 annual salary. Their charities range from the Albanian Agricultural School to Commonwealth College, an institution for agricultural and social teaching in Arkansas.

"I have only one life," Justice Brandeis once said, in explaining his charities, "and it's short enough. Why waste it on things

I don't want most? And I don't want money or property most. I want to be free."

Every autumn at the beginning of the court term Brandeis takes a new secretary recommended to him by Felix Frankfurter from the graduating class of the Harvard Law School, and each spring he launches his secretary on a career of his own. A friend once remonstrated with the Justice for putting himself to the trouble of breaking in a new secretary each year, but Brandeis replied: "It's good for me. It keeps me from getting lazy."

The Justice has a musty office one flight above his living apartment where his secretary works. He himself does most of his writing in a tiny room just off his own downstairs living room. It is almost bare, containing only a desk, a chair and a couch with a steamer rug on which the Justice catnaps when he is drowsy. But there is a view from his window which spreads out over the city of Washington, far beyond the swanky residences of Hoover and Woodrow Wilson to the Washington Monument, the Lincoln Memorial and the sloping banks of the Potomac.

Sitting before that window, Brandeis has written some of the most stirring opinions in court history. He writes them all in pencil, correcting and revising over and over again until they are perfect. He is the oldest member of the Court now, and is approaching his eightieth birthday, but he carries more than his share of the Court's work. During the 1936 term he wrote sixteen opinions, which was thirteen more than Van Devanter, four more than Butler, and one more than Sutherland. When he has finished an opinion it is a model of clear English and a logical presentation of facts. Brandeis has never been tripped up on an error of law. Those who disagree with him must do so on point of view. They cannot do so on the facts.

Neither can they challenge his scrupulousness in matters of personal honor. When the precedent-setting case of the District of Columbia minimum-wage law came before the Court in 1923, Brandeis voluntarily disqualified himself from sitting because his daughter was a member of the board that administered the act. When the Oregon minimum-wage statute, which he had helped to draft, reached the Court, Brandeis again withdrew—conduct in marked contrast to that of some of his colleagues.

Tall, thin, slightly stooped, with high cheekbones, deep-set eyes, and snowy-white hair, he is one of the most striking figures on the bench. Despite his age, he continues in fairly good health, thanks in part to the constant vigil of Mrs Brandeis, who warns all dinner guests that they must leave at nine. The Justice retires early but is an early riser and is a firm believer that there is a mysterious relationship between sunlight and the potency of man. He is at his desk by six every morning, and on his birthday not long ago Jim Landis found him working at five.

Every spring the Justice looks forward to getting up to his summer home near Chatham on Cape Cod. Here he lives as simply as he does in Washington and comes nearer to fulfilling the actuality though not the theory of President Roosevelt's horse-and-buggy criticism. For though the Brandeis summer home is three miles from Chatham, he has no automobile, though his daughter Susan has one just across the road.

The Justice believes in old-fashioned means of locomotion in other respects. Recently when Charles Taussig of the National Youth Administration visited him on a yachting cruise, Brandeis remarked that in his younger days he had found the best means of travel around the shores of Cape Cod was by canoe. It was a simple matter to keep close to land, the Justice explained, and it was easy to beach your canoe if a storm came up.

And true to his conviction that efficiency does not necessarily mean a happier life, he added:

"And the best part about it was that you knew you were doing it all yourself."

The only concession Brandeis has made to efficiency is a set of rolling bookshelves which on a sunshiny summer's day can be pushed out on his wide veranda overlooking the sea. They are filled with volumes of Supreme Court reports, and Morris Ernst once asked: "Why do you have those books around, Mr Justice, when you write them yourself?"

Whereupon the Justice, without response, dug up some pam-

phlets on savings-bank insurance and handed them to Ernst. He
explained that the value of the savings-bank insurance which he
inaugurated in Massachusetts increased 30 per cent during the
first quarter of 1936, while that of the regular companies went
down 13 per cent. The founding of this insurance system he
considers the greatest accomplishment of his life.

Probably the most beautiful friendship which ever existed on
the Supreme Court was that between Louis Brandeis and Oliver
Wendell Holmes.

When Holmes was still on the bench, the two men drove to
and from the Capitol together every day in a rented automobile,
and after he retired they took walks in the late afternoon when
the weather permitted. It was on one of these occasions that
Holmes, then ninety-two, paused to gaze in frank admiration
at a beautiful young girl who passed them. He even turned to
look at her as she continued down the street. Then, turning to
Brandeis, he sighed: "Ah! What wouldn't I give to be seventy
again!"

Holmes was a prodigious reader, but his taste ran to the classics and general literature. He was also enormously fond of
paper-backed French novels, which he read by the score, heap-
ing them in piles on the floor of his library as he consumed them.
To counteract this "low literary" taste, Brandeis once informed
Holmes that he would send him some worth-while summer reading.

Several weeks later a large box sent by the Library of Congress
reached Holmes at his Massachusetts home. He had his servant
take off the lid, and he scanned the upper layer of books. They
dealt with workmen's-compensation acts, insurance laws, labor
codes and similar subjects. Holmes read the titles.

"John, put this box down in the cellar," he ordered his servant
and returned to his paper-backed novels. In the fall Holmes
sent the box of books, untouched, back to the Library.

Justice Holmes played an important personal role in the lives
of the Nine Old Men. He was a focal point, a common meeting

ground, someone they all loved, even two such diametrically opposite characters as McReynolds and Brandeis. They all came to see him, even Mrs Mahlon Pitney, widow of the Justice whom Sutherland succeeded. Once, on one of her visits, Mrs Pitney poured out a sad tale about a robber who had backed up a truck to the rear door of her vacant home and carted away all the furnishings. However, the police had caught the culprit, Mrs Pitney continued, and put him in jail. There she went to visit him in his cell.

Mrs Pitney talked at great length to Justice Holmes about her meeting with the thief.

"I tried to find out how ever he had embarked on a career of crime," she explained. "I tried to point out the error of his ways, and I hope it did some good. I think I must have talked to him for *two hours.*"

"Poor man, poor man," nodded Holmes sympathetically.

Justice Holmes delighted in reminiscing about the Civil War, in which he fought for three years, having been promoted from the rank of lieutenant to lieutenant-colonel and having been wounded three times: in the breast at Ball's Bluff, in the neck at Antietam, and in the foot at Fredericksburg.

"It wasn't bad—when you were on the general staff," he used to say. "The officers got champagne for dinner, but what I really liked were those great big cocktails before breakfast."

Actually, Holmes abhorred war, and his fondest ambition was to make some slight contribution toward keeping the United States out of another war.

After he retired from the bench at the age of ninety-one, Justice Holmes gaily told his friends that for the first time he was really enjoying life. While on the Court, he complained, he had to work too hard. Once when he was about to drive out to Winchester, Virginia, to see the famous apple blossoms, a court messenger arrived with an opinion to be read.

"The goddamned fertility of my colleagues will kill me," he exclaimed as he canceled his trip.

During recent days of bitter internal strife among the justices of the Supreme Court, Brandeis has retained his poise and does not indulge in personal malice. No matter how fierce the debate inside the Court, he remains cool and collected. Even toward Justice McReynolds, who opposed his confirmation and who has cast snarling aspersions on his religious faith, Brandeis remains mild-mannered and on the surface friendly.

Once, while visiting in the Brandeis home, Professor Walton H. Hamilton of Yale told this story to a group of the guests, including the Justice. A lawyer from Wyoming, with the picturesqueness of a cowboy and an even more picturesque method of speech, was arguing a case before the Supreme Court while Justice Holmes still was on the bench, and despite a most impassioned appeal to the Court, full of the language of the frontier, he lost. As he concluded, Holmes, who sat on the right of Hughes, leaned over and in one of his loud, hoarse whispers said:

"Can't we hear that old bird again?"

The clerk of the Court heard the remark and afterward advised the cowboy lawyer that, if he applied for a rehearing, it might be granted. This was done. In the rehearing, the lawyer opened his appeal to the Court with these words:

"I come to you as John the Baptist saying 'Repent ye, repent ye.'"

Whereupon Justice McReynolds, who was enjoying the performance almost as much as Justice Holmes, leaned forward and said:

"But are you not aware of what happened to John the Baptist?"

"Yes, I am quite aware," was the immediate response. "He lost his head through the influence of a harlot. But I know the Supreme Court would not be so influenced."

At this point in Professor Hamilton's narration of the story, Justice Brandeis, who had been listening, came to the defense of his colleague.

"I do not believe that Justice McReynolds made such a remark," he said. And, turning on his heel, he walked out.

Justice Brandeis is an old man now and unconsciously perhaps has been training Stone and Cardozo to carry on the fight when he is gone. He conserves his energy carefully now, and after the drag of the winter looks forward a little more eagerly to his summer in Cape Cod.

But, despite his age, the old crusading fervor still is there. Less tenacious warriors would have surrendered long before, been content to pass their declining years dozing peacefully on the side lines. But not Brandeis. The philosophic calm of age and long experience is there, the calm that prompts the defense of a colleague no matter how diametrically opposite his colleague's views. But behind it all, behind those deep-set, piercing eyes, the old Brandeis is still crusading.

It is not a crusade for any group or class. Brandeis has no idea of the class struggle. Labor unions fall in the same category as corporations, if they are big. They tend to crush out individualism. And Brandeis' crusade is for the individual.

Perhaps the finest exposition of economic democracy ever handed down from the Supreme Court was Brandeis' dissent in the Oklahoma ice case, in which he said:

"I cannot believe that the framers of the Fourteenth Amendment, or the states which ratified it, intended to leave us helpless to correct the evils of technological employment and excessive productive capacity which the march of invention and discovery has entailed. There must be power in the states and nation to remold through experimentation our economic practices to meet changing social and economic needs. . . . Denial of the right of such experimentation may be fraught with serious consequences to the nation."

But despite the challenge in those words, Brandeis read them in a listless voice. The crusading fervor was not there. But in the chain-store decision, it was another story. Then it was another Brandeis speaking, a Brandeis with all the passion and vigor of his turbulent, crusading youth. For now he was rendering a decision against bigness, against the chain stores which threatened to crush the life of the small merchant.

Brandeis is the greatest legalist on the Court. But to him law is a means to an end. He looks first at the long-range objective and its relation to wages, hours, production, capitalization, profits, then he figures out the legal steps to justify that objective. In other words, the objective is based upon the economic factors involved. The law by which it is achieved is just a trick of the trade.

Or, as Judge Joseph C. Hutchinson, of the United States District Court, Texas, describes judicial method: "Having heard the cause and determined that the decision ought to go this way or that, he [the judge] then takes up his search for some category of the law into which the case will fit."

"You should be kind to the bankers," Brandeis told Ferdinand Pecora during the latter's investigation for the Senate Banking Committee. "Bankers are not men of ingenuity. It's always the lawyers who develop the chicanery."

But when it was suggested that the lawyers instead of the bankers be investigated, Brandeis replied:

"That would be useless. Who would do the cross-examining?"

On the bench Brandeis is just as prejudiced as his reactionary colleague, Justice Butler. Both are attempting to disseminate from the bench the philosophy they preached and practiced before they rose to fame. Their methods are the same. Their objectives are totally dissimilar.

"Property is only a means," says Justice Brandeis. "It has been a frequent error of our courts that they have made the means an end. . . . Instead of amending the Constitution, I would amend men's economic and social ideals."

That is the difference between Brandeis and Butler. Butler has spent his years on the Supreme Court proselyting to protect property. Brandeis has spent his years crusading to better men's economic and social ideals.

And through the hosts of young disciples who gather round

him, through his hints to those in high office, through his economic writings which Roosevelt paraphrased in his inauguration speech, and, most of all, through the masterful logic of his opinions, the unquenchable crusading fervor of Louis Brandeis will live and bear fruit long, long after he has passed away.

CHAPTER IX

The Dummy Director

WILLIS VAN DEVANTER, dean of the Supreme Court in length of service, has three claims to fame.

He is a fanatical reactionary. He is a fanatical dry. And he is afflicted with what psychiatrists call "neurotic pen," described in the vernacular as "literary constipation."

Only one decision has emanated from Justice Van Devanter in twenty-six years which could be classed as liberal—an opinion upholding the investigation powers of the Senate in the case of Mal Daugherty, brother of the malodorous Harry M. Daugherty of Harding's Ohio Gang. With this one exception, Van Devanter has not deviated from a course of rigid, impervious reactionism.

Regarding the Justice's second claim to fame, it was Van Devanter who rendered the Court's decision upholding the constitutionality of the Eighteenth Amendment, by the extraordinary procedure of giving no reason for the conclusions reached. It was Van Devanter also who decreed that a liquor prosecution in a state court, following one in a federal court for the same identical offense, did not violate the constitutional prohibition against double jeopardy. And finally it was Van Devanter who authored the Court's opinion in the famous case of Dr Lambert confirming the alleged right of Congress to set itself up as a medicinal authority. Dominated by the dry clerical hierarchy, Congress had enacted a law limiting medicinal prescriptions of whisky to a pint per patient for every ten days—and Van Devanter upheld it. The only instance in which Van Devanter ever deviated from his fanatical dry views was in concurring with a Canadian judge that compensation should be given to the American bootlegger-owners of the Canadian rum-rummer *I'm Alone,* sunk 225 miles off the Louisiana coast by the United States Coast Guard.

Van Devanter's third claim to fame is the fact that during the six years since 1930 he has handed down only twenty-two opinions, while during the same period the Court wrote a total of 963 opinions, and Brandeis, Hughes, Roberts, Stone and Cardozo averaged about twenty each, every year. Van Devanter's record during the last six years follows:

In 1930 he wrote five opinions, then dropped to one each during the years 1931 and 1932. In the latter year, *More Merry-Go-Round* exposed his extreme paucity of expression, and the next year he pushed his opinions up to nine. In 1934, however, he dropped back to three, and as if exhausted by the effort wrote nothing in 1935. Finally, with a terrific spurt, he produced three opinions in the latter months of the 1936 spring court term. Notice of the impending publication of this book was published just before the spurt.

Orally, Van Devanter is fluent, precise and uninhibited. In the Court's secret deliberations none of his colleagues excel him in clarity or succinctness of expression. Even Justice Brandeis, who vigorously disagrees with him, once remarked that if a stenographer could be present to take down Van Devanter's words, the Court would get as able an opinion as any he takes six months to write. But when Van Devanter sits down to put his thoughts on paper he goes through weeks of mental torture. He writes and rewrites. In the end he turns out an able opinion, couched in readable literary style—but the birth pangs are prolonged and prodigious.

Chief justices under whom Van Devanter has served make allowance for this strange neurosis, and more recently for his increasing physical infirmity. And Van Devanter has sought to make up for his lack of literary productiveness by contributing his considerable knowledge regarding questions of court history, procedure and jurisdiction.

No matter what Van Devanter's views may be, no matter how radically they may differ from those of other justices, whatever he says commands their respect and attention. Brandeis, despite differences of opinion, constantly pays tribute to his usefulness. He is one of the ablest members of the Court and one of its hardest workers. He has an active and analytical mind. He knows every case thoroughly. The entire Court defers to him on questions of jurisdiction. He is an excellent trial judge, keeps every detail of oral argument in his mind, so that when a lawyer gets his case badly twisted Van Devanter has been known to lean forward and straighten him out.

However, Van Devanter, despite his ability, despite his usefulness, seldom has deviated from a viewpoint as outmoded as the law of the six-shooter which governed Wyoming in the days when Van Devanter practiced there.

Willis Van Devanter was born in Marion, Indiana, in 1859, just before the Civil War started, and at an earlier date than any other justice save Brandeis, who is three years older. His father was a successful attorney who could afford to send his son to college, and after graduating from De Pauw University and taking a law degree at Cincinnati in 1881, young Van Devanter settled down in the home town to join his father's law firm. However, John W. Lacey, a youngster from the Territory of Wyoming, had come East for his education, married Van Devanter's sister and, returning to Wyoming, sent back glowing accounts of the opportunities for a young lawyer in the West. So Van Devanter, then only twenty-four, took his boyhood sweetheart whom he had just married, and headed West. It was a trip which was to have important repercussions not only upon the life of Willis Van Devanter but upon the economic and social legislation of the United States.

Wyoming at that time was one of the wildest and least developed territories in the Union. There was little law, few lawyers, and much battling over its vast and unexplored area. Red-men fought with land-grabbing whites, claim stakers with claim jumpers, cattlemen with rustlers, sheepmen with cattlemen, while the Union Pacific Railroad laid its hands on everything in sight.

Young Van Devanter very soon showed how shrewd were his pecuniary instincts by aligning himself with the most powerful forces in the Territory. Wyoming's political boss was Francis E. Warren, a wealthy cattle rancher, at that time territorial governor, later to become senator, chairman of the powerful Senate Appropriations Committee and father-in-law of General Pershing. Associated with Warren was another wealthy rancher, Clarence D. Clark, also destined to wield influence in the United States Senate.

But Warren and Clark were merely the vassals of the Union Pacific Railroad. It ruled the Territory. There was no Interstate Commerce Commission at that time, and the rates on cattle, sheep and ore were what the railroad wanted them to be. Its word was law. Its word was law in regard to transportation and in regard to land. It owned most of Wyoming. The federal government had brought more than one action against it for restoration of the land it had stolen, but the Supreme Court which Van Devanter later was to adorn held against the government.

So Willis Van Devanter, after a short period of reconnoitering in Wyoming, fastened himself to the coattails of Warren and Clark on the political side, and the Union Pacific Railroad on the economic side. Fortunately for him, both the politics of the Territory and the railroad were going in the same direction—in fact they were joined in unholy wedlock.

Senator Warren boosted Van Devanter up the political ladder with a speed only possible in those reckless, carefree days of the frontier. At the age of twenty-six, and although he had then been in Wyoming only two years, he was appointed a commissioner to revise the territorial statutes. At twenty-seven he was made city attorney of Cheyenne. At twenty-eight he was elected to the territorial legislature, and at the age of thirty he became chief justice of the Wyoming Supreme Court.

It was at this point that Van Devanter's prestige became sufficient to attract the attention of the Union Pacific. An ex-chief justice was a powerful person to fight the battles of the road, so Van Devanter resigned from the bench and, with his brother-in-law, established the firm of Lacey & Van Devanter, which attracted as clients some of the wealthiest land-grabbing corporations in the West, among them the Frontier Land & Cattle Company, the Powder River Cattle Company, the Moorcraft Ranch Company, the Springvale Ditch Company, the Searight Cattle Company and, of course, the Union Pacific.

Simultaneously Van Devanter kept his hand on the political affairs of the new state (Wyoming entered the Union in 1890). He became chairman of the Republican State Committee of Wyoming, later Wyoming representative of the Republican National Committee, and during the great Bryan-McKinley battle of 1896 he ranged the state on horseback to keep Wyoming in the Republican column. And although the temptation held forth by Bryan of free silver was too much for a mining state, Wyoming went over to the Democrats by a narrower margin than any of its Western neighbors.

Van Devanter's efforts deserved reward, and perhaps what was more important, Senator Warren and the Union Pacific needed a man in Washington. What could have been more appropriate, therefore, than that Willis Van Devanter should become Assistant Attorney General in charge of legal cases for the Public Lands Division of the Interior Department? How strategic was this position from the viewpoint of the Union Pacific Railroad can be gathered from the report of Commissioner Sparks of the Land Office a few years before Van Devanter joined that organization. He pointed out that the Union Pacific had fraudulently appropriated coal lands of inestimable value, that "nearly the whole of Wyoming and a large portion of Montana" had been fraudulently possessed, and that after possessing them, the

Union Pacific had turned round and sold 7,000,000 acres without any patent from the government.

The young man who now took over all legal work arising from these cases was the ex-attorney for the Union Pacific Railroad.

In recent years, Justice Van Devanter has won the reputation of being the friend of the Indian; and there is no doubt that his early days in the Interior Department gave him a knowledge of, and certain sympathy toward, Indian problems far beyond that of his colleagues. In the Interior Department, however, Van Devanter was anything but the friend of the red man and appeared personally in the Lone Wolf Case to champion an act of Congress providing for the sale of Indian lands to homesteaders at $1.25 per acre. This land had been guaranteed by treaty to the Kiowa, Comanche and Apache tribes "as long as grass grows and water runs," but Van Devanter argued that an act of Congress superseded a treaty, although according to international law it is exactly the reverse.

Van Devanter continued in this key position for six years, and then, in 1903, Senator Warren gave him another boost up the ladder and got Teddy Roosevelt to appoint him judge on the Eighth Circuit Court of Appeals. Here Van Devanter was in an even more strategic position to pass on Union Pacific legal squabbles. Here it was also that Van Devanter met Pierce Butler, then a practicing attorney in St Paul and a frequent advocate before the Circuit Court. The two men struck up a friendship which has continued, and ripened with each Sunday at the golf course at Burning Tree, until the two are probably the closest friends on the Supreme Court.

Seven years later, in 1910, Taft appointed Van Devanter to the Supreme Court. Senator Clark, who by that time had become chairman of the Senate Judiciary Committee, immediately recommended unanimous confirmation. He and Senator Warren had sent their man to the top.

Van Devanter was not confirmed, however, without at least one word of warning as to what was in store for the country.

William Jennings Bryan, against whom he had campaigned so ardently, issued a statement calling attention to the fact that Judge Van Devanter was the "man who gave a decision giving to the Union Pacific land along its right of way amounting in value to millions of dollars; he is the judge who held that two railroads running parallel to each other for two thousand miles were not competing lines, one of those roads being the Union Pacific."

Bryan referred to two decisions handed down by Van Devanter when he was on the Eighth Circuit Court of Appeals in which he not only lacked the good grace to step aside when his former clients came up for trial, but handed down decisions in their favor.

In view of this it is not surprising that during later years, when Justice Stone has stepped aside on sugar cases involving his former law firm, and while Justice Brandeis has stepped aside on child labor cases involving his daughter, where railroad cases are concerned, Justice Van Devanter has clung tenaciously to the bench. He was one of those to set aside the North Dakota state tax against the Great Northern Railroad in 1936, the Railroad Retirement Act in 1925; to rule that a return on investment of only 6.26 per cent in the Baltimore & Ohio case is confiscatory; and to favor higher valuation for railroads and other utilities in all cases coming before the Court.

On the bench, Van Devanter has remained what he was in private life—a corporation lawyer. Not once has he faltered. Not only have his votes always been on the Tory side, but, in those few instances that he has written opinions, they have been among the most reactionary in the history of the Court. They have included the ruling that a state has no power to fix the weight of bread, the invalidation of the federal gift tax, the decision that the federal government cannot tax the salaries of judges, and the opinion in the leather workers' case which puts strikers in approximately the same category as Wyoming cattle thieves.

Justice Van Devanter also appears to have taken particular

delight in massacring state laws passed to control the utilities; and when the people of West Virginia passed an act giving themselves priority rights in regard to their own natural-gas resources before export to other states, Van Devanter threw out the law on the grounds that it interfered with interstate commerce. But since 1933, when Van Devanter found the Roosevelt administration was regulating utilities through federal legislation, he has suddenly become the champion of states rights and claimed that the federal government was infringing upon their prerogative.

Probably no justice of the Supreme Court has handled such a varied and romantic array of legal cases as Willis Van Devanter when he was practicing attorney. All sorts of murder and cattle-thieving cases came to him during his early days in Wyoming. One of them was that of Tim Horn, notorious bad man, whom Van Devanter defended after he had killed Willie Nickell. Horn had been hired by cattlemen to guard their herds and, in doing so, had shot one of the rustlers. Van Devanter secured his acquittal. Later Horn was convicted in connection with another murder and hung.

Another even more spectacular case which Van Devanter defended was that involving a gang of Texas gunmen imported by Wyoming cattle ranchers to stop raids on their cattle. In doing so they shot two of the alleged thieves, and it required federal troops to round up the Texans and bring them to trial. Van Devanter handled their defense so cleverly that the entire band was acquitted.

Van Devanter is not the vigorous and dramatic young lawyer he used to be. He has mellowed, but he has not grown more tolerant. Nor has age increased his sense of humor. When the gold cases were before the Supreme Court, Edward J. White, counsel for the trustees of the Missouri Pacific, was defending the constitutionality of the act and pointed out that the preamble of the Constitution contains a "general welfare" declaration that gives Congress the power to determine what shall constitute currency. To emphasize his contention, White read the section of the preamble to which he referred.

"But that is not all there is to the preamble," snapped Justice Van Devanter. "There is more to it than what you have read."

"Of course," replied White, "and I wouldn't think of attempting to deceive this Court on the contents of the Constitution."

All of the justices laughed—except Van Devanter.

Van Devanter does have a faint spark of humor in his soul, though it gleams rarely. Harry Blair, now Assistant Attorney General in charge of Public Lands, virtually the same position Van Devanter held, once sat in Van Devanter's law course when the latter taught at George Washington University. And after arguing an Indian-lands case before the Supreme Court, Blair happened to meet the Justice at a dinner and remarked:

"Well, I'm still going to class under you, Mr Justice."

"Yes," replied Van Devanter, "but this time I'm not the only one marking the papers."

The Justice has two sons, one an investment broker in Washington, the other the manager of the newly acquired Van Devanter farm near Ellicott City, Maryland. A namesake, Willis Ballinger, whose father practiced with Van Devanter when he was in charge of public lands, has become one of the most liberal members of the New Deal which the Justice excoriates.

In his younger days, Van Devanter was an enthusiastic horseman and big-game hunter, but now the greatest exertion he permits himself is a round of golf every Sunday with his old friend Pierce Butler. He has become more aloof from the world as he has grown older and since his wife passed away. He did manage, however, to take his sister on a trip to Russia during the summer of 1935, where he got a doleful picture of Soviet progress from Ambassador Bullitt and spent his time on the way back reading the translated works of the Italian sociologist, Pareto, intellectual godfather of Fascism.

The greatest tragedy in Van Devanter's life was the death of his wife, the boyhood sweetheart who went West with him half a century ago. She became ill in the Black Forest of Germany during the summer of 1934, and when word of her death reached Van Devanter he fainted. He has not been in good health since and has talked of resigning, though, like the other reactionary justices, he cannot bear to leave the bench with the New Deal still running rampant over the old law of "to the victor belong the spoils" which he served and cherished in the old days of the Wyoming frontier.

Van Devanter's career on the Court is in striking contrast to that of the man whom he succeeded as dean. For twenty-one years he and Justice Holmes sat side by side. As the years passed, Holmes became ever more tolerant and understanding of change and the need for change. Van Devanter, clutching grimly at the past, sank deeper into the slough of stultification. Holmes, his senior by twenty years, carved out an imperishable niche in judicial annals with an undiminished stream of decisions and ringing dissents. Even during the three months preceding his resignation in January 1932, Holmes wrote six opinions, which was three more than Van Devanter has produced in the last two years. In the year prior to his retirement, Holmes delivered twenty-two decisions, twenty-one more than the much younger Van Devanter.

Holmes resigned because he felt he was growing too feeble to carry on his share of the Court's work. Van Devanter, with the advent of the New Deal, brushed aside his failing health, to sit, unproductive but obstructive, in the path of government progress.

When it comes to any public intimation regarding his views on the New Deal, Justice Van Devanter has been as silent as the tomb. But in the privacy of his home or of the Court's closed-door deliberations, he has been as relentless in his denunciation as Al Smith or Herbert Hoover—though more effective. He has flayed and castigated the Roosevelt regime in bitter, scalding words. In his home he has paced the floor, hurling anathemas. In the Court he has been the mainstay of his reactionary colleagues in supplying them with precedents to justify their death-dealing decisions. To the one-time McKinley campaigner, the war on the New Deal has been a holy jihad, and he has cited precedents and justifications with crusading fervor.

This fierce antipathy, however, did not restrain Van Devanter from accepting monetary largess from one of the Roosevelt agencies—the Agricultural Adjustment Administration—which subsequently he declared to be a violation of the Constitution. And although the Justice came forward with a belated statement to the press that he had returned the last crop-benefit payments to the AAA, those he received during the first two years never were returned.

Revelation of this inconsistency came about in an unusual way. Just before the Supreme Court handed down its decision a report leaked to the press that Justice Van Devanter was on the AAA rolls and that a telephone call had come through to expedite his check. Secretary Wallace, when questioned about this, refused to discuss it. And when newspapermen endeavored to trace the matter down to the clerical division charged with sending out AAA checks, it was discovered that all data regarding payments to Van Devanter had been taken from the files and sent to Wallace's office. Finally, on April 8, 1936, just three months after the AAA decision was announced, Carlisle Bargeron published a story in the Washington *Star* that Van Devanter had received AAA checks. That afternoon, the Justice summoned the press and admitted that he had received benefit payments for wheat-acreage reduction on two farms owned by Mrs Van Devanter in Montana. After Mrs Van Devanter died, he said, her estate had gone into probate, and he was without authority to return government checks being paid to it.

"While it is true that ultimately I might benefit when the estate is settled, I had no choice as executor," the Justice explained. "After the act was invalidated, however, I felt that, since I held against the law, the checks should be returned."

Therefore, two checks, for $14.97 and for $45.35, received on January 7, one day after the AAA was declared unconstitutional, were returned by Van Devanter to the AAA.

A few weeks later Frank Mondell, former Congressman from

Wyoming and, like Van Devanter, one of the leading henchmen of Senator Warren, published his memoirs. In them appeared the following:

"On the fifth of May, 1918, I was invited to Senator Warren's
office and there met the Senator and our mutual friends, Justices
Van Devanter and Van Orsdel. [The latter, also a Wyoming
Republican henchman of Warren's, is Justice of the United
States Court of Appeals for the District of Columbia.] The situ-
ation was discussed at length, and it was agreed that Senator
Warren would reconsider his declaration to stand for re-election
and that I should issue a statement with regard to the same."

The Brooklyn *Eagle,* commenting upon this disclosure, observed:

"Mr Mondell sets out therein that justices of the United States
Supreme Court and the United States Circuit Court of Appeals
thus indulged in directing Republican politics in Wyoming."

It was a naïve observation. For thirty years judicial robes have
no more diminished the arch-Republicanism of Willis Van
Devanter than the winds and the rains have fertilized the bleak
mountains of Wyoming.

CHAPTER X

The Lame-Duck Senator

JUSTICE SUTHERLAND and Justice Van Devanter have much in common. Both are extremely conservative, and both owe their conservatism to a Western pioneer era which molded their youth. Both are ardent prohibitionists. Both are Old Guard Republicans. Both are courteous, likable gentlemen, and both, in contrast to some of their reactionary colleagues, get along perfectly with the liberal justices with whom they are in frequent legal disagreement.

But there is an outstanding difference between the two men: Van Devanter has brains. Sutherland has not.

According to Thomas Reed Powell, indiscreet Harvard law professor: "Justice Sutherland is a very able man. An old lady at the Chevy Chase Club told me so."

Sutherland is rather an attractive and scholarly-looking person. Tall and slender, with a neatly trimmed gray beard covering a mild face, he is a sweet human character. Once during a summer recess—always very much occupied by the justices in reviewing hundreds of writs in preparation for the fall opening of the Court—Sutherland was the only justice in the city, and the attorney for a youngster convicted in Chicago for violation of the Volstead Act sought him out. The attorney wanted Sutherland to grant a petition for a writ of error which would serve as a period of delay. Sutherland took the petition and spent three minutes looking it over. Then he handed it back.

"I'm sorry I can't grant this," he said. "I only wish I could. It is the most courteous request ever made to a court. If lawyers only realized that we are busy and would write what they have to say in two pages instead of ten . . . I really wish I could grant this. I should like to bring this petition to court to show the Bar the real way to present a case. But you haven't a leg to stand on, and my opinion is fixed. I should be glad to have you see the other justices, however. They may view the case differently. You can reach Justice Brandeis, the nearest, at Chatham, Massachusetts, and Justice Holmes is near him in Beverly Farms. The others are much farther away."

Sutherland maintains this agreeable manner through all court debates. He never gets irritated as does Butler. He never sulks as does McReynolds. He never tries to influence another justice. He retains his poise no matter what happens. But to change Sutherland's set conviction on any economic question, one might just as well talk to the moon.

This sweetness of disposition makes Sutherland all the more effective. The dynamite-laden reaction which falls from his mild, scholarly lips creates a more profound impression upon a gullible public than the hotheaded blasts of McReynolds or Butler. Sutherland can wrap the poison in a pill of sweet and sonorous pontification. "Peace is a sweet and holy thing," he informed the world in the Bland-MacIntosh citizenship case. "There are few finer or more exalted sentiments than that which finds expression in opposition to war." Following which benediction he proceeded to bring his legal meat axe down upon any citizen who would not bear arms in any war, aggressive or otherwise, into which any plundering politician blundered the country.

Partly because he has remained on good terms with the liberal wing of the Court, partly because he takes great pride in his constitutional law, Sutherland long has been chief opinion writer for the conservative majority. Writing majority opinions requires a peculiar knack. The duller it is, the more it is wrapped up in ponderous legal platitudes, the more likely it is to reconcile the diverse views which usually exist even among the majority justices. If the opinion is too sharp on certain points, it will come back with question marks and objections noted on the margin. For every member of the Court, especially those of the conservative wing, is wary about letting certain points of law be written into an opinion which may be cited as precedent against them in the future.

Mr Sutherland is a past master at the trick of writing an unpopular opinion not well grounded on law; that is, saying nothing, but saying it in as many words as possible. Judge George C. Hutcheson describes this as "bewordling" an opinion. "For, while a judge may be," he says, "he cannot appear to be unreasonable. . . . Therefore by the practice of logomachy do I bewordle my opinion."

No other member of the Court, with the possible exception, in recent months, of Justice Roberts, has such a gift for voluminous prolixity. So the subtle Mr Hughes, too well aware of Sutherland's amiability, his faculty for compromise, his aptitude for righteous phraseology, his solemn, scholarly face and his inability to realize that he is being imposed upon, chooses him as the spearhead of the reactionary attack. Sutherland glories in his role. And without contributing a great deal to the actual formation of the majority's conclusion, he has established a record for writing the most unpopular opinions handed down by the Court.

The Justice is seventy-four years old now, and the younger, more energetic Roberts is beginning to pick up the lance of the reactionary majority. For George Sutherland is old even beyond his advanced years. He was old in everything save years even before he came to the Supreme Court. He has spent all his life in a past generation, an age that is no more—the frontier. He went West to practice the law of the West, the law which concerns itself with the land, with minerals, with grazing rights and which favored him who came first and took most.

And Sutherland—his manner of thinking, his law—dates back to those days that are dead and gone. His economic and social theories are as up to date as the moldy opera house, the gilded saloons, the crumbling shacks which once made up the thriving mining metropolis of Cripple Creek.

Born in Buckinghamshire, England, Sutherland's family brought him to Utah with Captain Horton Hought's wagon company of Mormon church colonists when he was only fifteen months old. That was in 1863, and Utah was only a territory. From that point Utah and Sutherland grew up together. After going East for a law degree at the University of Michigan, Sutherland formed an alliance with the Mormon-Old Guard Republican machine which has been profitable to both ever since. A faithful, plodding party wheel horse, he was elected to the first Senate after Utah was admitted to statehood in 1896 and four years later was promoted to the House of Representatives in Washington, where he served only one term, returning in 1905 for two terms as senator. In the Senate, Sutherland was known for his inoffensive good nature, his extreme conservatism, his unswerving party regularity and his long and dreary dissertations on the Constitution to which no one paid any attention with the exception of one man. He was Warren Gamaliel Harding, a senatorial colleague who, perhaps because he rarely listened and because he himself knew little of such things, thought the scholarly-appearing Utahan a very erudite man. This fact was to play a very important part in the life not only of George Sutherland but of the American people.

Sutherland was a member of the Senate Judiciary Committee when Louis D. Brandeis came up for confirmation as associate justice. He had heard that Brandeis was at one time retained by Louis K. Liggett in a case contending that chain stores did not violate the Sherman Anti-Trust Act. This, Sutherland considered inconsistent with Brandeis' anti-trust views, and although the committee already had finished extended hearings on Brandeis, Sutherland asked that the matter be reopened. This was done, but after hearing one witness the committee sent the appointment back with a renewed recommendation that it be confirmed.

During his twelve years in the Senate there was nothing which came up involving Reed Smoot, prohibition, and beet sugar which Sutherland did not favor; and nothing involving La Follette and the progressives which he did not oppose.

"Within the last few years the United States of America has become the field of operation for an amiable band of insurgent soothsayers," was the way he described the progressives to the Senate galleries, "who have been going up and down the land indulging in cabalistic utterances respecting the initiative, referendum and recall and divers and sundry other ingenious devices for realizing the millennium by the ready and simple method of voting it out of its present state of incubation. They direct our attention to the clouds flying above the far Western horizon, upon which the flaming finger of the Oregon sun has traced in radiant and opalescent tints glowing pathways, shining minarets, stately temples and castles and palaces, pinnacles of gold, caves of purple . . ."

Meanwhile Sutherland saw to it that the citizens of Utah were given more than their quota of lush jobs in Washington, kept such a tight rein on the Mormon-Republican machine that Utah was one of the two states to go for Taft in 1912, attended every Republican National Convention from 1900, and in every conceivable respect was a good party man. Party regularity, however, was not enough. Utah is a long way from Washington, but eventually the folks at home got wise to their colorless representative in the Senate, and in 1916 Sutherland lost out to that unintellectual Democrat, William H. King, who had been his classmate at Brigham Young University and the Michigan Law School, and later became his law partner at Provo.

For a time Sutherland returned to a highly remunerative practice of corporation law, got fees of $50,000 in at least two cases he argued before the Supreme Court, and delivered a dreary series of lectures at Columbia University on "Constitutional Power and World Affairs," later published in book form. In 1920 he became the personal adviser of the one man in the Senate who had genuine esteem for his dull harangues on constitutional law, and as the "Colonel House" of the Harding administration spent several months in Marion, Ohio, helping the Republican presidential nominee with his front-porch campaign. In return, Harding, who always took care of his friends, appointed Sutherland, a lame-duck senator, to the Supreme Court. The people of Utah had rejected him as a member of the highest legislative tribunal, and now Warren Harding elevated him to a life job passing upon the legislative acts of his former colleagues.

Symbolically, the message from the President carrying Sutherland's appointment was received by the Senate while dealing with a handful of private raids on the Treasury. Senator Nelson of Minnesota, chairman of the Senate Judiciary Committee, immediately asked for unanimous consent, saying that Mr Sutherland was so well known to all members that no other course was necessary. In this manner, Sutherland was unanimously confirmed.

Future generations of senators were to regret that hasty action. But Warren Harding, were he alive, would have been proud of his appointee. For Justice George Sutherland, faithful to all the Harding administration stood for, has done as much to cripple labor legislation and block state efforts to control business as any man in the history of the United States. It was Sutherland who wrote the 1923 opinion outlawing the minimum wage, citing as an "extraneous circumstance" the fact "that the employee needs to get a prescribed sum of money to insure her subsistence, health and morals." Even the conservative Chief Justice Taft dissented. It was Sutherland who, in the 1927 journeymen stonecutters' case, granted employers an injunction against union stonecutters because they refused to work on stone shipped into their territory. It was Sutherland who, in the Baltimore Street Railway case of 1930, ruled that a fare fixed by the state permitting the utility a 6¼ per cent rate of return was "confiscatory" and that the company was entitled to a return of 7½ per cent or more. It was Sutherland who, during the tragic depression days of 1932, handed down the majority opinion outlawing Oklahoma's attempt to establish order in the ice industry. It was Sutherland also who checked Oklahoma's attempt to use the power of taxation to promote co-operative farming. The state legislature passed an act providing that cotton gins owned by individual operators had to have licenses to operate, while cotton gins owned by co-operatives did not. Sutherland declared this legislation to be unwarranted discrimination against the individual capitalist.

It was Sutherland again who, in 1927, upset the New York law prohibiting ticket scalpers from making a profit of more than fifty cents per ticket. This, the learned Justice considered to be arbitrary and paternalistic interference with the right of free bargaining, and in a 5–4 vote decreed furthermore that the theater was not "clothed with public interest." Having set up this precedent, it was Sutherland again who leaned heavily upon it in writing the opinion upsetting the laws of twenty states limiting exorbitant fees charged by employment agencies for helping workers get jobs. Again it was Sutherland who wrote the opinion in the Liggett drugstore case annulling a Pennsylvania law requiring drugstores to be owned by licensed pharmacists. And finally it was Sutherland who handed down the opinions in the MacIntosh and Bland cases denying citizenship to those two distinguished foreigners, one of whom had fought in the World War, because they would not give an advance pledge to bear arms in any and all wars in which the United States might engage.

To those who applaud Mr Justice Sutherland as one of the great bulwarks of the *status quo,* there are just two black marks in his long career. One is his opinion proclaiming that the seven Negro boys condemned to die for the Scottsboro "rape" case were not given a fair trial; the other is his opinion upholding the freedom of the press in the Louisiana newspaper-tax case.

In both of these, Mr Sutherland championed the guarantees of personal liberty under the Bill of Rights in such a way as to appear in conflict with most of his previous legal philosophy.

And yet, within his own narrow limits, Justice Sutherland is consistent and faithful—faithful to the pioneer philosophy upon which he was nurtured. It was a philosophy of take what you could; give the other fellow an opportunity to fight and talk for it—but take. And once it was yours, keep it.

As a youngster on the frontier, Sutherland believed in the right of trial by jury, the right of free speech and the right of the revolver to defend one's property. And he still believes in them today. Thus he understands individual freedom but not economic freedom. He believes in the right of the Negro boys to have a fair trial at Scottsboro, and he also believes in the right of the elevator girl in the District of Columbia to bargain for her five dollars a week without the protection of a minimum-wage law. The revolver of frontier days has been turned into property-protecting opinions by the Supreme Court; but Sutherland cannot understand why the elevator girl should need protection.

He is consistently for personal rights until they clash with property rights; then it is a different matter. This was made all too clear in the two recent cases involving freedom of the press. In the first, the Minnesota Gag Law, in 1931, Sutherland sided with the minority in claiming that the "states shall be untrammeled and free . . . to prevent abuses of the liberty of the press." The Minnesota case involved the right of newspapers to criticize state officials. But the Louisiana newspaper-tax case in 1936 was different. Here property more than the freedom to criticize was involved. Here newspapers were taxed on the basis of circulation, thereby hitting the larger newspapers, more critical of Huey Long. And with property involved—highly valuable newspaper property which had criticized a "dangerous" demagogue at that time threatening to out-Deal the New Deal ideas of Mr Roosevelt—Mr Sutherland suddenly became the champion of free speech. Where once he concurred that the state of Minnesota had every right to censure the press, he now denounced the alleged attempt to the same end on the part of Louisiana.

Several years ago, when the late Justice McKenna still was a member of the Court, Felipe Espil, now Argentine ambassador in Washington, was a guest in the Justice's home and was much interested in his extensive library. It contained some of the finest works to be found in any law collection, but also, lying upon McKenna's reading table, were the *Nation* and the *New Republic*. Curious, the young diplomat asked his host how he happened to read these liberal papers.

"The chief danger to a man in my position," Justice McKenna replied, "is that as we grow old we lose our once-youthful perspective. I read those magazines in order to escape, if possible, that danger."

Justice Sutherland is as old as Justice McKenna now, and not in good health; but he makes no effort to keep his perspective, nor does he retire from the Supreme Court. He talks constantly about his ailments and the medicines recommended to cure them. And some years ago he did get so far as to talk of leaving the Court. In 1930 his secretary, having taken a law degree, told the Justice that he wanted to resign in order to establish a law practice of his own. But Sutherland asked him to stay another year, at the end of which he said he planned to retire. But as the years have rolled on, and Justice Sutherland has remained, it almost seems that he has taken as the guiding scripture of his life, a speech he once delivered in the Senate:

"It is not strange that, in the universal fever of haste, government itself should be swept by this mad spirit of impatience which has given rise to the new Apostle of Reform, whose demand is that we shall abandon the methodical habits of the past and go careering after novel and untried things."

A quarter of a century has passed since he delivered that speech, and Justice Sutherland, despite age and health, still sits, black-robed and solemn, athwart the path of the Apostle of Reform.

CHAPTER XI

The Hermit Philosopher

Dᴜʀɪɴɢ a visit to Washington in the winter of 1935, Carl Sandburg, Illinois poet and biographer of Abraham Lincoln, expressed to Congressman Maury Maverick of Texas a desire to meet Justice Cardozo.

"There is a really noble and brilliant public official," Sandburg enthused. "Not only is he a great judge, but he is a great poet. His books are among the finest writing in American literature. I've admired Cardozo for years, and I'd like to talk to him."

Maverick offered to arrange a meeting and the next day took Sandburg to Cardozo's office. Sandburg, in his hearty, vigorous manner, threw compliments all over the place, while Cardozo, quiet and gentle, lauded the genius of his guest and spoke of the pleasure he had derived from reading his poetry. Suddenly, Sandburg asked Cardozo if he would like to hear a poem he had just written, and, flushed with pride, launched upon this recitation:

What is a judge? A judge is a seated torso and head sworn before God never to sell justice nor play favorites while he umpires the disputes brought before him.
When you take the cigar out of your face and the fedora off your head in the presence of the court, you do it because it is required from those who are supposed to know they have come into a room where burns the white light of that priceless abstraction named justice.

*What is a judge? The perfect judge is austere, impersonal, im-
partial, marking the line of right or wrong by a hairsbreadth.
Before him, bow humbly, bow low, be a pilgrim, light a candle
For he is a rara avis, a rare bird, a white blackbird, a snowwhite
crow.*

*What is a judge? A featherless human biped having bowels,
glands, bladder, and intricate blood vessels of the brain,
One more frail mortal, one more candle a sudden change of
wind might blow out as any common candle blows out in
a wind change
So that never again does he sit in his black robes of solemn im-
port before a crowded courtroom saying two-years ten-
years twenty-years life for you or "hanged by the neck till
you are dead dead dead."*

*What is a judge? One may be the owner of himself coming to
his decisions often in a blur of hesitations knowing by what
snarled courses and ropes of reason justice operates, with
reservations, in twilight zones.
What is a judge? Another owns no more than a little finger of
himself, others owning him, others having placed him where
he is, others telling him what they want and getting it,
others referring to him as "our judge" as though he is
measured and weighed beforehand the same as a stockyards
hog, others holding him to decisions evasive of right or
wrong, others writing his decisions for him, the atmosphere
hushed and guarded, the atmosphere having a faint stockyards perfume. . . .*

Sandburg, totally oblivious of the presence of Maverick and
Cardozo, was now thundering at the top of his lusty voice. The
Justice, who after the first few lines had become rigid, was by
now white as a sheet. Maverick sat paralyzed in an agony of
helpless sympathy. He knew the reason for Cardozo's blanched
face. His father had been a notorious Tweed Ring judge, forced
from the bench on charges of corruption.

But Sandburg, unaware of this chapter in the life of his host, thundered on:

Take that cigar out of your face. Take that hat off your head.
And why? why? Because here we are sworn never to sell justice
and here burns the white light of that priceless abstraction
named justice.

> *What is a judge?*
> *He is a man.*
> *Yes, after all, and no matter what,*
> *and beyond all procedures and investitures,*
> *a judge is nothing more nor less than a man—*
> *one man having his one-man path, his one-*
> *man circle and orbit among other men*
> *each of whom is one man.*
> *Therefore should any judge open his mouth*
> *and speak as though his words have an*
> *added light and weight beyond the speech*
> *of one man?*
> *Of what is he the mouthpiece when he speaks?*

Maverick groaned. But Sandburg continued:

> *Of any ideas or passions other than those gath-*
> *ered and met in the mesh of his own per-*
> *sonality? Can his words be measured forth*
> *in so special a realm of exact justice in-*
> *structed by tradition, that they do not re-*
> *late to the living transitory blood of his*
> *vitals and brain, the blood so soon to cool*
> *in evidence of his mortal kinship with all*
> *other men?*[1]

Sandburg concluded, as triumphant and pleased as a boy who has just won a prize in oratory.

[1]From *The People, Yes* by Carl Sandburg. Copyright, 1936, by Harcourt, Brace and Company, Inc.

"Judge," he shouted, "what do you think of that?"

"It was a magnificent recitation, Mr Sandburg," replied Cardozo, smiling wanly. "But aren't you somewhat sweeping in your condemnation? I don't think it is fair to denounce the entire judiciary."

"Why not, Judge? They are destroying the country. They are cruel, they are inhuman, they are corrupt."

"What you say may be true of certain police judges or justices of the peace who do not realize their responsibility, but I do not think that is true of judges of record . . ."

"Judge," insisted Sandburg, "take my word for it, they are all no good. None of them are worth a damn. If they are not crooked they are ignorant, and most of them are both."

Throughout the conversation, Cardozo never raised his voice, gave no sign of his inner emotions. Sandburg continued to elaborate aggressively on his theory that all judges are infamous, and when finally he rose to leave, the two men parted as cordially as they met. But a certain sadness in Cardozo's tone, unnoticed by Sandburg but clear to Maverick's ear, showed that a secret emotion had been stirred.

Justice Cardozo's forebears on his mother's side came from Portugal to America in 1654, more than a century before the ancestors of his "early American" colleagues, McReynolds, Van Devanter and Butler, who opposed his appointment to the Court. Two of those ancestors were Revolutionary fathers; a maternal great-grandfather, Benjamin Mendes Seixas, having been a captain of infantry in Washington's army, and a great-great-uncle, Rabbi Gershom Mendes Seixas, having been so ardent a patriot that when the British occupied New York he refused to remain in the city and moved to Philadelphia, taking his entire congregation with him. Later, he officiated as rabbi at the inauguration of George Washington. Still another ancestor was the first Jew to be made a trustee of Columbia University, at that time King's College.

For two centuries this line of distinguished patriots and cultural leaders continued unbroken. Then occurred a lapse. Judge Albert Cardozo, father of the Justice, was a member of the infamous Tweed Ring. He was Tammany's judicial seal of sanctity. No steal against the public by the bosses or by the vested interests, especially the Vanderbilts, was too raw for him to approve. His conduct was so flagrant that finally the New York City Bar Association preferred five charges of malfeasance and corruption against him, and in order to escape impeachment he resigned.

His father's ill fame had a profound psychological effect on young Benjamin. It intensified his natural tendency to shrink from worldly things. Simultaneously, there was fired in his soul a deep compassion for the lowly and the weak. The Justice never speaks of his father, but today, when a stinging denunciation of corporate interests comes from his pen, it is the memory of his father that applies the lash. Much of Benjamin Cardozo's life has been an attempt to atone for his father's sins.

Another person also played an important part in molding the viewpoint and character of Benjamin Cardozo—his sister. Nellie Cardozo was a brilliant and charming woman who devoted her entire life to her brother. Their mother died when he was nine, and she assumed responsibility for his upbringing. She tutored him, kept house for him and continued to be a mother to him far beyond his youth, in fact until she died. There was a deep and abiding love between the two, and when, during the last years of her life, Nellie Cardozo became bedridden, Benjamin gave up his friends and beloved books to spend all his leisure by her side.

Undoubtedly Cardozo's devotion to his sister is the chief reason he has never married. Undoubtedly, also, her love inspired his deep reverence and chivalry toward women—a chivalry which few men, either married or single, have developed to the same degree.

Justice Cardozo's chivalry is apparent on the bench, where his sympathies invariably lean toward women. It was Cardozo who laid down the dictum that a deserted wife has the right to draw living expenses from the bank funds of her husband. Raffaele de Stefano abandoned his wife and child, and when she went to court to obtain access to his bank account he pleaded infringement of his constitutional rights under the "due process" clause. Cardozo brushed aside this claim as immaterial. "The law," he declared, "does not stand upon punctilios if there is a starving wife at home." It was Cardozo also who checked the efforts of Bud Fisher to renege on an alimony agreement. The famed Mutt and Jeff cartoonist was curtly ordered to pay up and shut up.

Never have his friends heard from Cardozo an off-color story or a word of innuendo against female virtue; nor would they dare indulge in the mildest form of ribaldry in his presence.

And although Cardozo is one of the most liberal men on the Supreme Court, his liberality stops on questions of morality. Owing chiefly to the influence of his sister, he will not go even as far as the pious ex-Senator Smoot of Utah, long unofficial censor of American morals, in admitting slightly risqué pictures and sexy literature into the United States.

A few years ago the Justice's secretaries, concerned about his lack of recreation, persuaded him to join them at the theater, where they saw Noel Coward's *Design for Living,* a hot bit of ultramodern sophistication in which Lunt and Fontanne were starring with barnyard gusto. The evening was not a success. The pained shock of the Justice was unescapable. But while there was a certain coolness in his conversation on the way home, he said nothing of a directly reproving nature to his young hosts. Miss Kate Tracy, the family housekeeper for more than a quarter of a century, however, was not as considerate of their feelings. Facing the unhappy culprits after Cardozo returned, she demanded indignantly, "What do you mean by taking our judge to see such a play?"

Miss Tracy, incidentally, rules the old Cardozo home on West 75th Street, Manhattan, with a kindly but firm hand, and has made herself the special guardian of the Justice's health. For many years Cardozo has suffered from valvular heart trouble, an illness that has serious recurrent periods, with periods of apparent health between. During the summer of 1935 Cardozo was so ill it was doubtful for a time whether he could return to Washington for the opening of Court. He is better now, but Miss Tracy watches over him like a brood hen and is particularly careful not to let him eat sweets, of which he is very fond, but which are banned by the doctor. Anna, the long-time family cook, has standing orders to serve no more of her cherished pastry concoctions.

Anna, however, who has the same feeling of protective tenderness toward the Justice so characteristic of all who know him, considers this rule a needless deprivation, and when she thought Miss Tracy's vigilance was relaxed, prepared an especially rich and tempting dessert. But the ever-watchful Miss Tracy discovered the secret confection and confiscated it. Instead she had Anna prepare a dish of lemon jello.

Cardozo offered no objection and dutifully ate what Miss Tracy decreed. But Anna was indignant over such harsh treatment of her beloved judge. And in her own way she figured out a method of reprisal against Miss Tracy. Every night for seven nights thereafter she served lemon jello for dessert. For six days the Justice submitted without protest. But on the seventh, he demurred.

"I think," he said gently, "I don't care for lemon jello this evening."

Unlike his close friend, Justice Brandeis, Cardozo is not a crusader. He did not win his spurs by deeds of daring in the public arena. His rise to the illustrious position he occupies in American jurisprudence was as undramatic as the life he leads under the watchful eye of Miss Tracy. The flame of righteous outrage against injustice burns as fiercely in his breast as in that of Brandeis. His grasp of modern economics is just as penetrating. His knowledge of the law is just as keen.

But the two men function in different spheres. Brandeis is a man of action, a reformer, a leader of causes. Cardozo is a philosopher, a legal recluse, a poet and dreamer.

To the public, Cardozo is known only as a great jurist. But in legal circles he is known as one of the greatest literary stylists to sit on the American bench. When Cardozo was teaching law at Columbia, a professor of English said of him: "He writes the most powerful English since Alexander Hamilton." His books, *Law and Literature and Other Essays, The Nature of the Judicial Process, The Growth of the Law,* and *The Paradoxes of Legal Science,* are legal classics; and his essay, "The Style of Judicial Opinions," is a masterpiece of prose and logic.

On the Supreme Court, Cardozo's genius in the written word has found expression in a number of memorable dissents. In *U. S.* vs. *Gus L. Constantine,* he upheld the right of the government to impose a special tax on illicit liquor dealers in dry states, aiming this caustic barb at the reactionary justices who overruled him:

"The judgment of the court rests upon the ruling that another purpose, not professed, may be read beneath the surface, and by the purpose so imputed the statute is destroyed. Thus the process of psychoanalysis has spread to unaccustomed fields . . ."

Again Cardozo dissented in the case of *J. E. Jones* vs. *Securities and Exchange Commission,* in which the Tory justices, under the guise of preserving personal liberty, stripped the SEC of authority to proceed against a suspected stock promoter if he withdrew his challenged application for registration. Again speaking for Stone and Brandeis, Cardozo lashed the decision with an epic of ridicule and logic:

"When wrongs such as these have been committed or attempted," he declared, "they must be dragged to light and pilloried. To permit an offending registrant to stifle an inquiry by precipitate retreat on the eve of his exposure is to give immunity to guilt; to encourage falsehood and evasion; to invite the cunning and unscrupulous to gamble with detection.

"If withdrawal without leave may check investigation . . . the statute and its sanctions become the sport of clever knaves.

"Appeal is vaguely made [by the majority] to some constitutional immunity, whether express or implied is not stated with distinctness.

"If immunity rests upon some express provision of the Constitution, the opinion of the Court does not point us to the article or section. If its source is to be found in some impalpable essence, the spirit of the Constitution or the philosophy of government favored by the Fathers, one may take leave to deny that there is anything in that philosophy or spirit whereby the signer of a statement filed with a regulatory body to induce official action is protected against inquiry into his own purpose to deceive.

"The argument for immunity lays hold of strange analogies. . . . The propriety of every question in the course of the inquiry being subject to the supervision of the ordinary courts of justice, is likened [Justice Sutherland in his majority opinion] with denunciatory fervor to the Star Chamber of the Stuarts. Historians may find hyperbole in the sanguinary simile."

Cardozo received his first education from his sister, aided by tutors, one of whom was Horatio Alger. The author of *Sink or Swim, From Newsboy to Bank President,* and other boyhood epics was a highly educated young man but was constantly getting into financial straits, and the Cardozos helped him out. In return he tutored young Benjamin, who was a voracious reader of his thrillers. Cardozo credits his admittance to Columbia University at the early age of fifteen to Alger's teaching. "My preparation for college," he told a friend, "was the work of Horatio Alger. He did not do as successful a job for me as he did for his newsboy heroes."

Despite the Justice's modesty, he was just as brilliant a student as Charles Evans Hughes and established about the same record. At nineteen he attained his master's degree and Phi Beta Kappa.

At twenty-one, after two years of law, he passed the bar examination with high honors. Cardozo never practiced commercial law, one of the things which Roberts, Butler and the rough-and-tumble practicing members of the Court hold against him. Almost from the start of his career he was a lawyer's lawyer. He was a youngster just out of law school when he made his first appearance before the New York Court of Appeals, which, next to the Supreme Court, is the most important in the country. Always diffident and shy, he was in an agony of nervousness while awaiting his turn. But afterwards the Chief Justice sent a note in his own handwriting, commending him for the brevity and clarity of his statement.

Cardozo soon won a wide reputation for his ability to argue difficult points of law before the Court of Appeals, and other attorneys employed him to handle this phase of their cases. Eventually, his practice consisted almost entirely of this super-legal work.

He was first appointed to fill a vacancy, then elected to the Supreme Court of New York in 1913 for the term beginning January 1, 1914. But before he had time to serve for more than a few days, the judges of the Court of Appeals demanded that he be delegated to serve with them under a New York state provision for the temporary appointment of a judge when the court's calendar is crowded. From a financial point of view, most judges are not enthusiastic over this honor, for the Supreme Court judgeship in New York City, although of lower rank, carries a salary of $25,000, while the Court of Appeals in Albany pays only $12,000. So unanimous was the demand of the Appellate judges that he join them, however, that he bowed to the demand and never left that court until he received his appointment to Washington eighteen years later. In 1917 he was regularly elected to a fourteen-year term, and in 1927, before that period expired, he was elected chief justice of the Court of Appeals.

The morning after election, when informed by his sister of his sweeping victory, Cardozo remarked:

"I am afraid that our good Italian citizens mistook the name Cardozo for that of one of their compatriots."

On the New York Court of Appeals, Cardozo spent the happiest years of his life. He delighted in the wide variety and humaneness of the cases which came before him and the comradeship of his associates. The personal and professional fellowship of the members of the Court of Appeals was unique. They were like a large and happy family. Cardozo's colleagues regarded him with a mixture of awed reverence and fatherly protection. They gently chided him for his arduous labors and secretly conspired to take him away for a few hours of recreation. No wonder that in 1927, when President Coolidge offered Cardozo the nomination as American jurist at The Hague, he vetoed it immediately.

Cardozo was first mentioned for the Supreme Court in 1922, when the place now held by Pierce Butler became vacant. The Dean of the Columbia Law School and other prominent lawyers urged Harding to appoint him, but the notorious Harry Daugherty was permitting no liberal jurist, no matter how able, to get by him to a place on the Supreme bench. When Justice Holmes retired ten years later the renewed demand for Cardozo's appointment came from men of every viewpoint, including such liberals as Senators Norris and Borah and such conservatives as ex-Senator James Watson and the late George Wickersham.

Hoover, however, was not at all enthusiastic.

To Justice Stone, to whom he broached the subject one morning after a medicine-ball workout, Hoover explained his reluctance on the ground that two New Yorkers already were on the Court—Hughes and Stone. Without hesitation, Stone offered to resign.

Hoover voiced the same objection to Borah when the Senator from Idaho pressed Cardozo's appointment at a White House reception. "Mr Cardozo," Borah shot back, "belongs as much to Idaho, or California, as he does to New York. It is not a question where the man comes from, but what he is, Mr President."

Hoover then raised another point. He expressed the fear that Cardozo's selection might add fuel to anti-Semitism in the country.

"Mr President," Borah replied, "there is only one way to deal with anti-Semitism. That is not to yield to it."

Several days later, Hoover telephoned to Borah to say that he was considering the names of two federal judges, one in New Mexico and the other in California. He asked Borah his opinion on the two men.

"If you appoint either of them," Borah replied, "I will defeat his confirmation."

"What is the ground of your objection?"

"Obscurity," was the terse answer.

Fearing another Parker or Hughes fight, Hoover finally swallowed his personal antipathy and appointed Cardozo.

Meanwhile, Justice Cardozo was just as anxious not to be appointed as Hoover was anxious not to appoint him. Walking through the streets of Albany with Herbert Cohen, confidential clerk of the Court of Appeals, at the time the appointment was definitely reported, they went over all the reasons why Cardozo should not and could not become a justice of the Supreme Court. By the time they returned to Cardozo's office they had planned a letter they would send President Hoover when they received his proffer of the justiceship.

Suddenly the telephone rang. Cardozo picked up the receiver, and Cohen heard his chief say:

"Why . . . yes, Mr President. Yes, Mr President."

With a dazed look, the new Justice of the Supreme Court hung up the telephone.

"Why didn't we realize," he said, "that he could use the long-distance telephone?"

So Benjamin Nathan Cardozo came to Washington and has been a little sorry he did so ever since.

Washington has been an aloof and uninteresting metropolis after twenty years among old friends in what was comparatively a village in New York State, and Cardozo finds himself alone and out of place. He is too shy to make new friends. He does not know how. Mr Hughes has gone out of his way to be kind to him, and Cardozo sees something of his two liberal colleagues,

Stone and Brandeis. But the brusque attitude of Butler and the deliberate hazing administered by McReynolds, who read a newspaper while the new Justice took the oath of office, deeply hurt his sensitive soul.

At a dinner party one evening, Cardozo was complaining that he loathed Washington and wanted to get back to his beloved New York. He could hardly wait, he said, until Court adjourned in order to get up to his summer home at Rye, New York. The subject changed, and a lady began telling how she had exchanged fur coats inadvertently with another woman at a restaurant. Cardozo brightened at this and said:

"I won a fur-coat case in New York in my younger days. My client, a woman, was so overjoyed when we won that she threw her arms around my neck and kissed me."

"Well, Mr Justice," interposed Seth Richardson, Assistant Attorney General in the Hoover administration, "in view of the type of practice you had, I don't wonder that you want to return to New York."

For the most part, however, Cardozo shuns Washington society. The only social recreation he really enjoys is being with young people and sometimes is enticed out to dinner by one of the court secretaries. At one of these, held at the home of Walter Gellhorn, secretary to Justice Stone, the conversation drifted around to President Roosevelt, and the Justice remarked that he had been awakened that morning by a great clatter of klaxons from the President's motorcycle escort going down Connecticut Avenue. Justice Cardozo added that he did not think any one individual, not even the President of the United States, was entitled to make all that noise and have so many guards.

"Didn't you have an escort like that when you traveled through New York?" someone asked.

"No," replied Cardozo. "The only time I ever had a motorcycle escort like that was when I went with an ambulance."

"Oh, Mr Justice," shot back Mrs Gellhorn in mock gravity, "I didn't know you were an ambulance chaser."

Aside from these rare parties, Justice Cardozo spends most of his time with his court opinions or his books. He is a tremendous worker, turning out more than his share of decisions, and during 1932—the year he was appointed—wrote almost as many opinions in the half court term which he served as did McReynolds in a whole term. Cardozo rises at six or earlier every morning, and if he has not court work on hand, he likes nothing better than plowing through a book of history or philosophy or even a volume of Greek. His personal law library in New York, containing books published as far back as 1730, he has now given to St John's College in Brooklyn, but he is constantly acquiring new books. He has a remarkable pair of eyes, enabling him to read for hours without fatigue, and he browses through every conceivable subject, including physics. His greatest enthusiasm is for engineers. "A bridge builder cannot guess," is one of his favorite sayings, and in his own work he exemplifies this love for the exact by his genius in seizing upon essentials, no matter how involved, and propounding them in brilliant, lucid language.

The Justice seems to remember almost everything he reads, and once when Charles Evans Hughes, Jr, who was his secretary, was asked how he liked the job, he replied, "It's the grandest in the world, but you might as well be secretary to an encyclopedia."

Cardozo has now moved from the Mayflower Hotel to an apartment house at 2102 Connecticut Avenue, partly to be away from the activity of downtown Washington, partly to be nearer his chief friend, Justice Brandeis. He takes no exercise now, having given up golf, which he tried to learn as a result of doctor's orders, but found himself to be the world's worst player. Now, even when he goes to visit Brandeis, only three blocks away, he orders his car.

Having reached the apex of his career, an apex achieved by only a handful of men, Cardozo summarizes his achievements with characteristic modesty:

"The years have taught me caution, though they may not have

taught me wisdom. In truth, I am nothing but a plodding mediocrity—please observe, a plodding mediocrity—for a mere mediocrity does not go very far, but a plodding one gets quite a distance. There is joy in that success, and a distinction can come from courage, fidelity and industry."

Justice Cardozo's chief "joy" is his work on the Supreme Court. He sits on the bench each Monday that Court is in session, an intent listener, the quietest of the group. His long, ascetic face, the shock of white hair falling across his fine, high brow, draw the eyes of the courtroom. Frequently he inclines his head to converse with Stone, who speaks not one word to his other neighbor, Sutherland, on his right. Cardozo has sat through hundreds of such sessions—perhaps thousands—twenty-two years in New York and Washington listening to the legal battles of states and cities and corporations and people—a parade of human conflict that has passed before him. Sometimes he seems a little tired of watching that parade.

"My chief job," Cardozo told an old friend after he came to Washington, "is trying to find out what was in a Congressman's mind when he wrote certain legislation."

But he sits on—watching, judging that endless parade of human conflict with "courage, fidelity and industry."

CHAPTER XII

Scrooge

T HE Supreme Court's greatest human tragedy is James Clark McReynolds. He is a tragedy not in regard to his legal opinions —they are no worse than those of certain colleagues—but in his relationships with mankind. Somewhere in James McReynolds' life some searing tragedy must have warped his soul. For not only can he not get along with his colleagues on the bench, he cannot get along with himself.

He is a tragic, lonely figure.

On one occasion several clerks and attendants of the Supreme Court, always inclined to see the clayish qualities of those in high places, got into an argument as to who was the stupidest justice on the bench. The debate narrowed down to Butler and McReynolds. Finally it was decided in favor of the latter, although one point never definitely was determined, namely, whether McReynolds is chiefly stupid or lazy.

Apparently, however, he is both.

Some years ago, McReynolds scarcely wrote an opinion. Years passed with practically no legal output from him. Finally, however, criticism in legal circles, which reached McReynolds' ears, plus the Taft-Hughes speed-up system, forced him to bestir himself, and he now turns out a moderate quota of work.

On one occasion, McReynolds' secretary complained that the burden of research he had to do for his employer's opinions was too great, that he needed an assistant. To this McReynolds re-

plied in effect: "You'll do this work alone and like it. Furthermore, if I weren't afraid the Chief [Chief Justice] would suspect
me, I'd make you write my opinions, too."

McReynolds' opinions are notorious for their sloppiness and
undoubtedly fall in the category Justice Cardozo once described
as "tonsorial or agglutinative, so called from the shears and the
paste pot which are its implements and emblem." In the middle
of an argument before the Court, McReynolds will stop the attorney and ask for an explanation of some point which is
perfectly intelligible to every other justice.

Indirectly McReynolds owes his appointment to the Supreme
Court to Brandeis; yet when the first Jewish justice took his
seat, no other member treated him with more disdain.

Woodrow Wilson had selected Brandeis as Attorney General
in his cabinet and almost immediately thereafter started for a
vacation in Bermuda, leaving behind a furor of protest led by
the Boston Bar Association. Wilson, afraid to face the criticism,
wrote Brandeis a letter asking that as a personal favor he with-
draw. Then, with the date of his inauguration approaching and
the office of Attorney General unfilled, Wilson turned to William
Gibbs McAdoo for advice. McAdoo recommended his old
friend and fellow Tennesseean, James Clark McReynolds.

McReynolds was then an obscure lawyer who had oscillated
between a highly respectable law practice in Tennessee and the
money-pots of Wall Street, with four years as Assistant Attorney
General sandwiched in between. His cosmic being was a cross
between a liberal and a reactionary, but with no great clash
between the two. His conflicting philosophies were not deep
enough for that. He had served as secretary to Howell E. Jackson, conservative Tennessee corporation lawyer, while the latter
was on the Supreme Court, and also he was a close friend of
Justice John M. Harlan of Kentucky, at that time the most liberal
justice on the Supreme Court. At one and the same time, also,
he was a lawyer, a real-estate operator, a teacher at Vanderbilt
University and the Reverend William Thomas Manning's right-

hand reformer in cleaning up Nashville's gambling and red-light districts.

McReynolds came to Washington when Teddy Roosevelt was President and Philander C. Knox Attorney General to fill the Justice Department shoes of the late James M. Beck, and, like Beck, graduated four years later to a profitable partnership in a Wall Street law firm. As Assistant Attorney General, McReynolds' record was neither brilliant nor reactionary—in fact, gave off faint sparks of liberalism; but certainly there was nothing in it to indicate that he would be an outstanding Attorney General. In fact, President Wilson soon found that the only thing outstanding about his cabinet member was his original friendship with William Gibbs McAdoo and his inability to be friendly, or even civil, to most of those around him. The problem of patronage gave McReynolds a large pain in the neck, and he antagonized every Congressman who came to see him about it. He even ordered Senator Norris and ex-Governor Joseph Folk of Missouri out of his office when they came to urge the prosecution of a trust-busting case against the New Haven railroad. And, in the end, he rowed with his old friend McAdoo to such an extent that the Secretary of the Treasury and the Attorney General communicated with each other only through the medium of the White House.

All this, plus the storm which arose over McReynolds' postponement of prosecution in the Caminetti white-slave case, caused Wilson to jump at the first opportunity to get rid of his inept and bellicose Attorney General. In later years Wilson was credited with the remark that the greatest mistake of his administration was the appointment of McReynolds to the Supreme Court. But at that particular time all he could see was his mistake in appointing McReynolds as Attorney General. So, when Justice Lurton died in 1914, he doubled the error by kicking him upstairs to the highest tribunal of the nation.

McReynolds, therefore, landed in the cabinet in place of Brandeis, and on the Court ahead of him.

And in that cloistered atmosphere he has been free to develop an ever-deepening reaction against all social and economic progress and to nurse a gnawing grudge against mankind.

For a man of his sheer ugliness of disposition McReynolds has come far.

During the period when the Court was housed in the old Senate Chamber, McReynolds refused to eat soup and crackers with the other justices in the robing room and went to the trouble of taking off his robes and going downstairs to the Senate lunchroom. When Justice Stone first came to the bench from the Department of Justice, McReynolds deliberately got up and left the conference room when Stone discussed a case. When Cardozo's appointment was being pressed on Hoover, McReynolds joined with Butler and Van Devanter in urging the White House not to "afflict the Court with another Jew." Later, when news of the appointment was announced, McReynolds snarled: "Huh, it seems that the only way you can get on the Supreme Court these days is to be either the son of a criminal or a Jew, or both." Stone was so shocked that he left the room. When Cardozo was sworn in, McReynolds read a newspaper, and when Justice Brandeis gave his famous dissent in the Oklahoma ice case to a crowded and intense courtroom, McReynolds pretended to be busy with his papers. When former Justice John H. Clarke retired from the Supreme Court, he told friends that one of his reasons for retiring was that he could not stand McReynolds.

McReynolds does not confine his rudeness to his colleagues of the Court. Once, however, he got a salutary lesson at the Chevy Chase Club, of which he is a member and at which he plays a slow and atrocious game of golf. Despite the fact that he was almost constantly in the rough, McReynolds made it a practice of refusing to let anyone play through him. The result was that whenever McReynolds was on the greens there was always sure to be a long line of irate players behind him, forced to take hours to finish nine holes.

On one occasion McReynolds, playing with Howland Chase, added to his usual insults by standing on the fifth tee directing the caddy where to find a lost ball and refusing to move off the tee or allow a member to play through him until the ball was recovered.

That was the climax. A group of members filed a complaint against McReynolds and demanded that Morven Thompson, chairman of the Golf Committee, call the Supreme Court Justice to account. Thompson, who had witnessed the scene, did so.

"Well, I've been a member of this club a good many years," McReynolds replied, "and no one around here has ever shown me any courtesy, so I don't intend to show any to anyone else."

Thompson, who had been deferential, now became indignant.

"Mr Justice," he said, "you wouldn't be a member of this club if it wasn't for your official position. The members of this club have put up with your discourtesy for years, merely because you are a member of the Supreme Court. But I'm telling you now that the next time there is a complaint against you, you'll be suspended from the privileges of the golf course."

Since then McReynolds has stepped aside.

There is another side to Justice McReynolds which few people have glimpsed, but those who have say it is human and kindly beyond belief. Perhaps it gleams more beautifully because it is so rare and hard to penetrate. Those who really know him—and they can be counted on the fingers of the hand—refer to him as "Old Mac" and say his sardonic bluster is chiefly for effect. If so, he has done it so constantly that he cannot divorce himself from the role. But he does show moments of mellowness, as with the late Oliver Wendell Holmes, whom he visited frequently during his declining years. When Mrs Holmes died, McReynolds, the terror of the Supreme bench, broke down and wept at her funeral.

And yet for years he was not on speaking terms with Holmes's closest friend, Justice Brandeis.

One day while McReynolds was riding to his office on a

Pennsylvania Avenue street car, a man got aboard in the last stages of intoxication. When the car lurched around a corner a moment later, he fell out in the aisle. McReynolds picked him up, helped him back to his seat and said:

"My friend, I see you are not feeling well. I'll just sit here and see if I can help you."

The Justice sat beside his charge until they reached the top of Capitol Hill, when he inquired where the man wanted to get out, and left him only after giving explicit instructions to the conductor.

McReynolds is not without a sense of humor and can enjoy a good joke even at the expense of his own kind. One such occurred when Robert Jackson, ablest of Mr Cummings' Assistant Attorney Generals, was arguing a case in which the government attempted to collect a tax from the estate of Malcolm MacFarlan of Philadelphia, who had transferred his property to relatives prior to his death. Jackson held that the defendant's advanced years indicated that he had his own demise in mind when he gave away his wealth.

"But," snapped Justice McReynolds, himself a Scotsman, "didn't you read the opinion of the lower court? It is shown there that this man was a hale and hearty Scotsman in his seventies."

"Yes, your honor," replied Jackson, "and that is the reason the government is so sure that this gift would have been made only in preparation for death."

Even McReynolds joined in the laughter. The Court handed down a unanimous opinion for the government.

McReynolds has a story of his own which he tells on the Scotch in his more mellow moments. A Scotsman, leaving a pub one night after imbibing freely, was approached by a Salvation Army lassie, who extended her tambourine for alms. The man dropped in a shilling and was about to pass on, when suddenly he turned and asked:

"What are you going to do with that money? What's it for?"

"It's for God."

"For God? Well, in that case give it back, because, my girl, I expect to see Him before you do."

During his early years on the bench, McReynolds was a queer mass of contradiction. For the most part, he lined up with the reactionaries. But on occasions as rare as his bursts of humor, a gleam of the past, when he was trust-busting Assistant Attorney General for Teddy Roosevelt, stirred the old man's soul, and he came out as a champion of human rights. Then he sank back into the slough again.

There was a day when McReynolds touched off a pyrotechnic display of rhetoric regarding the sacredness of the Bill of Rights, in dissenting from the majority in the Carroll case. In this his colleagues held that an automobile could be searched for liquor without a warrant—but McReynolds claimed otherwise. Then he reversed himself completely by joining with the majority in the Olmstead case, which permitted prohibition agents to tap telephone wires.

Again McReynolds personally wrote the opinion in the case which held that Massachusetts could not tax income from patent royalties, on the ground that patents and copyrights are granted by the federal government; only to turn round and support a decision giving authority to the state of New York to tax income from copyrights which also are granted by the federal government.

Justice McReynolds' economic theory is not dissimilar from the Brandeis passion to break up all big business and go back to the horse-and-buggy days of town merchants and small manufacturers. He hates bigness, which is probably one reason he hates the New Deal. But theory is as far as he goes. Whereas Brandeis will excuse bigness when it takes the shape of a co-operative or a labor union organized for the benefit of the masses, McReynolds draws no such distinction. Bigness is bigness, and his Tennessee fundamentalist soul revolts against it.

There is one hate regarding which McReynolds has been consistently faithful—his dislike of all things pertaining to tobacco.

It was when he was a young lawyer with the firm of Cravath, Henderson & de Gersdorff in 1907 that he was drafted by the Roosevelt administration to prosecute an anti-trust case against the Duke Tobacco Company. He was then forty-five years old. His prejudices had not yet congealed. He had spent four years under Teddy Roosevelt as a reasonably forthright Assistant Attorney General in the Justice Department. And he gave the Duke Tobacco Company all of the vigorous vituperation that he has since thrown at the New Deal. "Commercial wolves and highwaymen" was what he called the corporation. "When has property illegally and criminally acquired come to have any rights?" he asked.

He did a far more effective job than did his colleague, Pierce Butler, called upon at about the same time to prosecute the meat packers. And, although McReynolds won a technical victory when the company was ordered dissolved, actually an innocuous settlement was arranged which now permits the glamorous Doris Duke to parade her picture over the front pages as the richest heiress of the century.

Probably there is no relation between tobacco smoke and the tobacco trust, but in Washington society McReynolds' hatred of tobacco is proverbial. No one who knows him would think of lighting a cigarette in his presence. Feminine guests at his Sunday-morning breakfast parties sometimes spend an hour of agony waiting to reach the freedom of the corridor outside, in order to get a lift with a Camel. Once when Roberts lit a cigar while the justices were in chambers, McReynolds scribbled a hasty note asking that he put it out. Tobacco smoke, McReynolds explains, makes him physically ill.

But in 1933, when Justice Stone and his liberal colleagues urged that the Court rule on the plea of minority stockholders of the American Tobacco Company to stop the preposterous bonus-grabs of George Washington Hill and other tobacco-company officials, McReynolds sided with Butler and the conservative majority against the complaining stockholders.

Probably the best insight into the guiding motive of McReyn-

olds' early days on the bench are his own words when appointed
Attorney General.

"I am opposed," he said, "to a strict regimentation of business,
and likewise to the ownership of business by government.
Therefore, I am trying to help bring about free working conditions or competition in business. I am not hostile to wealth, nor
to men who are doing business openly and fairly. Neither do I
enthrone those men who have gained wealth by unjust practices. I want to see prices natural, and not unnatural—to see them
fixed by the laws of trade, and not by combinations among the
producers."

With this two-directioned economic philosophy, it was a simple
matter for McReynolds to slide more and more in one direction;
so that, long before the New Deal, he had become unalterably
opposed to progress, and, except when it came to tobacco, was
the unalterable enemy of the underdog. In the Jensen case he
ruled that an injured stevedore could not recover damages under
the New York Workmen's Compensation Act, on the ground
that his work was of a maritime nature and, therefore, under the
exclusive jurisdiction of the federal government. As this jurisdiction was not then exercised, the stevedore was left unpro-
tected. But when Congress sought to overcome this technicality
by enacting a statute making compensation laws applicable to
dock workers, McReynolds led the Court in holding that Congress had no authority thus to transfer federal power. Later he
wrote the decision that injured longshoremen could not secure
damages in the absence of an act of Congress specifically apply-
ing to them. Again, in the 1931–32 term, McReynolds joined in
the Hughes opinion which nullified the administrative features
of the Longshoremen's and Harbor Workers' Compensation
Act, which Congress had passed in an effort to overcome the
Court's persistent obstruction.

Long before the New Deal, also, McReynolds joined enthusiastically in the states'-rights obstructions thrown up by his
conservative colleagues. He wrote the decision annulling the
Wisconsin law which taxed gifts by rich donors within a certain

time of their death, and also the opinions outlawing the Minnesota and Missouri acts taxing bonds and bank accounts of nonresidents. These last two decisions reversed a previous ruling of the Court written by Justice Holmes.

The climax of McReynolds' reactionarism came in 1936, when he confided to a friend: "There is only one movement in this country which I consider dangerous to it and which must be destroyed at all hazards. That is the labor movement."

McReynolds is a bachelor, tall, slender and has a face with such a Satanic look that in it there is a certain charm. It has a definite appeal for women, and in his quiet way the Justice is quite a ladies' man.

Largely in order to avoid White House dinners during the New Deal, McReynolds has established the reputation of not going out in Washington society. But this is mere fiction. There is nothing the Justice loves more than a quiet party with his intimate friends, especially if those friends include a sprinkling of debutantes. McReynolds' big hour each week comes with his Sunday-morning breakfast parties, which are among the most exclusive in the Capital. Those invited include: Mrs Jacob Leander Loose, of Kansas City Loose-Wiles biscuit fame; Judge and Mrs Robb of the District of Columbia Circuit Court; Judge Marion DeVries, formerly of the Customs Court; with a few others. And on a spring or summer morning they will sit down on the balcony of the Justice's new apartment and partake of hot cakes and sausage, cooked by his faithful housekeeper and served by Harry, his Negro handy man. All mention of the New Deal or court matters is carefully avoided.

For years McReynolds was expected to marry Mrs Camilla Lippincott, an attractive widow, in whose company he was frequently seen, and he narrowly escaped being named in a divorce case between an army officer and his wife.

One of his recent feminine admirers is Mrs Jacob Leander Loose. After John Chamberlain wrote for *Fortune* a series of personality sketches on the Supreme Court, the publishers received the following note from Justice McReynolds:

"Gentlemen:
For some months you have been sending me your literature. Send it no more."

In forwarding the letter to the editorial department, the circulation department added this postscript: "Gift subscription of Mrs Jacob Leander Loose."

No matter what his record on the Supreme Court, McReynolds will always go down in history as the Attorney General who checked the use of the Mann Act for blackmail purposes. While he was serving in the Wilson cabinet, F. Drew Caminetti, son of the Commissioner of Immigration, together with Maury I. Diggs, former state architect of California, escorted two high-school girls to Reno, Nevada, and subsequently were charged by them with violation of the Mann Act. The case was patently what Professor Powell describes as "nonpecuniary interstate fornication," and McReynolds, who thought the Mann Act should not apply to noncommercialized vice, let prosecution of the case slide over to the autumn term. Immediately there was a hue and cry of "political favoritism," and McReynolds was the object of bitter attack. Eventually Caminetti was convicted and the conviction sustained by the Supreme Court. But the Tennessee wrath of McReynolds was aroused almost to the peak later attained during the New Deal. Regardless of public opinion, he determined to strike back. Seizing a case where a woman in Pittsburgh attempted to take advantage of a man for escorting her across a state line, McReynolds charged the woman with blackmail, took personal charge of the case and convicted her. There has been no attempted blackmail since.

McReynolds comes honestly by his indomitable determination to resist progress. For years his Scotch ancestors resisted progress in that part of Tennessee and Kentucky where the same

English and Scotch folk songs have been sung with the same dialect for almost two centuries. Religion has not changed. Moonshining has not changed. Attitude toward the law has not changed. And James Clark McReynolds, son of a small-town Kentucky doctor and plantation owner, has not changed.

Born during the Civil War in the days of slavery, horse-and-buggies and a more popular conception of Santa Claus, McReynolds recently attended a Christmas party given by a Washington couple for their eight-year-old daughter. The Justice, standing in front of a huge open fireplace and surveying the little girl with her abundant gifts, said:

"Well, well, this must have been the chimney that Santa Claus came down for you."

The young lady, puzzled but polite, made a noncommittal reply, but later asked:

"Mother, who is that old gentleman? Doesn't he know I'm eight? Why did he want to tell me that old-fashioned story?"

But the folks back in Tennessee have looked on their old neighbor a little disapprovingly since his TVA dissent, when he made it all too plain that he considered Santa Claus unconstitutional when it came to federal millions for the Tennessee Valley. On this point, however, McReynolds was consistent. For as a student at Nashville he wrote an editorial in the Vanderbilt University *Observer* entitled "Southern Sycophants," in which he castigated the trustees of Southern colleges for accepting funds from Northern endowments.

McReynolds also has been consistent in his attitude toward one of the most moot questions of the Roosevelt administration —gold. Here again he doesn't believe in Santa Claus. He is a traditional gold Democrat. Even as far back as 1896, when Bryan's free-silver theories were rocking the country, McReynolds, then only thirty-four years old, ran for Congress from Tennessee on an old-fashioned gold platform, ensuring certain defeat rather than endorse the monetary "heresy" of William Jennings Bryan.

Those who heard McReynolds raging from the bench against

the gold decision probably did not realize it, but they were listening, not to a Supreme Court justice, but to the Tennessee politician who split his party wide open forty years before, now grown increasingly old and bitter.

McReynolds made no effort to conceal his rage. His face crimson, his eyes burning fiercely, he almost shouted his words at a shocked court chamber.

"Acquiescence in the decision just announced [upholding Roosevelt's devaluation of gold] is impossible," he snarled.

"It seems impossible to overestimate the result of what has happened today. It is not too much to say that the Constitution is gone.

"The guarantees to which men and women heretofore have looked to protect their interests have been swept away. The powers of Congress have been enlarged, and we stand as a people stripped of the very fundamentals.

"The people expected these gold clauses to protect them against a debased currency. A debased currency is nothing new. Nero undertook to exercise that power. Six centuries ago, in France, it was regarded as a prerogative of the sovereign. . . .

"This is not a thing I like to talk about. God knows I wish I didn't have to. But there are some responsibilities attaching to a man on this bench to reveal to the bar, in all its nakedness, just what has been done; and the minority refuses to use mere generalities or a multitude of words to distract the mind from the issues involved.

"Just men regard repudiation and spoliation of citizens by their sovereign with abhorrence; but we are asked to confirm that the Constitution has granted power to accomplish both. . . . Not only is there no permission for such actions; they are inhibited. And no plenitude of words can conform them to our charter.

"Under the challenged statutes it is said that the United States have realized profits amounting to $2,800,000,000. . . . To such counterfeit profits there would be no limit; with each new debasement of the dollar they would expand. Two billions might be ballooned indefinitely—to twenty, thirty, or what you will.

"Loss of reputation for honorable dealing will bring us unending humiliation; the impending legal and moral chaos is appalling."

It was not merely McReynolds' words—though they were harsh enough; it was the manner in which they were delivered. Probably it was the most scathingly sarcastic harangue ever delivered from the bench of the Supreme Court.

Just thirty years before, James Clark McReynolds, then a young admirer of Teddy Roosevelt's trust-busting activities, had stood before the court in the Duke Tobacco Company case, and in words almost as vitriolic proclaimed:

"There are some of us who have hoped for a peaceful solution of this great question under the law as declared by the courts. But if, in the light of the facts here presented, this Court shall decide that this defendant has not violated the law, then our hopes are a dream."

The same belligerency was there, the same sarcasm, but today James Clark McReynolds is on the other side of the fence.

The Justice grew increasingly sour after the gold decision. Some of his conservative colleagues wavered occasionally in their antipathy toward the New Deal, but not McReynolds. Hughes went over to the liberal side on the minimum-wage and municipal-bankruptcy cases. Even Butler, Van Devanter and Sutherland sided with the New Deal when it came to upholding the TVA. But McReynolds remained immovable. His vote on all New Deal measures was 12 to 0. There was not one he favored.

So he became grimmer and grimmer. The sense of humor which once gleamed occasionally for a few intimates flickered and almost disappeared. Not only did he refuse to attend White House functions, but even at Gridiron dinners McReynolds deliberately turned his back when the entire assembly rose in tribute to the President. And when the Federal Trade Commission took over the Rochambeau Apartment, forcing him to abandon the suite he had occupied for half a lifetime, he became even more embittered.

One day, in keeping an appointment with his dentist, McReynolds arrived breathless and irate. Plumping himself down in the dental chair without even removing his hat, the Justice said:

"Doctor, I don't know what this country is coming to. Do you know what happened to me downstairs? I was just coming in the door when a man accosted me and said: 'Hey, Chief, want to buy some contraceptives?'"

Even this, it seemed, he blamed on the New Deal.

One day, after McReynolds had joined in tossing out the AAA, he was about to enter his suite of offices in the new Supreme Court building and noticed that a set of numerals—128A—had been placed on his door. Glaring at the figures for a moment, he beckoned to a guard.

"What's that for?" he demanded.

"They are your room number, sir."

"I know that. But what's the 'A' for?"

"That's the serial letter, sir. That's what the plans call for. Each office has a serial letter."

"Have it taken off—at once. I don't want any of this damned alphabet stuff around me!"

McReynolds is more lonely than ever now. Even his old friends, Justices Butler and Van Devanter, find him so crotchety that they see less and less of him. They even transferred their golf from the Chevy Chase Club to Burning Tree in order to get away from him. McReynolds has about given up his golf, but still goes duck shooting, though always alone. Not even his best friend, Judge DeVries, whose wife died some years ago, ever has gone with him. In the summer McReynolds mopes around Washington wondering what to do with himself. Sometimes he wanders off to Europe, sometimes to California to visit his brother, or his sisters in Tennessee. But always he is glad when Court reopens in the fall. It gives him something to do.

McReynolds feels the antipathy which so many people have for him. It upsets him. But he takes pains not to show it, and he could not change his manner even if he would. He feels age and loneliness creeping in on him and sometimes he has considered resigning from the bench, retiring from its abuse, its stormy debates, to a comfortable pension and obscurity. But then he remembers his grim, self-appointed role of mowing down every act and deed of the New Deal; of destroying the labor movement. And so he hangs on—a lonely, tragic figure.

CHAPTER XIII

Hot Oil

Lawyers appearing before the Nine Old Men on behalf of New Deal legislation have advanced many theories as to why their cause so consistently was lost. There is the theory held by Jerome Frank and many other liberal legalists around Mr Roosevelt that if the constitutionality of the recovery measures had been tested during the first full flush of Roosevelt popularity, the Supreme Court would have handed down a different story. Then there is the theory that if the ebullient General Johnson had not tried to bring every tailor shop, beauty parlor and gold-fish hatchery in the United States under the strident wing of his Blue Eagle, the NRA never would have come to unconstitutional grief. And there is the further theory—as will be developed in a subsequent chapter—that had not President Roosevelt eaten too many cherries on a certain Sunday afternoon the entire history of the NRA and the Supreme Court might have been different.

All this, of course, is interesting only in historical retrospect; and in the end, at least five of the Nine Old Men probably would have voted just exactly as they did no matter whether the President ate cherries or persimmons, or whether the test cases were brought late or early.

No matter what the outcome might have been, however, it is undoubtedly true that never since the days of Harry M. Daugherty had the Department of Justice been so poorly equipped to handle even routine defense of government legislation as during the early days of Franklin Roosevelt's administration. And no inquest of the New Deal's legislative deaths would be complete without noting the effect which Thomas J. Walsh's amorous romance with a virile Cuban widow had upon the New Deal. The Walsh honeymoon left the seventy-four-year-old Senator dead on the floor of his railroad compartment, and Franklin Roosevelt without an Attorney General. It also transformed the Justice Department from what promised to be the most forthright branch of the New Deal to the most tragic conglomeration of political hacks recently assembled in Washington.

Homer Stillé Cummings, who stepped into Walsh's shoes, is a good-natured gentleman, with a charming manner, a membership in the Elks, the Odd Fellows, the Eagles and the Masons, a fair knowledge of law and a sense of humor which keeps cabinet meetings convulsed. He also chairmanned the Democratic National Committee during part of the futile 1920 campaign to elect Franklin Roosevelt Vice President of the United States. In fact, Homer made the speech which led to Roosevelt's nomination, and Franklin has not forgotten him. Mr Cummings, also, has acutely developed the political custom of not forgetting one's friends; so that when Jim Farley, hard put to it to place all of the deserving Democrats who had boosted Roosevelt "Before Chicago," sent them over to the Justice Department, Homer nearly always obliged. In fact, due to the yen of Henry Wallace, Harold Ickes and Fannie Perkins for pristine unpolitical purity in the personnel of their departments, Mr Farley found himself sending more and more political deadweight over to the Justice Department, until the obliging Homer was loaded to the gunwales.

Homer's attitude was understandable. He is old and human and kindly. He has seen much of life and much politics come and go. He had been in Jim Farley's shoes himself; and he knew that party organization is built on the motto: "To the victor belong the spoils." To his credit it should be noted that

Homer has now cleaned out his Justice Department, so that it is one of the most efficient in the New Deal and in 1935 terminated 713 cases as against 83 in the last year of Mr Hoover. But in those early days he was so ultra-obliging that when Jimmy Roosevelt sent down to Washington the mayor of Gardner, Massachusetts, a young man overburdened with enthusiasm for Roosevelt and underburdened with a knowledge of the law, Homer made him an Assistant Attorney General, one of the highest offices in the Department, where he served for more than one month without knowing enough to take the oath of office—though later he developed into a first-class executive. Again, when Senator McAdoo of California desired a berth for the garrulous and grossly inept A. V. Dalrymple, Homer made him Director of Prohibition, where he caused so much commotion that eventually he was dropped.

Then there was the case of Pat Malloy, an oil operator from Tulsa, Oklahoma, whom Jim Farley sent round to be Mr Ickes' Assistant Secretary of the Interior. But Mr Ickes felt that his Department had smelled too strongly of oil during the Teapot Dome days, and so Farley offered Pat the post of Assistant Secretary of War. On that particular day, however, the Oklahoman had drowned his sorrow so deeply in Maryland rye that he rejected the job; though a day or two later he realized what he had done and came back. Jim was compassionate. Pat Malloy was loyal. He had organized the state of Oklahoma for Roosevelt. So Jim went to Homer Cummings and, much to the amazement of all Washington, Homer rewarded Pat with the important post of Assistant Attorney General in charge of the busiest section in the Department—criminal and tax cases.

Perhaps Homer was omniscient. Poor Pat Malloy died a short time later, a victim of acute and continued alcoholism.

Homer was not so omniscient in the case of J. Crawford Biggs, his Solicitor General. This office almost equals that of the Attorney General in importance, for it handles all cases before the Supreme Court, and the Solicitor himself usually pleads personally before the Court. For this post, Felix Frankfurter urged Dean Acheson, former secretary to Justice Brandeis and one of the most brilliant young lawyers in Washington. Simultaneously, Josephus Daniels urged the appointment of Biggs, a North Carolina attorney of rare Southern charm and doubtful ability who had handled cases for Daniels' Raleigh *News and Observer*.

Politics being politics with Homer Cummings, Biggs got the job. Acheson became Under Secretary of the Treasury, a position for which he was not at all qualified and subsequently resigned to win various Supreme Court cases against the New Deal.

The appointment of Biggs was the beginning of the New Deal's legal downfall. He chose to make his first appearance before the Supreme Court in a murder case. This, in itself, was a shock to the Nine Old Men. Such cases rarely come before them, usually are of minor importance, and always are argued by the bright young men who assist the Solicitor General.

This case was that of the army doctor, Major Charles A. Shepard, convicted by a jury of poisoning his wife. He had appealed, and the conviction had been sustained. Shepard was now appealing from this ruling, and the issue centered on the question of the admissibility of deathbed statements.

J. Crawford Biggs, appearing before the Court personally, began his argument with a redundant declamation to the effect that he would discuss two points. And with this weighty pronouncement out of the way, he proceeded to orate at great length, ardent fervor and extraordinary aimlessness. After a half-hour of rhetoric, the Court began to fidget. Finally Chief Justice Hughes interrupted:

"Mr Solicitor, you said you would discuss two points. You have used up forty-three minutes and so far have touched only on one. Do you plan to discuss the other?"

"Certainly, Mr Chief Justice, certainly," was the cheerful reply. "How much time have I left?"

"You have two minutes. We will give you three in addition to that. You will please finish in that time."

Under Biggs's backwoods legal guidance, the New Deal started out by losing more cases than it won. This was during the days when Mr Roosevelt was enjoying the peak of his popularity, long before the avalanche of unconstitutionality was hurled from the Supreme bench.

And finally it became apparent even to the complacent Mr Cummings that either the grandiloquent Mr Biggs would have to be sacrificed or else the Department of Justice be reconciled to losing even its relatively minor suits before the Court. So an easy way was sought to get J. Crawford out. It was discovered, after considerable research, that the District of Columbia needed an additional judge for its United States Court of Appeals. One of its judges, Charles H. Robb, was old and sick most of the time, but would not retire because he was two years under the retirement age of seventy. So a bill was introduced creating a sixth judge, and Biggs was slated for the job. But, much to the regret of the Justice Department, Congressman Blanton, Texas' self-appointed watchdog of the District of Columbia, decided that the Court of Appeals did not need an extra judge and killed the bill. Mrs Roosevelt even invited Mrs Blanton to lunch at the White House, but it did no good. Tom remained adamant, and in the end the President eased Mr Biggs into a trusteeship to protect the investments of the Reconstruction Finance Corporation in the Wheeling and Lake Erie Railway. This was something of a step down when it came to dignity, but the pay is good—$10,000, exactly the same as Solicitor General's—and it takes very little of J. Crawford's time.

Mr Biggs's undramatic exit took place in March 1935, just about the time Mr Cummings and the President began to wake up to the fact that plucking favorable decisions from the Nine Old Men was in no way comparable to securing nourishment from the proverbial bowl of cherries. The first storm warning that the Nine Old Men had not been wholly converted to Mr Roosevelt's philosophy came on January 7, 1935, when Chief

Justice Hughes read the majority decision in the hot-oil case. That decision passed almost unnoticed by a nation still relatively enthusiastic over Mr Roosevelt; and yet it laid the basis for undermining the most important work he was attempting to do.

Under the red sand of east Texas lies the largest oil field in the world. Discovered in the late twenties, it was opened up full blast when the depression was settling its black wings over America. The field is unique, not only in respect to its size but because its rich crude oil set a record for flowing to the surface without pumping. Some of the wells gush ten thousand barrels an hour, giving east Texas enough production in a week to supply the entire nation a year.

But even more unique is the fact that this oleaginous monster was largely owned by small independents—cotton farmers, town plumbers, filling-station operators and wildcatters of all descriptions. Of course, when the enormity of east Texas' wealth dawned on the big companies, they tried frantically to buy up lease rights, but it was too late.

All they could do was sit by and watch the small independents reap profits—and, what was more important, reap them as fast as they could. Controlled production was nonexistent, and their oil flowed so furiously and they sold it so rapidly that the market plummeted from three dollars to ten cents a barrel.

This, if it continued, could mean only one thing—almost certain bankruptcy for the big companies. There seemed to be absolutely nothing they could do about it. The supplies of east Texas appeared inexhaustible, and all the big companies could do was stand by and stare with glassy eyes as millions of barrels of black oil, oozing from the sands of east Texas, threatened to put them out of business.

It was precisely at this moment, at the depth of the oil depression, that an angel arrived in the person of Franklin D. Roosevelt. The oil companies at first did not recognize him as such; but when in lieu of wings he unfolded a plan, the now famous and defunct NRA, the oil tycoons got to their feet, rolled up their striped trousers and galloped to Washington. There they found the President and his Secretary of the Interior in a receptive mood. They had determined to halt the "outrageous waste of our natural resources"; and, although it may not have been uppermost in their minds, incidentally save the lives of the Rockefellers, the Mellons and the Harry Sinclairs. Straight at east Texas was aimed the oil code, endorsed, in fact even drafted, by the major companies. The plan was ingeniously simple. The state of Texas already had evolved the pro-ration system supposed to hold the big oil wells to a fixed quota per month. But the authorities either did not or else could not police the field, with the result that hundreds of thousands of barrels were being shipped out of the state in excess of the quota.

This was called "hot" oil, a term filched from gangsterdom and meaning "illicit." Therefore, the plan evolved by the potentates of petroleum, together with their heaven-sent friends of the New Deal, was to refuse transportation to "hot oil." If Texas could not bottle up the wells, then the federal government would cut off tank-car facilities and pipe lines, which, as well as the railroads, fall under the jurisdiction of the Interstate Commerce Commission.

So an oil code along this line was drafted. Into it was tucked a seemingly harmless provision, later to become famous in New Deal history—Section 9c—by which Congress authorized the President or his agents to prohibit the shipment of oil in interstate commerce when that oil was produced in violation of any state law. This was a delegation of power by Congress considered not unusual and rarely subject to legal attack. Certainly when the President, at Hyde Park on August 29, 1933, gave Secretary Ickes the go-ahead signal, there was not the slightest suspicion on the part of anyone that this was to be the wedge which the Nine Old Men would drive into the entire structure of government regulation.

Simultaneous with the signal from Hyde Park, Louis Glavis's Bureau of Investigation agents encamped all over the east Texas field, a commission was set up to check bills of lading against quotas, and regulation went into effect with a boom. The flow of "hot oil" out of Texas dwindled to a dribble, prices shot up, oil was pegged by the major companies at one dollar a barrel, the government looked on approvingly, competition was killed, the major companies had the upper hand again, and all was well in the world of oil once more.

But not entirely.

Immediately there came a tremendous squawk from the small independents. Their quotas cut practically to nothing, they were making far less than under the old free-for-all system, despite the price jump from ten cents to one dollar. Just as the small independent in many other businesses suffered under the NRA, so many of the smaller oil companies were squeezed into bankruptcy. It was all part of the NRA theory of eliminating "wasteful competition." But the political consequences of that elimination were so terrific that they threatened to wipe out the entire NRA structure—and later did.

Also the major companies, which had prayed for, written and been saved by the oil code, now began to view it as a dubious blessing. Chiefly they were skeptical regarding the power they had placed in the hands of the government. What increased their skepticism was the speeches of their oil administrator, Harold L. Ickes, regarding conservation of the natural resources. Mr Ickes appeared to be taking his job much too seriously.

"In a real sense," he said, "oil is liquid gold banked in the vaults of Mother Earth. If it were gold actually lying in a bank we would not think of drawing a thousand dollars' worth of it every morning and throwing it off the end of a long pier into the ocean. Yet this liquid gold which we call oil is being wasted on an even greater scale."

Furthermore, Mr Ickes appointed a Natural Resources Board which began to study the problem of inefficient oil equipment, of flooding the world markets with cheap oil, of overcrowding wells on flush territory, the wastage of tremendous quantities of gas blown into the air at the wells' mouths, and the underground loss of oil through the seepage of water or its leakage into unrecoverable strata. This looked to the oil men like the beginning of highly undesirable government meddling in their business, and even the big companies, at one time prayerfully grateful for New Deal intervention, but now fully recouped and confident, began to sour. Their opposition was further increased by the election of James V. Allred as governor of Texas, pledged to enforce the state hot-oil law, but opposed to the all-embracing NRA. Finally, and perhaps most important, the big companies had taken advantage of the tight place in which the oil code put the little fellows to buy up some of their east Texas wells at bargain-counter prices. Thus the fall of 1934—about one year after the oil code had saved the industry—found the Rockefellers, the Mellons and the Sinclairs looking around for some way to get out from under.

The answer came from an unexpected source.

The Panama Refining Company, a tea-kettle outfit and one of the most confirmed violators of the Texas statutes, had brought suit against the government for unconstitutionally interfering with its oil production. It hired F. W. Fischer, a lumbering, cigar-chewing, backwoods practitioner, generally known in Texas as "Big Fish," who argued before the lower federal courts that the ban upon the shipment of hot oil—backbone of the oil code—had the effect of direct regulation of production, over which the federal government never had had, and never should have, control. This struck a sympathetic note with Texas jurists, steeped in the doctrine of states' rights, and injunctions were issued immediately restraining Mr Ickes from further enforcement of his oil code. These were reversed by the Circuit Court of Appeals, however, and the case finally came before the Nine Old Men in December 1934, just about the time the big oil companies decided they wanted no more of government regulation.

Big Fish Fischer bought a frock coat, wiped the red mud of east Texas off his satchel shoes and took a train for Washington. It is doubtful if he realized he was off to do battle for the greatest enemy of his client, the big oil companies. It is doubtful also if any one of the several million American motorists had any idea whatever that the prices of their oil and gasoline were at stake. It is even doubtful whether any one of the New Deal executives, at that time jubilant over the tremendous vote of confidence given Roosevelt in the 1934 congressional elections, had the vaguest notion that the first vital nail was being driven into their reform legislation. Certainly the newspaper editors had no realization of it. They did not even publish the photographs which Big Fish Fischer considerately had taken and sent round to newspaper offices.

The government's side of the case was handled by Harold M. Stephens, one of the few men of ability in the Justice Department, and in preparing his brief, Moses Huberman, one of Stephens' assistants, dug up the original executive orders making the oil code effective—a piece of thoroughness which lost him the case. For in the executive order of September 13, 1933, one of the most important provisions was omitted. This was the second paragraph of Section 4 of Article III, and the nubbin of the code. It provided that, if any oil producer exceeded the quota allotted to him by the state, he would be deemed a violator of the code. According to the text issued by the Petroleum Board, and according to the text circulated throughout the oil fields, and according to the only text available to the oil operators, this key paragraph was in the code. And yet in the executive order as signed by the President of the United States, this paragraph did not exist. Therefore, it was not law.

A stenographer or a linotype operator had dropped this important provision, a suit had been fought all through the district and circuit courts of the United States, and not until a year later was the omission discovered.

This lack of clerical exactitude in publishing NRA codes was to play an important part also in the Schechter sick-chicken case. The fact was that, during those early days when the Blue Eagle was spreading its all-embracing wings over the entire country, few people knew exactly what was in the codes. They were OK'd at the White House, sometimes at the rate of a dozen a week, following which the Secretary of State tacked an executive order on the press-room bulletin board declaring the code to be effective. The original, with all its voluminous appendices, was placed in the files of the State Department, and no one ever saw it again.

Stephens discovered the omission of this key paragraph in September 1934, just one year after the Panama Refining Company initiated its suit. Obviously no one else had noticed the error. Big Fish Fischer certainly had not, or he would have made the most of it in his argument before the lower courts. Nor had the district judge nor the Circuit Court of Appeals noticed it. Moreover, it was extremely unlikely that any of the Nine Old Men, concerned only with the briefs before them, would notice the omission. However, Stephens recommended that, as a matter of honor, the omission be pointed out to the Supreme Court, and this he did.

It proved the deciding factor in losing his suit.

Aside from Stephens' disclosure, the government case seemed airtight. To prove that the control of oil was properly interstate commerce, Stephens showed that the sudden opening of a new field quickly diverted rail traffic from the old stripper fields to new areas, closing down entirely the old wells which were unable to compete with new gushers. He also showed how states had been unable to control production because of competition between themselves; and how oil was no respecter of state or property boundaries but flowed to the wells operated by whichever producer was able to pump it out the fastest.

But none of this mattered after Stephens disclosed to the Court the omission in the executive order of September 13, 1933.

This was a heaven-sent opportunity for Big Fish, and he made the most of it. Impromptu oratory is his forte. And he described—with some justice—the confusing broadsides of Executive Orders which flooded the oil fields. He embroidered on the snooping activities of Glavis' men from the Interior Department. He told how the operators in east Texas had no idea what the oil code was one day and what it was the next.

And he climaxed this by shouting that there was no law because even the original executive order was defective in its most important part.

Reaching into his hip pocket, he pulled out a dog-eared pamphlet and waved it above his head.

"There be the law, y'r honors," he cackled, imitating a federal agent, "in the hip pocket of a dep-yew-tie administrator! And no one else knows what it is!"

It was shrewd showmanship, and when Stephens started his main argument, the justices could hardly wait to heckle him regarding the missing paragraph.

"Are the codes being published?" asked the Chief Justice.

"Yes," Stephens replied, "there's a set of nine volumes, and also pamphlets available for every code. Furthermore, there is no statute requiring their publication. They are published merely as a convenience to the public."

To this Justice Van Devanter took vigorous exception. He claimed that the publication of executive orders was mandatory by law.

"No, your honor," countered Stephens. "'The law requires the publication neither of presidential proclamations nor executive orders, although, as a matter of practice, proclamations are published."

"Is there anything being done by the government toward getting these orders published?" asked Justice Brandeis.

"Yes, a committee has just been appointed to establish a federal gazette which will publish all orders daily."

What Stephens did not add was that, although such a committee had been appointed, the White House had killed its work. The committee, instigated by Erwin F. Griswold of the Justice Department, and including Stephens and John Dickinson, then Assistant Secretary of Commerce, had worked for weeks on the idea of an official gazette which would publish all executive orders, proclamations and other government decrees. But when they sent their proposal to the White House, Stephen Early, secretary for press relations, killed it on the ground that it would compete with the *United States News,* published by the President's bitter critic, David Lawrence. Roosevelt, presumably, never saw the recommendation.

So in order to get White House approval—which, incidentally, came an hour or so after the hot-oil argument—one of the government lawyers had tipped off Justice Brandeis to interrogate Stephens. This, however, was an unnecessary precaution. The cross fire of questions leveled at him from the Court was the hottest of any New Deal case during the entire year.

Stephens, who now has been elevated to the United States Court of Appeals of the District of Columbia, one step below the Nine Old Men, countered as best he could that the mistake had been rectified and that no prosecutions would be made during the year that the paragraph had been missing from the executive order.

But it did no good. There was something about the picture of the government trying to enforce a code, one important section of which did not exist, that got under the skin of liberal and conservative justices alike. Justice Brandeis was especially incensed. There had been stories from the oil fields of the highhanded methods employed by federal agents, of espionage by the undercover men of Louis R. Glavis. Furthermore, Brandeis is the champion of the little fellow, and in east Texas, the small wildcatter, for the first time in history, had been getting a break at the expense of the Sinclairs, the Mellons and the Rockefellers. Brandeis knew that the oil code had been a godsend to the big oil companies, and he is the enemy of bigness. In this Justice Stone went with him.

The reactionary members of the Court instinctively opposed the NRA, although Hughes and Roberts were inclined to tread gingerly, especially when it came to hot oil. Justice Roberts, attorney for the government in the Teapot Dome oil scandals, was all too familiar with the cutthroat competition of the oil industry. He knew how oil, without controlled production, could be drained from one leasehold to another; he knew how rapidly the nation's reserves had been exploited in the past; and, most of all, he knew how precious the Navy considered the reserves it was holding for the use of its fleet. Chief Justice Hughes was even more familiar with the part which oil played in the defense and industrial life of the nation. As Secretary of State, he had sent peremptory notes to Great Britain and France demanding for the United States equal exploitation rights in the League-mandated territories of the Near East. As Secretary of State, also, he had put all his weight behind the drive of Standard Oil to secure drilling privileges in the Dutch East Indies; and was all too familiar with the instructions sent by the State Department to diplomatic and consular officers: "The vital importance of securing adequate supplies of mineral oil both for present and future needs has been forcibly brought to the attention of the Department. . . . You are instructed to lend all legitimate aid to United States citizens or interests which are seeking mineral-oil concessions."

Other reactionary members of the Court also are ardent militarists, but uppermost in their minds in the hot-oil case was, not the necessity of controlling one of the most priceless of the nation's resources, but the necessity of curbing the growing power of the federal government, and particularly the man at its head. This, added to the crusading zeal which flamed in the eyes of two of their liberal colleagues, left no doubt whatever regarding the outcome of the hot-oil decision.

The decision came on January 7, 1935, and was rendered by Chief Justice Hughes, despite the fact that he once had served as attorney for Standard Oil and the American Petroleum Institute, both vitally interested in this case. Because of the missing paragraph, Mr Hughes refused to pass on the validity of the petroleum code, and thereby struck the severest blow of all. For New Deal lawyers had staked everything on their belief that the Court would find the control of petroleum production to be the regulation of interstate commerce and therefore constitutional. It was the best case they had on this point, but now the Chief Justice deliberately sidestepped the issue.

Having done this, he proceeded to grope for some constitutional reason for killing Section 9c, the heart of the code, and found it in the thesis that Congress had delegated undue authority to the President—a point which Big Fish Fischer, in arguing the case for the oil companies, had mentioned hardly at all.

Mr Hughes, however, went through the entire history of congressional delegation of power, and at first his citation of precedents made it appear that the government was going to win. He pointed out that in 1809 Congress had delegated power to the President to invoke an embargo against France or Great Britain, when, in his judgment, those nations trampled upon the neutrality rights of the United States. This delegation of power was upheld by the Supreme Court. Mr Hughes then cited the McKinley Tariff Act of 1890 delegating to the President the power to suspend articles from the free list when foreign nations were found to be discriminating against the United States; and another act in 1897 giving the Treasury Department power to establish standards for purity in tea; and an act in 1899 giving the Secretary of War the power to decide when bridges were obstructions to navigation, and to remove them. These delegations of power also were upheld by the Supreme Court. He even cited the Interstate Commerce Commission and its power to fix railroad rates; and the power of the Secretaries of the Interior and Agriculture to make rates preserving the public forests and to regulate sheep grazing; and the flexible tariff act, in which Congress gives the President power to raise or lower tariff rates. All these also were upheld by the Court.

Mr Hughes might have cited also a law which he himself had pushed through Congress while Secretary of State in 1922, delegating to the President the power of embargoing shipments of arms to Latin-American nations suffering from the disease of revolution. He did not cite this, however—possibly because Congress gave no greater guide to the President in diagnosing the highly controversial question of what is revolution than it gave him in regard to hot oil.

Summarizing, the Chief Justice maintained that, in the cases which he cited, Congress had set forth general rules regarding the delegation of its power. "The Court," he said, "has recognized that there are limits of delegation which there is no constitutional authority to transcend. We think that Section 9c [of the NRA] goes beyond those limits. . . . If Section 9c were held valid, it would be idle to pretend that anything would be left of limitations upon the power of Congress to delegate its law-making function."

To the naked eye of the ordinary layman it was difficult to see what specific limitation Congress placed upon its delegation of power in the cases Justice Hughes cited which it did not place upon Mr Roosevelt in the regulation of oil. But the ordinary layman was not armed with a microscope looking for legal loopholes with which to justify his own personal convictions. The fact was that eight of the Nine Old Men were outraged at the slipshod manner in which the oil code was administered.

Justice Cardozo, who had sat dispassionately through the whole argument, handed down a dissenting opinion in which he said that the phrases "to eliminate unfair trade practices" and "to conserve natural resources" were adequate to guide the President. But no one else agreed with him.

It was the first time in the history of the United States that an act had been declared unconstitutional because the legislators handed away part of their power. However, the dictatorial powers of President Roosevelt had been stopped.

Nearly two years later—July 1936—the petroleum industry petitioned the Federal Trade Commission, asking that it set up a code of fair practice to take the place of the NRA which it had helped to junk.

CHAPTER XIV

Joseph and His Brethren

W<small>HEN</small> the Nine Old Men declared the National Industrial Recovery Act unconstitutional they passed judgment, not on the fact that four Jewish boys in Brooklyn sold a few crates of sick chickens in violation of the poultry code, but upon a chapter in the history of the United States as important and as bizarre as any since the Civil War.

The writing of that chapter revolves chiefly around a colorful ex-cavalry officer named Hugh S. Johnson—and, in a very minor way, around a bowl of cherries. It goes back to the days right after the banking crisis of 1933 when Roosevelt called an emergency session of Congress which, in turn, passed the Wallace-Tugwell Agricultural Adjustment Act, and then waited for Senator Wagner of New York to draft a National Industrial Recovery Act calculated to set industry on its feet. Working with Wagner on this were John Dickinson, at that time Assistant Secretary of Commerce; Jerome Frank, then counsel for the AAA; Isadore Lubin, Commissioner of Labor Statistics; Simon H. Rifkind and Leon H. Keyserling, Wagner's secretaries. Their original idea was to establish an organization for the regulation of only a dozen, or at the most fifteen, basic industries of the country—coal, oil, lumber, steel, and so on. But in the course of their work they heard that an ex-army officer named Johnson had an office in the State Department and was working on a similar plan. So they went over to see him.

Johnson, then a mysterious, behind-the-scenes figure, had been active during the campaign as the representative and adviser of Bernard Baruch, donor of $70,000 to the Roosevelt war chest, and as such had formed a close friendship with Professor Moley, and when the latter became Assistant Secretary of State, he gave Johnson an office in the State Department with Robert K. Straus, son of the ambassador to France, and with the subsequently famous Miss Frances Robinson as his secretary.

What Johnson and Moley had prepared was a very vague plan modeled after the War Industries Board on which Johnson had served with Baruch during the war. The entire Johnson draft covered only one page and a half and aimed at a quick pick up of business through public works rather than any long-term regulation of industry.

In the end the Johnson idea of public works was grafted onto the Wagner-Dickinson-Frank plan for the regulation of industry, and after a dozen other authors had their hand in it, including Donald Richberg, the National Industrial Recovery Act finally was rushed through Congress. No sooner had it passed than Professor Moley, genuinely fond of Johnson and anxious also that the President recognize the campaign contribution of Baruch, persuaded Roosevelt to appoint the General its administrator. But Moley was not able to put across the General's further appointment as Administrator of Public Works. This job went to Harold Ickes, Secretary of the Interior. The General gnashed his teeth and protested indignantly, but it did no good. And then, having been thwarted in getting the job which he himself inserted in the NRA, he began pumping up that part of the bill which did not originate with him—the regulation of industry—and which did not particularly fit into his economic philosophy. He pumped it up with such gusto that it soon became the most important part of the whole national-recovery thesis. Overnight General Johnson, all his life a rugged business individualist, assumed the pose of a fervid, crusading regulator of big business. And on a cruise down the Potomac one Sunday, he sold the President on the Blue Eagle.

In those glowing salty words for which he has since become famous, Hugh Johnson recalled the gasless Sundays of war days and mapped a campaign by which he would arouse the entire nation to a pitch of patriotic fervor against any violator of the Blue Eagle.

The President was on the crest of the wave in those days. Whatever he touched turned to success. Furthermore, he is inclined to be smitten with the same disease chronic in the make-up of General Johnson—superenthusiasm. So without giving the idea any real thought, he bestowed his blessing. Whether he really meant to OK all of the General's grandiose program perhaps never will be known. The President has a bad habit of nodding his approval to many visionary schemes chiefly to get rid of their authors, and his treatment of Johnson may have been in that category.

But in Hugh Johnson he was dealing with a man of action. And having secured at least a provisional go-ahead signal from the President, Johnson rushed before the National Emergency Council and in equally glowing language unfolded his plan for a national boycott of any firm violating the codes of the Blue Eagle. The council, however, was not as amenable as the President. Several of its members pointed out that this was not wartime, that the country could not be kept at a pitch of patriotic fervor. Johnson countered by describing in detail the gasless Sundays, how no law was necessary to enforce them, how anyone venturing forth in his car was ditched by the Sunday crowds. Again his colleagues on the council pointed out that the United States, at that time, was menaced by a foreign enemy, that such incentive today was lacking. All of which only caused the General to burst into another stormy harangue that he could mobilize public opinion, avoid any test in the courts without the incentive of an enemy knocking at the gates.

In the end most of the council decided that the best way to get rid of Johnson was to agree with him. They counted upon going to Roosevelt behind the General's back and getting a presidential veto. So when the council vote was taken, only two opposed the General: Secretary Wallace and Professor Tugwell, who held a proxy for Secretary Ickes.

But afterward Johnson called Ickes on the long-distance telephone and raised so much verbal hell that the Secretary of the Interior stalled, said he was not familiar with what had happened and withdrew his vote.

Big issues sometimes turn on fleabites. The fate of nations has been decided by drummer boys. In this case, however, it was a bowl of cherries. The President had eaten them just before the stormy meeting described above, and they made him sick. The newspapers said that he was confined to his bed with a cold, but that was not the case. The peerless leader was suffering from diarrhea.

And when the various members of the cabinet who had resolved to kill Johnson's Blue Eagle behind his back tried to slip in to see the President, they were balked. General Johnson is a fast worker. And they were balked just long enough for him to transform the NRA from its original plan of regulating only a dozen key industries to a Frankenstein monster with a hard-riding cavalry officer at the controls bent upon regulating and regimenting the entire economic life of the nation.

From that point on there should have been little doubt in the mind of anyone even remotely familiar with the Nine Old Men as to how they would view the constitutionality of the Blue Eagle.

There was the Jerome Frank school which argued, with Mr Dooley, that the Court goes with the elections and advocated an immediate test of constitutionality while the country was in the first flush of enthusiasm over Roosevelt recovery measures. Then there was the Felix Frankfurter school which argued that the NRA was too unwieldy, too big, too tyrannical, sure to fall afoul of the Court unless given time to perfect its faults, smooth out its cumbersome and inefficient machinery.

Professor Frankfurter knew what he was talking about as far as Justice Brandeis went, and General Johnson should have known it, too. For, on one occasion, a friend took him in to see

Brandeis, and despite the fact that Brandeis did not know he was coming, they had a very frank talk. Brandeis told Johnson that in his opinion the NRA had gone much too far, might become a boomerang against the small independent businessman, and said that the same end which Johnson sought through all his intricate regulatory machinery could have been accomplished by three relatively simple measures: the abolition of child labor, a minimum wage and maximum hours. This, Justice Brandeis felt, would eliminate unfair competition, increase wages, thereby increase purchasing power and bring back prosperity.

But Johnson was back in the days when, as author of the selective draft, he was mobilizing five million men to fight the war to end war, to make the world safe for democracy. Now he was mobilizing the uncounted millions of industry and of commerce to fight the war to end unfair competition, to make the world safe for both labor and employer. To hell with the consumer! Power had gone to his head, and instead of seeking ways to restrict it, he was looking for more codes to conquer.

He soon found them over in the Agricultural Adjustment Administration.

The National Industrial Recovery Act provided that the agricultural codes—that is, codes for the agricultural industries such as canning, meat-packing, tobacco and poultry—could be administered either by the Secretary of Agriculture or the NRA administrator, according to the will of the President. Therefore when Gardner Jackson, Jerome Frank and a little group of liberals in the Consumers' Division of the AAA objected to the consumer-be-damned attitude of Johnson's old friend and partner, George Peek, then administering the AAA, Johnson made a blustering demand of the President that he take over the AAA codes. And he got them. He got all of them except the package bee code, which, for some strange reason as mysterious as the package bee itself, remained in the gentle hands of Henry Wallace.

Had this transfer not been made, there never would have been a Schechter case, for with the transfer Johnson inherited the task of maintaining fair competition in an industry which never yet has drawn an honest breath.

In Greater New York there are between 300 and 400 wholesale poultry dealers who supply between 10,000 and 12,000 retailers. The city uses about two hundred carloads of chickens a week and is easily the nation's largest market. From all over America come the carloads, from California, Wisconsin, Massachusetts and points in between—10,000 cars, 216,000,000 pounds a year. It is no petty business.

It is not only big, but is particularly suited to racketeering. Nowhere could be found a more happy setting for racketeers— thousands of small Jewish shopkeepers, millions of Jewish chicken eaters, and hundreds of Jewish wholesalers. A few Jewish gangsters find nice pickings here. For years they have been working one kind of racket or another in the poultry business—indeed, the word "racket" as used in its slangy sense originated here. But it wasn't until swarthy Joe Weiner and his colleague, Arthur "Toots" Herbert, came along shortly after the war that the racket was systematized and set up in an A1 perfect working order.

Mr Weiner, through cash and threats, got himself elected to the key position of head of the kosher butchers' union. This union traces back to the days of Abraham and sinks its roots deep in the immovable soil of religious ritual. Every chicken must be killed with a single sweep of a special ritual butcher knife while an ordained rabbi chants an ancient incantation. The butchers are called *Shoctim* and get $65 a week, a rabbinical salary for which they can thank their untiring boss "rabbi," Joe Weiner.

Mr Arthur Toots Herbert is head of the Local 167 of the International Brotherhood of Teamsters, Chauffeurs, Stablemen and Helpers. This union performs the business of unloading chickens from freight cars, boxing them in coops, loading the coops onto trucks, hauling, unloading, and subsequently moving chickens sold into retail to their final destination—the local butcher shop.

These two guildsmen had much in common, as they themselves perceived. They saw that by a little strong-arm and considerable co-operation they could control the entire business. Weiner's domination over the butchers gave him an unbreakable grip on the killing of fowl; while Toots Herbert, with his rule over local transportation, had an unbreakable grip on the source of supply. They got together.

The Metropolitan Poultry Feed Corporation, owned by Weiner and Herbert and a few other union delegates, was organized in March 1930, and it wasn't long till they had a monopoly on the business of supplying feed to the poultry dealers in Greater New York, despite the fact that its prices averaged about 50 per cent higher than competitors' prices. The new business soon became extremely lucrative, in spite of the intense competition existing before its organization. Weiner, who allegedly paid $4,500 for his forty-five shares of stock, soon received nice dividends of $150 a week, or $7,800 a year, a return of more than 173 per cent on his investment—if he ever made one in the first place. The other stockholders fared equally well, though their services were trifling. It was pure shakedown.

The method of forcing marketmen to buy from them was absurdly simple. If the marketman refused, extra workers were ordered on the job by the union heads, greatly in excess of the marketman's needs. If he still refused to buy or to hire more *Shoctim,* a strike was called. It wasn't long until he succumbed.

Another neat racket the Weiner-Herbert team worked out was the coop racket. The New Jersey Coop Company was formed to supply coops for transporting poultry from the railroad terminals to the slaughterhouse markets. This also was a monopoly, a juicy one. Its rentals ran around $1,000,000 a year. Each coop was rented for $1.00 a trip, upon the return of which in good condition the marketman was refunded 35 cents, making a net rental of 65 cents. A single coop could be used 200 times in the course of sixteen months, making the aggregate net rental from one coop in sixteen months around $130. Since the coops were purchased from manufacturers for $1.55 each, sometimes as low as $1.00 each, the gentlemen stockholders sat back for four years and drew "salaries" of more than $60,000 a year.

All but four of the marketmen in Greater New York used the New Jersey Coop Company's services, despite its exorbitant rentals. And one who dared purchase coops from independent sources was that enterprising merchant, Joe Schechter. Joe ordered fifty new coops from a box company, but when the truck appeared at his place next morning his union workmen would not unload them. The driver waited three or four hours and, while he was waiting, a union delegate appeared, telling Schechter he could not buy the coops. During the ensuing argument, the driver left his truck unguarded, and when he drove away with the coops he noticed something wrong with the truck. An inspection at a garage disclosed that two cups of emery powder had been poured in the oil. The engine was ruined.

As a result of this incident, Joe Schechter was summoned as a government witness when the anti-trust division of the Justice Department began an investigation of the New York poultry racket, six years before the NRA ever was heard of. State and municipal authorities for years had made half-hearted attempts to clean up the New York poultry racket, without success. Then, in 1929, the federal government stepped in and began collecting evidence against Joe Weiner, Toots Herbert, *et al.,* for violation of the Sherman Anti-Trust Law. Thus it was that Joe Schechter first became involved in federal litigation, though this case had no direct connection with his later rise to fame as the man who broke the NRA.

The Schechter brothers were four—Joseph, Alex, Martin and Aaron—and in the poor Jewish section of Brooklyn known as Brownsville, where the kosher butchers of the city work in filth, blood, and chicken feathers, they operated jointly a prosperous pair of smelly chicken companies known as the A. L. A. Schechter Company and the Schechter Live Poultry Market, Inc., engaged in wholesaling live or dead fowl to retail storekeepers. Joe was the oldest. Stocky, medium-sized, he was the boss of the busi-

ness. With his three shrewd young brothers, he had brought
the business up from a small stand to the largest wholesale
chicken market in Brooklyn.

The Schechters were unwilling witnesses for the government
in the racketeering case. Joe and his brothers were scared. Walter
L. Rice, indefatigable attorney for the Justice Department,
finally got Joe to testify before a grand jury, but he did not
dare put him on the witness stand in open court. He just would
not talk.

The government tried the gangsters three times. In the first
case—1931—ninety defendants were named, and Rice got sixty-
eight convictions. A general injunction was issued against their
restraint of trade plus mild jail sentences.

But the racketeers did not take the injunctions seriously and
soon not only were back at their old game but had perfected it.
They divided Greater New York into five sections, with the
wholesalers in on the conspiracy this time. Each wholesaler was
given thirty or more retailers as exclusive customers. Prices were
raised at once. Whereas the wholesaler had been working on a
margin of four cents a pound before, the net was jumped almost
overnight from twelve to eighteen cents a pound. The wholesalers in turn were forced to pay the corrupt union leaders one
cent a pound tribute for a "protection" fund. This fund netted
Weiner and his friends $2,000,000 a year. The increased prices
to retailers, which the wholesalers grabbed, amounted to $12,-
000,000 a year, paid by the Jewish housewives of New York
whose religion forced them to eat only kosher fowl.

Once again—in 1932—the government stepped in. This time
101 racketeers were hauled into court, again on a charge of
conspiracy to restrain and monopolize trade. After a trial of five
weeks a sweeping decree was entered against 99 of the
defendants, permanently enjoining them from allocating customers, fixing prices, or intimidating or interfering with the freedom of purchasing, handling, selling or slaughtering poultry.

This decree was appealed to the United States Supreme Court,
where the racketeers pleaded that their acts were not an inter-

ference with interstate commerce, and therefore their racketeering could not be restrained by the federal government.

But the Nine Old Men did not agree with them. They held that their acts *did* affect interstate commerce, and the injunction was emphatically sustained. This was extremely important. It was the furthest the Court ever had gone in its interpretation of the interstate-commerce clause.

Also it set the precedent upon which the Government based its hope of victory in the Schechter case one year later.

Into this strange bit of Americana, the graft-infested, racket-ridden Jewish poultry business in New York, came General Johnson's big idea, NRA. And like all the other New York poultry dealers, the Schechter brothers signed up as supporters of the poultry code and tacked up the Blue Eagle.

Vitally interested in this code were all the poultry farmers of the nation. For New York sets the prices for the country. To the 6,000,000 poultry farmers it is what Wall Street is to the investor—the capital of a one-and-a-quarter-billion-dollar industry.

The poultry code had innumerable restrictions and regulations in it, among them an anti-racketeering clause, though by 1933 racketeering was fairly well stamped out. The sweeping injunctions, sustained by the Supreme Court, had accomplished that. Joe Weiner was in jail shortly afterward for two years on a contempt-of-court charge for violating the injunctions, while Tootsie Herbert was cooped for six months.[1]

Other provisions of the code outlawed the sale of diseased fowl, fixed hours of work, wages, etc., and sought to protect farmers by compelling commissionmen to sell "the run of the coop," that is, in coop lots with no selection of birds permitted.

It didn't take Joe Schechter and his brothers long to see the advantages of breaking the code. And it didn't take enforcement officers long to catch them. They were caught selling large quan-

[1] Weiner's two-year sentence was the severest ever decreed for contempt of federal court, the judge being angry when Joe broke the injunction the second time. Longest previous sentence was a year and a day.

tities of diseased chickens to the colored trade in Brooklyn. So great did their business in consumptive chickens become that, coupled with that of several other wholesalers, it caused Brooklyn to become the dumping ground of sick chickens for the whole United States. The Schechters also were accused of other violations, including failure to observe "run of the coop" regulations, and were indicted altogether on ten classes of violations, with sixty separate counts against them.

Joe retained a little hawk-nosed Jewish lawyer named Joseph Heller to defend them, and the case was heard before Judge Marcus B. Campbell in the United States District Court in Brooklyn, a jury trial, with Walter Rice up from Washington to argue the government's side. It was just one of thousands of code-violation cases instituted all over the land, and the Justice Department lawyers had no idea it was to make history. Rice was very careful nevertheless to introduce plenty of evidence on the interstate-commerce angle just in case it should wend its way up to the Nine Old Men. Purposely Rice showed that 99 per cent of the chickens slaughtered in New York came from outside the state.

One of the counts against the Schechters was selling diseased chickens. And Rice told how an agent had followed a Schechter delivery truck to a retail shop, how the agent had bought an "egg-bound" bird, and then went on to show how such sales of poultry, unfit for human consumption, tended to affect in geometric proportions the flow of interstate commerce in poultry. He tried to prove that if 2 per cent of the poultry sold in the city was unfit, sales in the city fell off 20 per cent and affected interstate commerce and the whole national price structure in that ratio. If a housewife bought a bad bird, she switched to beef and told her friends about it; and they switched to beef, the 2-per-cent expanding to a 20-per-cent drop in business in the area. The testimony showed that the Schechters sold thousands of pounds of unfit poultry, indeed made a practice of dealing in it.

This was the backbone of the government's case.

Rice finished, and it was Joe Heller's turn. In his Brooklyn-Hebrew accent he told the jury how he had known the Schechter boys since they were children, that they came of fine parents and a good home, that they were honest men. As his reminiscences waxed fervent, tears began to roll down Joe Schechter's fat cheeks.

". . . End eef you sent them to jail," wailed Joe Heller, his voice a full octave above its normal range, "eet will ruin their lives!"

Exhausted, he slumped in his chair, pulled out a handkerchief and he, too, began to weep.

Joe Schechter got up to get a drink. Someone asked him why he had cried.

"Vell, I'll tell you"—he grinned sheepishly—"I felt so sorry for mine counsel, I couldn't help it."

After three weeks of trial, Judge Campbell, a Republican, gave the jury a strong charge favoring the New Deal, and it filed out. It remained out twenty-three and a half hours. When it came in, the foreman had bad news for Joseph and his brethren. They were found guilty on seventeen counts. Joe was ordered to jail for three months, Alex two, Martin and Aaron one month each. The four brothers and their two companies were fined $7,425, and they were locked up in the federal building, Brooklyn, until they could arrange bail.

The rise of the Schechter boys to fame was well under way. Never before noticed in the world's shifting kaleidoscope, even relatively unimportant in their own world of cackling chickens and housewives, the Schechters now were destined to make headlines around the globe.

On appeal to the United States Circuit Court of Appeals, their case suddenly became important. Certain people along Park Avenue and Broadway began to take an interest. In the Circuit Court they were again turned down. More people became interested. Joe Heller labored over his lawbooks in Manhattan, determined to rank his name alongside that of Daniel Webster. He was going to prove that the NRA was illegal, and he was going to do so single-handed. He didn't need any help. He would write the names of Heller and Schechter a mile high upon the mind of the nation, and he worked night and day for the big test.

Then something happened. Suddenly Joe Heller became associated with one of the greatest corporation law firms in Manhattan—Cravath, de Gersdorff, Swaine & Wood. Joe Heller's associate counsel, it was announced, was to be Frederick Wood, victorious attorney for the Baltimore & Ohio Railroad in the gold-clause cases.

Just who had induced and was paying Cravath, de Gersdorff, Swaine & Wood to enter the case was not known. Joe Heller merely announced that he was "overworked" and needed assistance.

It was about this time that those who were piloting the legal course of the New Deal became increasingly aware that, as far as the Supreme Court was concerned, they were facing a fight which might wreck all the machinery of industrial regulation which Roosevelt had erected.

The hot-oil decision was the first warning of what was to come. This, it is true, was followed by favorable decisions in the gold cases, but no one who understood the extent to which Wall Street would have been disrupted by an unfavorable decision on gold had any idea at all that Hughes and Roberts, big businessmen at heart, would let down the New Deal on gold.

The general public may have been lulled into security by the Court's decision on gold cases; not the legal Brain Trust. Just after the hot-oil case, it got a special court warning in the Wilshire oil case which no one else noticed and which sent cold shivers of apprehension down their vertebrae.

The Wilshire case was certified up to the Supreme Court by William Denman, a friendly Roosevelt-appointed judge on the Circuit Court of Appeals in California who thought that by hastening a test case on the NRA he was doing the New Deal a favor. But some of the Nine Old Men, equally friendly to the

New Deal, sent the case back on the grounds that all the records were not complete. Actually they knew what its fate would be and wanted to avoid a test until sentiment was more favorable.

Donald Richberg, then guiding the destinies of the Blue Eagle, caught the signal. Immediately he withdrew the Belcher case, even though it was already placed on the Supreme Court docket. This was a test of the lumber code, the most meticulously drawn in the entire NRA, and the NRA's most carefully prepared case. But it had one bad fault psychologically. The lumber code was so meticulously drawn, so tightly administered, that it completely regimented the lumber industry, accentuating just the points to which the liberals on the Court were emphatically opposed. Brandeis, Felix Frankfurter warned, never would swallow it. Also, it became known that during the preceding summer Justice Stone had planned to build a garage on his island retreat in Maine, only to find that the price of lumber was so high that he swore he would not buy one stick of lumber as long as the industry was regimented by the NRA.

Furthermore, just at that particular time, all of the nation's small storekeepers, all the small manufacturers, every mechanic able to rent a machine shop and hire a couple of other mechanics were protesting to high heaven against the Blue Eagle. This is the pet stratum of society to which Justice Brandeis listens. It is also the stratum of society to which the Senate progressives— both Democratic and Republican—listen with cupped ears. And the complaints from the little fellows back home were amplified until they echoed upon the floor of the Senate with a mighty roar. Senator Borah delivered a diatribe against the NRA. Senator La Follette followed him. Even George Norris, loyal to almost everything Roosevelt had done, fidgeted rebelliously as anti-NRA sentiment reverberated from back home.

And although General Johnson finally asked Clarence Darrow to investigate the grievances of small businessmen and recommend steps for alleviation of their ills, it made no dent upon the growing conviction of the country and of Congress that the NRA had gone much too far and that the Blue Eagle should have stuck to the original Wagner-Frank thesis of wrapping its wings only around a dozen or so of the nation's basic industries. By the winter of 1935—when the Belcher case was dropped—this conviction was so firmly fixed in the minds of most senators that they passed a resolution extending the life of the Blue Eagle for a further trial period of only ten months. By this time, furthermore, Felix Frankfurter and others in a position to read the minds of some members of the Court were convinced that there was no chance of securing Supreme Court approval of the NRA until after it had gone back to Congress and been revised on a permanent basis.

In other words, Brandeis, Stone and Cardozo, the three men most likely to be open-minded about the NRA, probably would not veto it if they were sure—through a second vote of Congress —that it was the accepted will of the people. But with small businessmen vociferously rebellious, and with the Senate willing to extend the life of the Blue Eagle only for ten months, Frankfurter reported that any immediate test of the NRA would be suicidal.

However, there were other factors to be considered, the most important being the morale of the NRA. Following Richberg's withdrawal of the Belcher case, there started a tremendous wave of code violation. If the administration was going to shun a test of code constitutionality, industrialists in every field argued, there was obviously no reason why they should live up to them. And they started a wholesale undermining of the codes right and left. At one time 17,999 cases of wage and hour violations and 4,000 cases of unfair trade practice were on the docket of the NRA Compliance Division awaiting action. NRA morale rapidly evaporated. Enforcement officers reported that without a test of the codes their work was futile, and the newspapers laid down a terrific barrage of criticism against the man who had replaced Johnson. Richberg, they said, was yellow, afraid of a showdown, wrecking his organization by his cowardice.

Richberg at that time was not a well man. Cruelly overworked, goaded by the press, harassed by a neurotic General who thought he still should be piloting the Blue Eagle, Richberg faced the alternatives of an immediate court test or of seeing his organization gradually crumple beneath him.

So, looking round for a test case, his eye fell upon Joe Schechter and his brethren. Their case offered two important advantages. First, the Supreme Court only one year before had passed upon the conviction of Toots Herbert and Joe Weiner, and in doing so definitely found that racketeering in the chicken industry of Brooklyn was in restraint of interstate commerce. Second, the Schechter attorneys had stipulated regarding the points in the case, thus obviating any necessity on the government's part to prove what the code was. This, because of the slipshod manner in which codes were filed at the White House and State Department—as discovered in the hot-oil case—might be embarrassing and difficult.

However, the Schechter case had one grave drawback. The Justice Department had brought a criminal action against Joseph and his brethren, and if their convictions were upheld by the Supreme Court, Joe would serve three months, Alex two, and Martin and Aaron one month each in jail. It was possible that some of the Nine Old Men might go along with the NRA if the Schechters were charged only with a civil breach of the law. But to send four insignificant Jewish poultry dealers to jail for violation of a system at which the big steel moguls were thumbing their noses was bound to grate upon the susceptibilities of the liberal judges, and New Deal legalists should have known it.

Nevertheless, faced with the rapid molting of the Blue Eagle's feathers, Donald Richberg took a one-hundred-to-one shot. He decided upon an immediate test of the NRA, and on April 8, 1935, the Department of Justice joined with the Schechter Live Poultry Corporation of Brooklyn in asking the Supreme Court for an immediate review of the latter's appeal.

The argument was heard in the old red-plush courtroom in the Capitol, and the Schechter brothers enjoyed it more than anyone else. Joe Schechter pushed his way through the crowd, only to be stopped by a guard.

"Who are you?" the guard demanded.

"Me?" Joe gasped. "You dun't know who I am?"

"No, who are you?"

"I am Joe Schechter!"

Joe regarded the black-robed justices a little nervously and slid into a seat. But Attorney Heller, soaring far beyond his wildest ambition, was not in the least awed. His East Side accent in fullest flower, he described the tribulations of his clients under the tyranny of the NRA; how customers walked into Joe's Brooklyn market and tried to take their pick of the chickens in the coops, but, alas, were compelled under the code to accept the first bird that came out of the coop; and told how the rabbis shrugged their shoulders at Joe and remarked, "Vell, if I kent have the chicken I vant from you, Joe, I go someplace else," which they did. . . .

Justice McReynolds, listening with grim interest, leaned forward and asked:

"And it was for that your client went to jail?"

In his inexperienced way, Heller drew an excellent picture of the interference in petty business which the NRA entailed. Probably he did more to win the case than the great Wood, who followed with a learned discussion of the interstate-commerce question. Stanley, Reed and Richberg divided the government's time, the latter painting an eloquent picture of the chaos sure to follow if the NRA were junked. He described the great social progress which the act had brought, and envisioned the collapse sure to follow an unfavorable decision.

Joe Schechter, overwhelmed by Richberg's speech, whispered to a near-by spectator:

"I hope they gives it a conviction, so NRA will stand."

Eventually the Nine Old Men filed out, to reappear on May 27, 1935—an eventful day in New Deal history.

The announcement of decisions began uneventfully, Justice Butler reading an opinion involving the New York Life Insurance Company. Justice Sutherland followed with a unanimous opinion that President Roosevelt had grossly exceeded his authority by removing William E. Humphrey from the Federal Trade Commission without cause. The New Deal had lost its first skirmish of the day.

Justice Brandeis then began a gentle and scholarly opinion branding unconstitutional the Frazier-Lemke Act. Although not a New Deal measure, this was signed by Roosevelt and permitted farmers to retain their land for five years despite mortgage foreclosure and with the privilege of paying the mortgage later at a new appraisal. This decision also was unanimous.

Then the Chief Justice began to read the opinion for which the courtroom waited. Using oratorical emphasis, and shifting about in his chair, Mr Hughes spent some time outlining the background of the Schechter case and describing the methods of moving poultry in New York. Ultimately he dropped this significant sentence:

"The defendants do not sell poultry in interstate commerce."

Richberg and Reed seemed to slump deeper in their chairs. They knew their case was lost. Just one year before, the same Nine Old Men, passing upon the conspiracy of Joe Weiner and Toots Herbert to interfere with the New York poultry trade, unanimously held that "unquestionably it [poultry] is in interstate commerce."

But now they held, with equal unanimity, that the Schechter sick chickens had "come to rest."

At his next press conference President Roosevelt, for perhaps the first time, lost his smile.

"The gravest question," he said, "revolves around the Court's interpretation of the government's powers over interstate commerce. These powers constitute the only weapon we have to fight conditions not even dreamed of a hundred and fifty years ago.

"When the Constitution was written, this country was in the horse-and-buggy stage. Almost ninety per cent of our trade was intrastate. There was no problem of earning and buying power. There was no social question, such as health, to be reckoned

with on a national basis. Ethics were different. If one fellow
could get away with skinning another fellow—well, that was all
right.

"But now things have changed. The country thought it was
solving its problems gradually on a national basis, but now its
attempted solutions are thrown back in the face of the American people, and the country is right back in the horse-and-buggy
stage where it started.

"The issue," concluded the President, "is second in importance
only to war."

Mrs Roosevelt sat beside him, calmly knitting a blue sock.

But the rest of the country was not so calm. With the press
and a good part of the public, the NRA was anything but popular. And the general exclamation escaping from a General-
Johnson-wearied public was: "Whoopee! Good for the Supreme
Court!"

The Nine Old Men are only human, and those hosannas rang
in their ears for a long time. Probably if the Schechter hosannas
had not been so loud, the story of the AAA and the New York
minimum-wage and the Guffey acts might have been different.

One year later, Joseph and his brethren, back in Brooklyn,
were wondering about the ultimate effect of what they had done
to NRA.

On the streets of London on the day of the Schechter de-
cision, the London *Express* blazed forth with these headlines:
"AMERICA STUNNED! ROOSEVELT'S WORK KILLED
IN TWENTY MINUTES."

And the *Express* appeared to be right. In some of the major
industries, volunteer codes were announced. But price cutting
started almost immediately, and with price cutting came wage
cutting and hour stretching, until, within a few months after the
Supreme Court's momentous decision, a study by the Commerce
and Labor departments showed that wages as low as $7 a week
were paid for forty hours of work in the suit-and-coat industry,
that in the retail jewelry trade wages dropped as low as $6

weekly, that three quarters of the grocery stores had junked all code standards, the employees in the retail lumber industry were cut to below minimum, that, in general, fair competition was abandoned and the sweatshop was back.

As for the Schechters, they lost the wholesale business which thrived during the days of the Blue Eagle, and one year later a "For Sale" sign was on the ten-room brick house in which they had lived for ten years. The mortgage was unpaid.

"The Liberty Leaguers sent us a lot of swell letters saying they appreciated what we had done," said Aaron, "but they didn't put any money in the letters."

"We got an offer to go on the stage. But we're businessmen, not actors," grumbled Alex.

Joe Schechter, eldest of the brothers, seemed more tolerant of the Blue Eagle.

"I honestly think," he said, "the NRA could have been a good thing if there had been safeguards against racketeering. That was what wrecked us."

Even Joe Heller, the attorney who fought so valiantly for the Schechters, was tolerant. "We need some kind of control of business," he said, "some kind of modified NRA."

"But what about that famous case you won a year ago?"

"Well, we all have our private opinions."

Meanwhile, the government once again charged Charles Herbert, brother of Toots, with terrorizing the New York poultry business.

CHAPTER XV

The Court Spills Alphabet Soup

Wʜᴇɴ Henry Wallace left Des Moines to become Secretary of Agriculture in the Roosevelt administration he packed in his suitcase the book he had written on the mathematical relationships and ratios of plant life; for Henry probably is the greatest specialist on breeding corn and the most ardent lover of growing things anywhere in the country.

He also took with him to Washington a conviction that somehow or other—even by subjugating his passion for growing things, if necessary—the discrepancy between farm income and industrial income must be erased. His father had gone to Washington as Secretary of Agriculture in the Harding cabinet twelve years before with the same conviction and his struggle to attain it—among other things his battle with Secretary of Commerce Hoover—killed him. It was the thesis of both Wallaces that whereas industry had flourished in a well-organized, tariff-protected market, tariffs meant nothing to a farm population faced with an annual unexportable surplus; and that their only hope of economic salvation was to organize and control production exactly as did the barons of the steel industry. Obviously the only way such organization could be accomplished among several million farmers was through the Department of Agriculture which Henry was about to head.

Henry went to Washington with these convictions, though he had to swallow hard to get them down sometimes, and when he

274

flew to the Southland to see the first rows of cotton being plowed under, he admitted afterwards that it almost made him sick.

Henry frankly did not like the destructive phase of the Agricultural Adjustment Act, and by the summer of 1934 he had announced that he "would not mind seeing the processing tax and acreage control abolished by 1936, if we have something better to take its place." All too cognizant of the gap between industrial and farm income, however, he warned that unless some such substitute were forthcoming, the farmers would soon face a "repetition of the 1932 situation."

Entirely aside from Wallace's personal convictions on crop control, it is certain that the Agricultural Adjustment Act was relatively free of politics. Its authors were Wallace himself, a New Deal Republican; Professor M. L. Wilson of Montana State College, a nonpartisan; Mordecai Ezekiel, a Harding appointee to the Department of Agriculture; together with Fred Lee, a Democrat, who served as legislative draftsman of the Senate during two Republican administrations.

How remote was any realization that the Supreme Court would find against the AAA can be gauged from what was happening at the White House at eleven-thirty on the morning of January 6, 1936, at the very moment the Nine Old Men were preparing to don their robes and announce their momentous AAA decision.

Roosevelt at that time was holding a conference on the Farm Tenant Bill, and sitting with him were Wallace; Will Alexander, who is Tugwell's right-hand man on tenant farming; Marvin Jones, chairman of the House Committee on Agriculture; and Lee Pressman, legal adviser to Tugwell. The President was explaining certain political reasons why he wanted the Farm Tenant Bill passed by the House of Representatives as soon as possible. Already passed by the Senate at the previous session of Congress, the bill provided for a billion-dollar corporation through which the government would buy land from the big landowners and help tenant farmers get established on it. Since the bill gave the plantation owners a chance to sell their land, and the tenants a chance to get land, everybody was for it. Even the big insurance companies, with mortgages on most of the cotton plantations of the South, saw salvation in the bill.

So, turning to Representative Jones, the President said:

"Marvin, what about getting hearings started by your committee within the next three weeks?"

"But, Mr President," replied Jones, "don't you think we had best not hurry? Remember we may have to pass some legislation for the AAA after the Supreme Court hands down its decision."

"I doubt it," replied the President. "I don't think we'll have anything serious to worry about."

Twenty minutes later Justice Roberts began reading the reverberating decision declaring the Agricultural Adjustment Act unconstitutional.

The President was not alone in being nonchalant about the test of the AAA. Up until a few months before the case came to the Supreme Court, a good many of the big processors were quite content to let the Agricultural Adjustment Act stay on the statute books until the cows came home. In fact, when William Morgan Butler first decided to test the constitutionality of the act in order to avoid paying processing taxes, there were very few processors, big or little, any place in the country who were not much more satisfied with the act, probably, than Henry Wallace himself.

That was quite early in the days of the New Deal—October 1933—before the AAA really got started. Butler's four Hoosac Mills once were extremely valuable properties and the chief industry in New Bedford, Taunton and North Adams, the three Massachusetts towns in which they are located. They had made Butler a millionaire several times over, had enabled him to contribute lavishly to the election funds of Calvin Coolidge, whose campaign he managed, and helped elevate him to the chairmanship of the Republican National Committee. Profits from the mills, however, could not win his election to the Senate despite the fact that Coolidge not only secured his interim appointment but even publicly urged his nomination, a gesture of friendship which Calvin indulged in only once during his years in the White House.

As late as 1933 the Hoosac Mills still were valued at around $10,000,000; but they had been steadily losing out to Southern competition, so that, even before Mr Roosevelt came into office, Butler had borrowed one million dollars from the First National Bank of Boston and during the first year of the New Deal did some unsuccessful dickering with the Reconstruction Finance Corporation for a loan of $2,000,000.

Failing this, and with the loan from the First National Bank falling due, Senator Butler executed a neat stroke of legerdemain and had his company thrown into bankruptcy.

There were some very significant facts regarding this bankruptcy that did not bear scrutiny in the full light of day. In the first place, the firm which asked for it was the Franklin Process Company, with offices at the same New York address as Hoosac Mills. In the second place, Hoosac Mills owed only $13,557 to the Franklin Process Company, of which it had a lien on goods amounting to $8,300—an infinitesimal balance to throw a ten-million-dollar corporation into bankruptcy. But far more significant was the part which Frederick H. Prince played behind the scenes. Fred Prince is the largest depositor and one of the largest stockholders of the First National Bank to which Hoosac Mills owed $1,000,000. He is also the owner of Armour & Company and has a large interest in Swift & Company, two meat-packing firms materially affected by processing taxes. Furthermore, as chief owner and president of the two railroads which provide transportation for the Chicago stockyards, his interests are inextricably interwoven with the meat-packing industry. Finally, the fact that Armour & Company was the biggest buyer from Hoosac Mills, purchasing large quantities of ham and sausage stockings, put Mr Prince in a powerful position.

Not only was he the chief creditor, but also the chief customer, all of which leads to the almost inescapable conclusion that Prince, secretly opposed to processing taxes, but not wanting his meat-packing companies to arouse the wrath of the farmer by opposing them openly, saw in the Hoosac Mills a chance to test out processing taxes without appearing in the picture himself.

At any rate one of his subordinates, James A. McDonough, an executive of Armour & Company, was appointed coreceiver, together with Prince's old friend, William M. Butler, whose receivership fees were now fatter and certainly more regular than the dividends due from the company. Furthermore, Hoosac Mills were now in a strong strategic position to procrastinate on payments of AAA processing taxes already piling up at the rate of $20,000 a month.

All this took place in October 1933, not long after the AAA was put in operation. But it was not until January 1934 that federal tax collectors discovered what had happened. At that time they could have collected the taxes anyway, had they desired, since by a decision of the Supreme Court in a case argued for the government by that bitter critic of the New Deal, the late James M. Beck, no injunction or legal action can interfere with the collection of taxes.

In this case, however, Jerome Frank, counsel of the AAA, was anxious to find a chance to test out the constitutionality of the Agricultural Adjustment Act and jumped at the opportunity offered by the Hoosac Mills. No further attempt was made to collect the processing taxes, and the first hearing of the Hoosac case took place in the United States District Court in Massachusetts on April 30, 1934. It attracted no great attention even in the world of big and little processors. There was not the slightest indication at that time that Mr Butler and his mills were to set historic legal precedents. The country in general was much too busy working itself out of the red of the Hoover depression. Nor did anyone pay any great attention when Judge Elisha H. Brewster, a Boston blue-blood who traces his ancestry back to Revolutionary days, who owed his appointment to President Harding, and whose brother is attorney for the Du Ponts, handed down an opinion favorable to the government. Judge Brewster said:

"I rule that the Agricultural Adjustment Act does not violate the provisions of the Constitution. . . .

"The act is assailed because it 'unlawfully delegates legislative power to the executive.' Regulations and executive orders with the force of law have been upheld, even where a violation resulted in a penalty. . . . It is significant that up to the present time no act of Congress, so far as I am aware, has been held invalid because it conferred legislative power upon an executive."

Judge Brewster did not know—in October 1934—that a few months later Chief Justice Hughes was to set a new landmark in the hot-oil case decreeing that Congress could not delegate power to the President except within narrow limits. So Judge Brewster proceeded at this point to cite a long list of decisions in which the Court had upheld the delegation of power.

"These cases," he said, "demonstrate that when Congress has gone as far as it reasonably can in declaring a policy, and the means to accomplish the end sought, leaving to administrative officers the filling in of details, the statute very likely will be upheld, even if no definite standards have been established, and though the functions are legislative in character. . . .

"The Constitution has restricted the power to levy taxes to two purposes, namely, payment of debts of the United States, and to provide for 'the general welfare of the United States.' *It is not within the province of the court to substitute its judgment for that of Congress upon the effect of a particular measure manifestly designed to promote the general welfare of the United States. . . .*"

Another nine months elapsed before Senator Butler could put the case of his Hoosac Mills before the Circuit Court of Appeals and get a decision. And by that time—July 13, 1935—the constitutionality of the AAA had become a question in which there was a genuine, and in some areas vital, interest. The drought of 1934 had boosted the price of farm commodities, catching the small meat packers and other small processors with no stocks on hand. The big processors, with ample stocks, made money from inventory appreciation, but the little fellows lost. In deference to this situation, federal tax collectors extended the period of grace for collection of processing taxes from 90 to 180 days. But when processors failed to pay at the end of this period, tax collectors got hard-boiled.

From that moment there began a barrage of court tests of the AAA. Judge Charles I. Dawson, arch-Republican federal judge of the western Kentucky district, even resigned from the bench after finding the Kerr Tobacco Act invalid and started a lucrative practice suing the United States on behalf of a score of small wheat millers and meat packers.

Most of the big processors, although still favoring the AAA, had grown somewhat apprehensive over the amendments to the act, at that time being pushed through Congress by the Department of Agriculture in order to provide for tighter regulation of the meat packers, the canners, and the millers. Their opposition, however, was centered chiefly on the bill, then pending in Congress, rather than on the basic theory of the act.

But more important than that was a growing belief, especially in the big industrial centers of the East, that food prices were too high and that the AAA rather than the drought had materially increased the cost of living. Furthermore, the Roosevelt administration had played directly into the hands of those fomenting this idea, by discharging a little group of rebels within the AAA—Jerome Frank, Gardner Jackson and Lee Pressman —who fought for the interests of the consumer and claimed that he was being squeezed between the farmer on the one hand and the big processor on the other. These men were discharged with a resounding thud of publicity known as the AAA "purge," and it created a distinctly unfavorable impression in consumer centers. This feeling was not reflected in the West or South, where the AAA still had powerful popular support, but unfortunately for the New Deal the Hoosac Mills case was being tried in New England.

Since Judge Brewster had rendered his affirmative opinion,

furthermore, the Supreme Court of the United States had handed down two momentous decisions decreeing unconstitutional the control of petroleum and of business through the NRA. And with the latter decision, almost the entire country had applauded enthusiastically, yelling: "Whoopee! Supreme Court! Give the New Deal the works!"

It was precisely at this moment that the Circuit Court of Appeals handed down its decision reversing Judge Brewster. The vote appeared to be on strict party lines. Justice George H. Bingham of Manchester, New Hampshire, a Democrat appointed to the court by Woodrow Wilson, voted for the constitutionality of the AAA. Justice Scott Wilson of Portland, Maine, and Justice James M. Morton, Jr, of New Bedford, Massachusetts (the city in which two of the Hoosac mills were located), both Hoover Republicans, declared unequivocally that the AAA was unconstitutional.

In rendering this opinion, the majority of the three old men injected a new legal angle into the case. They said:

"The taxes imposed are not warranted under the federal Constitution in that they were imposed for the unlawful purpose of regulating and restricting the production of cotton in the several states, which is an unwarranted interference with matters solely within the control of the respective states and is violative of the powers reserved to the states under the Tenth Amendment."

This part of the decision attracted no great attention then, but much was to be heard of it later.

From that moment on, the AAA was flooded with all sorts of suits and restraining orders, a total of 1,700 being entered against it to prevent the collection of taxes. From that moment on, also, the Justice Department pushed a final test of the Hoosac Mills case in order to obtain a clear-cut decision regarding AAA constitutionality, and finally Chief Justice Hughes set December 9, 1935, as the date for argument.

There now took place one of the most intensive mobilizations of business and agricultural forces ever before witnessed in a

Supreme Court case. Almost every important farm organization and processing firm in the country lined up on one side or the other. John W. Davis wrote a brief for P. Lorillard & Company, plus the entire tobacco industry. Ex-Governor Nathan Miller of New York obtained permission to file as *amicus curiae* for the National Biscuit Company, representing the bakers. Briefs also were filed for the American Nut Company and the General Candy Corporation, representing the candy industry; for the General Milling, International Milling and Pillsbury Companies, representing the millers; the National Association of Cotton Manufacturers for the cotton industry; also the hog processors and the Farmers' Independence Council, accused by Senator Black's Lobbying Committee of being connected with the Liberty League. All these were in opposition to the government.

On the other side of the case, Fred Lee, an author of the Agricultural Adjustment Act, filed a 140-page brief for the American Farm Bureau Federation, while briefs also were filed by the League of Economic Equality, the Mountain States Beet Growers' Association, the Texas Agricultural Association and the Farmers' National Grain Association.

Those on the immediate firing line were Solicitor General Reed of the Justice Department; Prew Savoy and Alger Hiss of the AAA legal staff; and, on the other side, Senator Butler and rotund Edward R. Hale.

Early in the case, however, Senator Butler decided that so momentous an argument required a more celebrated and powerful pleader than the relatively obscure Mr Hale. And so he selected, as his chief legal gun, George Wharton Pepper of Philadelphia. Butler had known Pepper in the Senate, to which they both had been appointed through the deaths, respectively, of Henry Cabot Lodge and Boies Penrose. Both Butler and Pepper, incidentally, were unable to persuade their electorates to continue them for any protracted period, though Pepper managed to hang on for one full term. Butler also had heard that Pepper defended a group of small Pennsylvania meat packers in a lower-court test of the constitutionality of the AAA and won. His retainer in these cases was $50,000 plus a percentage of the processing taxes which he saved his clients, so that Mr Pepper was not averse to more such cases and agreed to divide with Mr Hale the time allotted for the Hoosac Mills argument before the Supreme Court.

There was another factor also which made Mr Pepper's choice particularly fortuitous from Senator Butler's point of view. Senator Pepper was not only personally acquainted with most of the conservative members of the Supreme Court, but he was an extremely close friend of Justice Roberts, regarded at that time as the key member of the Court who would swing the decision one way or the other. Both had graduated from the University of Pennsylvania, both subsequently taught in its law school, and both had taken a leading part in the legal and civic affairs of the city. Not only were they close friends, but Pepper had suggested Roberts' name to Calvin Coolidge as Teapot Dome oil prosecutor and subsequently to Hoover as justice of the Supreme Court.

What could be happier, therefore, from the point of view of Senator Butler and all those interested in nonpayment of processing taxes than that the old friend of Justice Roberts represent them before the Supreme Court?

Mr Pepper is reputed to have received for his services one million dollars in fees and percentages of taxes saved his various clients. If this is so, he earned it. For from the point of view of capturing the conservative wing of the Supreme bench, he put up a masterful performance. It was not a legal argument, it was an appeal to human psychology, and Pepper had studied it out very carefully indeed.

Senator Pepper makes an imposing appearance. He is tall, angular, square-shouldered, bushy-browed. With this he affects a humble hesitance of speech calculated to indicate careful deliberation of thought. Actually, the ex-Senator from Pennsylvania can be as glib as a carnival pitchman. But the pseudo uncertainty is effective, just as it was for the late Will Rogers, and Pepper used it for all it was worth in pleading before the Nine Old Men.

"I affirm first," he said, "that the processing exaction is not in its nature the exercise of the taxing power of the United States, but is wholly regulatory in character, and is part of a nation-wide scheme for the federal regulation of local agricultural production; and second, that if that scheme as a whole is unconstitutional as an invasion of the reserved powers of the states, then the whole scheme falls and the processing tax falls with it. . . .

"Congress has said in so many words, 'We exact from the processor a sum equal to our estimate of what the farmer should be receiving in addition to his present income.' . . . If I am right in my analysis, it is about as clear a case of exaction masquerading as a tax, but really regulatory in its character, as I think has ever come before this Court. . . . If it is going to be possible for the federal government to offer pecuniary reward to the farmer under conditions such that he cannot very well afford to decline, you get a situation where he sells his freedom for a mess of pottage and disavows his allegiance to that state which, under the Tenth Amendment, is entitled to control his production."

This was the main legal thesis running through the Senator's argument, as indeed it was the main thesis of the opinion subsequently handed down by his friend, the Justice from Philadelphia. Time after time Pepper came back to the financial coercion of the farmer, the Tenth Amendment, the right of the states to regulate all things not otherwise expressly provided in the Constitution.

"As far as the vocal majority [of farmers] are concerned," he continued, "you might get a closer approach to unanimity if you were to poll college students on the question, 'Do you favor a continuance of the allowance from father?' . . .

"The United States should not be entitled to a thrill of moral satisfaction merely because it has robbed Processor Peter to pay Producer Paul. . . ."

Pepper is a leading Episcopal churchman, and in closing he put a note of prayerful righteousness in his voice:

"And I pray Almighty God," he said, "that not in my time may 'the land of the regimented' be accepted as a worthy substitute for 'the land of the free.' "

And then he broke down and wept.

It was superb showmanship, and any student of human psychology watching the faces of the Nine Old Men during Pepper's act could almost tell what the result would be. To Van Devanter, who had spent his life on the free and "unregimented" plains of Wyoming; to Sutherland, who pioneered the frontier in Utah; to Butler, who had spent his life arguing for free and unregulated railroads; and to Roberts, perhaps for other reasons, Pepper's argument had a telling effect. Obviously they were delighted with his appeal. The three liberals did not look particularly pleased.

The face of Chief Justice Hughes alone remained inscrutable.

When Homer Cummings was a young and idealistic student at Yale, he wrote a poem, one verse of which read:

> "In after years should troubles arise,
>   To cloud the blue of sunny skies,
>   How bright will seem thro' Memory's haze,
>   Those happy, golden bygone days."

Forty-four years later, as Attorney General during the hectic legal years of 1935–36, Homer had occasion to remember those lines.

However, not even he, nor any one of the many legalists around him, dreamed that the Nine Old Men would throw out the Agricultural Adjustment Act with the resounding thud they did. Most New Deal legalists, including the President, were firmly convinced that the Court would not throw it out at all; it was far too popular with the great and vocal mass of the farm population. But there were some who felt that the Court might take a crack at "undue delegation of power" by Congress to the executive, as Judge W. H. Kirkpatrick had done in the case of the small Pennsylvania meat packers. This, they knew, could easily be amended by Congress. There were some, also, who felt that the Court might hold that the processing taxes were for social rather than revenue purposes, and therefore invalid.

But with the exception of Paul Jackson, one of the gloomiest members of the Justice Department, no one dreamed that the AAA would be thrown out on the basis of the Tenth Amendment and the contention that regulation of agriculture is a state rather than a federal function.

As the days progressed, however, and no decision came down from the temple of justice regarding the fate of the AAA, it began to be bruited about that the Nine Old Men were engaged in one of the stormiest debates in their sometimes stormy career. The Chief Justice, it leaked out, wanted to avoid a 5–4 decision on so vital a question affecting thirty millions of the farm population of the United States. Mr Hughes had been more active politically and more recently than any of his conservative colleagues, and he still had the habit of keeping his ear to the ground for popular reverberations. Also he cherished, beyond any of the others, the prestige of the Court. And he knew that to throw out the AAA by one vote would wreak almost irreparable damage to that prestige.

Mr Hughes wanted to avoid such a calamity. But, being unable to avoid it, he switched his vote to the majority, thus increasing the margin of difference from one to three votes. Six-to-three certainty would make a better impression on the country than five-to-four, especially when two of the minority votes came from Jews.

This news fell upon the surprised ears of the minority, especially Justice Stone, on Saturday, December 28, just three days before New Year's Day. It meant that Stone, rather than Hughes, would write the minority opinion, and it also meant that he must write it in two days if he was to keep a promise he had given to his family to attend a reunion in Massachusetts on New Year's Day. Stone asked the Department of Agriculture to keep its library open all Sunday in order to obtain from it certain material which he wanted, and by Monday night he had finished the minority opinion and was ready to leave for New England. It was an opinion destined to make history in the annals of the Court.

Both opinions were handed down one week later—January 6, 1936. Members of the Agricultural Department, anxiously awaiting the verdict, knew when they arrived at the mausoleum of justice that the decision would be announced that day and that Justice Roberts would participate in it. For Mrs Roberts, always on deck when her husband is to play a stellar role, was present. They did not know, however, which way the decision was to go.

Just what motivated the majority in its selection of Justice Roberts as its spokesman is best known to themselves. Usually it is customary for the Chief Justice to render the opinion when he is on the majority and when an important case is involved. But in this instance, obviously, Mr Hughes did not feel enthusiastic over the majority's position.

Many felt that Roberts' close friendship with Senator Pepper should have persuaded the Justice to take a less conspicuous part in the case. But, whatever the motives which put him forward as majority spokesman, he did a superb job. Thirty years of jury pleading have made Roberts the most effective spokesman on the Supreme bench. Furthermore, he goes to great pains to perfect the delivery of his opinion, rehearsing it in advance to a point where he does not once glance at the sheets of paper before him. Finally, Roberts also has the gift, so important in an opinion certain to meet with popular disapproval, of wrapping the unpalatable portions in a maze of immensely impressive legal verbiage.

This was what he did in rendering the AAA decision. His opinion totaled a little more than seven thousand words, of which the first forty-four hundred were spent in a high-sounding declaration of the principles at issue and a discussion of the conflicting theories of Hamilton and Madison over the general-welfare clause of the Constitution. It was the contention of Alexander Hamilton that Congress had the power to spend money for the general welfare even beyond the point that it had power to legislate. James Madison, on the other hand, claimed that the congressional power of expenditure could go no further than its power of legislation.

For more than one hundred years this question has been one of ardent debate by constitutional lawyers and never has been settled by the Supreme Court. Or, to use the more diplomatic language of Justice Roberts: "This Court has noticed the question, but has never found it necessary to decide which is the true construction."

Once when preparing his brief in the case of *Massachusetts* vs. *Mellon* testing the constitutionality of the Maternity Act, Solicitor General James M. Beck wrote: "This honorable Court has evaded this question for one hundred years, and it is now high time that it decided it." Beck was persuaded by his colleagues to drop this from his brief; but the Supreme Court did not then or subsequently rule on this historic debate until Justice Roberts stepped forward with his AAA opinion.

He decided it. The decision went in favor of Hamilton.

There was a very good reason for that decision. In the first place, if Roberts had sided with Madison it would have meant that some of the most important functions of the federal government would have ended. It would have meant the end of co-operation between Washington and the states for the fighting of forest fires, for the suppression of insect pests, for the eradication of hoof-and-mouth disease, and for the distribution of seeds. It would have meant the end of maternity grants to states for expectant mothers. It would have meant the end of grants for the building of roads. It would have meant the end of a good part of the work of the Department of Agriculture. For, while the federal government cannot regulate these things by legislation, it can spend money for them, according to the Hamilton theory, without violating the Constitution.

Roberts might have dodged a decision on this delicate question had it not been for one other highly important factor. He knew that Chief Justice Hughes, when a practicing attorney, had appeared before the Court in the Federal Land Banks case and submitted a masterful brief supporting the Hamilton theory. And in presenting the case for the AAA, Solicitor General Reed very cleverly used a good part of the Hughes brief to show that the government had the right to make benefit payments to farmers in return for crop reduction.

Roberts also knew that, for one reason or another, Chief Justice Hughes, after the AAA case first was argued, was very much inclined to side with the government. His vote was important. So Justice Roberts for the first time in one hundred years settled this long-standing debate regarding the spending powers of the government—and settled it the way Hughes had argued. Eventually it brought the Chief Justice over to the side of the majority.

But then, having accepted the Hamilton theory, Roberts proceeded to put limits on it that would have made Alexander Hamilton vomit. Roberts had decreed that Congress could spend money on things which it is not permitted to regulate; but now he further decreed that, in doing so, Congress cannot spend money in such a way as to purchase regulation. In other words, when the Department of Agriculture signed a contract with a farmer for the reduction of acreage in exchange for benefit payments, it was purchasing regulation in a manner unjustified by the Constitution. And the difference between purchasing maternity care, the fighting of forest fires and the building of good roads on the one hand and the reduction of crops on the other was, according to Justice Roberts, the fact that the states were not compelled to accept the grants offered by the federal government. Farmers, he contended, were. Justice Stone later cited figures showing that many farmers spurned benefit payments and prospered, but his figures, apparently, cut no ice with the majority.

And then, to clinch his case, Justice Roberts launched into exactly the same argument put forward so skillfully by his old friend George Wharton Pepper, namely, that the AAA was a violation of the Tenth Amendment reserving to the states all "powers not delegated to the United States."

Previous to the debates on the AAA, the Tenth Amendment had been an almost forgotten paragraph in our charter of government. Even the law schools ignored it. But Justice Roberts dusted it off and ceremoniously brought it forward. Wholly apart from any question of general welfare, he said, "the act invades the reserved rights of the states. . . . From the accepted doctrine that the United States is a government of delegated powers, it follows that those not expressly granted . . . are reserved to the states or to the people. To forestall any suggestion to the contrary, the Tenth Amendment was adopted."

Then, ignoring completely the attempts made by individual states to control agriculture—always thwarted by their complete inability to agree on how much of a commodity each should produce; and ignoring also the absolute inability of thirty million widely scattered farmers to organize for control of production, Roberts warned of the horrible precedent the AAA might create for decreasing the production of shoes—apparently quite oblivious of the fact that in major industries production is already self-regulated.

Finally he closed with a peroration which almost paraphrased the sentimental jury plea against regimentation made by Mr Pepper.

"The expression of the framers of the Constitution . . . may be searched in vain," he said, "for any suggestion that there exists in the Constitution authority whereby every provision and fair implication from that instrument may be subverted, the independence of the individual states obliterated, and the United States converted into a central government exercising controlled police power in every state of the Union."

The day after Justice Roberts' opinion was rendered, his daughter Elizabeth received first prize in a Junior League art exhibition. Her painting was entitled "Vegetables."

The dissent of Justice Stone, on behalf also of Brandeis and Cardozo, was not delivered with the same impressive flourishes. It was brief and to the point.

take potshots at the Nine Old Men. They heard about it, and that's why they voted as they did."

What they heard, however, was the rumbling of public resentment against the concentration of greater power in the hands of nine men than their ancestors had permitted in the hands of the royal governors of the colonies.

A few months after the historic AAA decision, two of the Hoosac mills, despite their victory and their nonpayment of processing taxes, were closed. And of the other two, one had abandoned the ancestral production of cotton for rayon.

CHAPTER XVI

Lynch Law

THE five-one-three decision that felled the Guffey Coal Act was a clear-cut case of lynch law.

The other New Deal measures axed by the Court had had an opportunity to function before their doom was pronounced. But not the Guffey Act. By the time this law was enacted the reactionary cabal on the Court had reached such a pitch of berserk fervor that they did not even wait for the statute to operate. They cut it down while the new coal commission created by the act was still hiring stenographers and arranging its new offices.

Justice Cardozo, in his caustic dissent on behalf of the minority, bluntly accused his Tory colleagues of precipitous action:

"The opinion of the Court," he declared, "begins at the wrong end. . . . Some [provisions of the law] may operate in one way as to one group, and in another way as to others, according to particular conditions as yet unknown and unknowable. A decision in advance as to the operation and validity of separate provisions in varying contingencies is premature and hence unwise. In *Steamship Company* vs. *Emigration Commissioners* the Court rules, 'The Court will not anticipate a question of constitutional law in advance of the necessity of deciding it.' . . . To adopt a homely form of words, the complainants have been crying before they are really hurt."

But by the end of the spring term of 1936 a majority of the

Nine Old Men were so blind in their hatred of the New Deal, so determined to wipe its legislation from the statute books, that they jumped at the opportunity to knife the Guffey Act even before it started.

If there was one industry in the country in dire need of compulsory stabilization it was the production of bituminous coal. For fifteen years it had been degenerating steadily into anarchy and chaos. Incredible overproduction and destruction of vital natural resources, cannibalistic competition, ferocious wage cutting, strikes, terror and bloodshed blackened its pages. Between 1920 and 1935 half a dozen congressional investigations were conducted and twice as many schemes proposed in an effort to find some method of introducing order and sanity into its business. And by the time the National Industrial Recovery Act, which brought the first breath of reason, was enacted, the industry had become a menace not merely to the operators and miners but to the national welfare.

This welter of turmoil was due directly to conditions resulting from the World War. The bituminous-coal industry was as much a victim of that conflagration as the shattered veterans at Walter Reed Hospital.

When Europe became a vast charnel house in 1914 the roar of its guns and the tramp of its armies soon echoed in every coal field in America. Agents of the belligerents stormed mine owners with orders. Any coal, good, bad or indifferent, they would buy. Output zoomed to record-breaking heights, pyramiding from 422,000,000 tons in 1914 to over 550,000,000 by 1917, when the United States entered the conflict. Prices kept pace with these soaring figures. Six months after the crack of the assassin's pistol at Serajevo, spot prices for soft coal had skyrocketed from $1.30 to $4.18 a ton, f.o.b. the mines.

Easy millions were to be made—and the operators lost no time in making them. New mines were opened by the hundreds. The total number of operating properties increased from 4,800 in 1914 to 9,000 in 1920. And with this tremendous plant expansion went an extensive technical perfection of production methods. Electric cutting machines, mine cars, mechanical loaders and other time- and labor-saving devices were introduced in an effort to keep pace with the mounting demand for coal.

With American entrance into the war, the combination of vaulting prices and the need for keeping the war industries adequately supplied with fuel quickly resulted in a crisis which the government met by enacting the Lever Act. This placed control of distribution, prices and labor relations in the hands of a federal agency, the Coal Administration. The latter acted with vigor and dispatch. It fixed a scale of rates, regulated distribution with a firm hand and compelled the operators not only to recognize the United Mine Workers but to enter into wage agreements with the union.

During the two years of this government-enforced stabilization, the coal industry enjoyed the greatest era of internal peace and prosperity in its history.

But the Armistice slackened the floodtide of orders to a snail's pace. Production dropped from a high of 579,000,000 tons in 1918 to 465,000,000 in 1919. Now, if ever, the value of enforced regulation, so strikingly demonstrated during the two previous years, should have been taken to heart. But the exact opposite was the case. The operators, with their eyes glued only on production charts, set up a yammer for the removal of government control. They demanded a restoration of "free competition" and the privilege once again of cutting each other's and the miners' throats in the old dog-eat-dog scramble for business.

In the spring of 1919 the Wilson regime bowed to this pressure from the owners and dismantled the Coal Administration.

There followed turmoil and dissension.

In order to keep from shutting down their greatly expanded properties the operators began to slash prices. Since labor constitutes approximately 65 per cent of the cost of mining coal, this meant wage cutting; and it took place on a large scale. Well-organized and militantly class conscious to a greater degree than other American workers, the miners pointed to the rising cost of living and threatened a nation-wide strike unless wage slashing were discontinued.

But the operators disregarded the warning, and in November 1919 450,000 miners staged a walk-out in twenty-two states. The industry was paralyzed; coal shipments dropped from 13,000,000 to 3,500,000 tons in one week. On the verge of winter, the nation faced an acute fuel shortage.

Attorney General A. Mitchell Palmer immediately rushed into the breach—on the side of the operators. Appearing before Federal Judge Anderson in Indianapolis, he asked for a sweeping injunction against the striking union miners.

And the judiciary, which seventeen years later was to lynch the Guffey Coal Act for exactly opposite legal reasons, granted the injunction. Judge Anderson issued the restraining order on the ground that the production of coal was an *interstate* industry and that the miners by striking were interfering with interstate commerce. But in his majority opinion pronouncing the Guffey Act unconstitutional, Justice Sutherland solemnly proclaimed that the production of coal is not an interstate business and therefore the federal government was without authority to regulate it.

The two opinions illustrate what is sometimes called the "shoe theory" of law—fitting the law to suit the particular case.

In 1919, when in order to curb labor it was expedient to declare the production of coal to be within the scope of interstate commerce, the judiciary had no difficulty in reaching such a conclusion. But in 1936, when it desired to strike down the hand of federal regulation, the judiciary found no trouble in holding exactly the reverse. Coal was now *intrastate* commerce.

But Palmer's injunction did not deter the miners. As long as the operators refused concessions, they remained on strike. After six weeks of this deadlock, with the coal supply of the country almost exhausted and with the railroads and industry facing stoppage, Wilson finally bestirred himself. He re-established the Coal Administration to regulate wages and prices, together with a special arbitration commission which in March 1920 increased basic rates of pay 27 per cent for a two-year period.

For two years the industry again enjoyed peace, but when time came for a renewal of the agreement, the operators balked. They claimed that competitors in the nonunion fields of Kentucky, West Virginia and Alabama were paying lower wages and thus were able to undersell them. When they insisted on a reduction in pay, the miners refused and again took to the picket lines. The ensuing fight in 1922 was violent and costly. The 450,000 bituminous miners who walked out were soon joined by 142,000 anthracite miners, and a few weeks later by railway shopmen. The triple-headed labor stoppage created nation-wide loss and confusion. The coal shortage caused prices to jump from two dollars to six dollars a ton, railroad service was disrupted and the nation's entire industrial system was thrown out of gear.

Under government pressure the operators finally backed down and agreed to another two-year renewal of the 1920 wage scale.

The renewal expired in 1924, an election year, and the Coolidge administration bestirred itself to prevent a strike. Due to quiet behind-the-scenes wire pulling on the part of Herbert Hoover, then Secretary of Commerce, there was negotiated the famous Jacksonville agreement, running for three years and providing a base pay of $7.50 per day. This compact was lived up to by the operators until early in 1926. Then certain bitterly anti-union companies in West Virginia and Kentucky, claiming they could not compete with larger firms, began repudiating wage contracts with the United Mine Workers. This wave of contract repudiation soon extended to adjoining fields, then to adjoining states and in a few months had spread like a virulent cancer throughout the industry.

The result was chaos and anarchy. With the stabilizing factor of a fixed wage level overthrown, the operators soon were at each other's throats fighting like beasts for business. And the diminishing margin of profit was taken out of the hides of the miners and their families. Wages sank to as low as $1.25 a day, and large users, such as the railroads, were able to buy coal at sixty to seventy cents a ton.

It was a buyers' paradise, and the railroads and big industrialists exerted every effort to keep it so. By secret economic pressure they forced those operators who were willing to co-operate with the United Mine Workers to break their contracts. And in Congress they blocked every measure designed to re-establish order and stability in the coal fields.

This insane cutthroat competition was suicidal alike to operators and workers. Scores of companies were forced into bankruptcy. Practically all operated in the red. Thousands of mines were abandoned, and the water which crept up the shafts meant that millions of tons of coal were lost to future generations. Mines decreased in number from 9,331 to 6,057, and the suffering among miners and their families was tragic in the extreme. Over 200,000 of them, or approximately half the men in the industry, were thrown out of work. In isolated regions whole communities were left to starve through the shutting down of the local mines.

And the operators, caught between the pinchers of their own greed and that of the big industrialists, made little effort to extricate themselves. It was left to the miners, through their union, the United Mine Workers, to try to save the owners from their own cupidity, incompetence and cowardice.

This role of rescuer on the part of the workers is one of the remarkable things about the coal industry. Time and again it has been the miners, fighting lone-handed and against desperate odds, who have struggled to save not only themselves but their employers.

The United Mine Workers now inspired an investigation of the big utility coal users, and in 1928 introduced a bill for the stabilization of the coal industry. But it got nowhere. Hoover, while a candidate for the presidency, promised the United Mine Workers to support the bill, but after election ignored his pledge.

The bursting of the Coolidge-Hoover boom struck a solar-plexus blow to the already punch-drunk coal industry. Consumption dropped from 535,000,000 tons in 1929 to 310,000,000 by 1932.

The steady disappearance of markets operated to intensify the fierceness and rapacity of competition among the owners to the point of piracy. Wages were cut so ruthlessly that it became a common thing for miners to find that after a week's work and various deductions they had a mere pittance in their pay envelopes. Tens of thousands were added to the already huge army of unemployed miners. The dues-paying membership of the United Miners fell to one third of its strength. And the industry in general sank deeper and deeper into the mire of ruin and despair.

This was the situation in April 1933, when President Roosevelt called the special session of Congress to enact relief and recovery measures. John L. Lewis, president of the United Mine Workers, and the most forceful leader in the ranks of labor, immediately saw the possibilities for the coal industry and swung into action. While the operators sat stolidly on the side lines and while the heavy-barreled executives of the American Federation of Labor milled round in leaderless confusion, the fast-thinking miner chief took steps to revive the old coal-stabilization bill. It was on the point of being reintroduced in Congress when Senator Wagner informed Lewis of the administration's NRA plan and asked his assistance in drafting the legislation. Lewis promptly withdrew his bill and co-operated in framing the New Deal measure.

The NIRA was still in the legislative mills when Lewis, grasping its possibilities, moved quietly but vigorously to make the most of its opportunities. Rushing organizers into the field, he regained 95 per cent of the old strength of the United Mine Workers before the NIRA was more than six weeks old.

Lewis, however, was the only A. F. of L. leader with the foresight to take such preparatory measures, and as a result of his strategy the miners not only derived more benefits from the NRA than any other labor group, but they were better able to protect their gains when the Supreme Court wiped out the Blue Eagle.

Lewis now was made a member of the NRA Labor Advisory Board, became one of General Johnson's most trusted advisers and was the chief conciliating force during the long wrangle of writing a coal code. After three months of exhausting effort, a code fixing price differentials and establishing a standard wage scale finally was put through by Lewis and a group of leading operators—J. D. A. Morrow, head of the Mellon-owned Pittsburgh Coal Company, James B. Francis, president of the Island Creek Coal Company, of West Virginia, and Charles O'Neil of Peale, Peacock & Kerry, Pennsylvania operators.

It was a Homeric accomplishment, and during the next twelve months the industry enjoyed a measure of peace and prosperity it had not known in years. Profits again began to appear on balance sheets, closed mines reopened, labor was paid a living wage and strikes and violence ceased.

But—the Garden of Eden had its Serpent, and the Blue Eagle its chiselers.

After the fearful losses and misery suffered by the industry during its seven years of "free competition" it would have seemed that the operators had learned their lesson and would have cherished the hard-won stabilization enjoyed under the code. A majority of them did. But there were just enough incorrigibles, chiselers and rabid anti-unionites to jeopardize the security and peace of the rest.

Taking advantage of the mounting agitation and resentment against the NRA, this minority began to sabotage. In the gunmen-ruled anti-union fields of Kentucky, West Virginia and Alabama this defiance was open. In the strong union fields of Pennsylvania, Illinois and Ohio it was undercover. A common trick to sell below code prices was to ship to a favored customer "hot" coal, about to burn through spontaneous combustion. The time of combustion, incidentally, can be calculated almost to the exact hour. The customer then complained that he had received damaged coal, and the coal operator, claiming that he had no more slack on hand, substituted good coal. The code permitted substitution for coal lost in transit or which started to burn.

Thus the customer got good coal for the price of slack, the shipping of "hot" coal being a mere subterfuge to permit the substitution.

There were various other subterfuges. Chiseling and violations in one area inevitably led to similar tactics in others, so that by the fall of 1934 code adherence practically had ceased and the industry was rapidly returning to anarchy and chaos. Again it was labor that moved to save the operators from themselves.

Foreseeing clearly that, if the existing wage contracts once expired, the operators would begin another mad price-cutting war at the expense of labor, and also having a strong hunch that the Blue Eagle was doomed for slaughter by the Supreme Court, Lewis launched a movement for a separate and permanent coal-stabilization act with sufficient teeth to make it effective. As a result, a committee of owners and miners was organized to study legislative plans and to draft a bill. Judge Warrum, counsel of the United Miners, went to England to examine its mining laws and, returning, collaborated with Jett Lauck, miner economist, and Lewis, to write what later became the Guffey bill.

The original bill was introduced by Senator Joseph F. Guffey, newly elected Democrat from Pennsylvania, in January 1935, five months before the Supreme Court declared the NRA unconstitutional. The bill consisted of two parts: Title I, price-fixing and labor provisions; Title II, creating a national bituminous-coal reserve.

This last provision did not originate with the miners. It was sponsored—of all people—by the Pittsburgh Coal Company, of which Andrew W. Mellon, Secretary of the Treasury under three Republican Presidents, is one of the chief owners. "Uncle Andy's" pronounced views against government ownership and regulation and for "economy" are well known and need no repetition here. But business is business, and a profitable deal with the government rings just as sweetly on the cash register as one with a private customer. The Pittsburgh Coal Company happens to own extensive coal lands, bought at fancy prices during the World War, which now have become a white elephant

on its hands. Nothing would be more welcome than unloading
them in the guise of a coal reserve on Uncle Sam.

So in the spring of 1934, when the coal code began to encounter
heavy sledding, an emissary of "Uncle Andy's" company called
on Secretary of the Interior Ickes and, playing upon his known
enthusiasm for conservation, proposed that the New Deal
initiate a coal reserve. Mr Ickes is an idealist. But also he is a
hardheaded businessman. His answer was an emphatic "No."

Later, when the miner-operator committee, inspired by Lewis,
began working on a substitute for the NRA, the Pittsburgh Coal
Company again trotted out its coal-reserve idea. Morrow, head
of the corporation and a member of the committee, insisted that
it be included in the proposed bill, and although Lewis was not
enthusiastic he acquiesced in order to obtain Mellon's powerful
support in the coming battle in Congress.

But in the end the conservation dreams of Mr Mellon's coal
company were knocked out by the Senate, and the Guffey Act
stood stripped of all except two all-important provisions, one
benefiting the operators, the other giving compensating benefits
to the miners.

The operators, on their side, were permitted to fix prices at
the mouth of the mine, and in return for this revolutionary concession they were to co-operate with the miners in fixing maximum hours and to permit the miners the right of unionization,
collective bargaining, freedom from using company stores and
company houses and other restrictions practiced in the coal
baronies of West Virginia, Pennsylvania and Kentucky.

The compulsory factor in the bill, which its enemies claimed
was unconstitutional, was patterned after the Bankhead Cotton
Control Act, and provided for a 15-per-cent tax on coal, of which
90 per cent was returned to the operator if he complied with
the coal code. Those who did not comply were taxed just the
same but did not get their 90-per-cent rebate.

It was an ingenious plan, first to preserve prosperity among
the operators, second to enable them to pass wage benefits down
to the miner. And at hearings held on the bill even while the

Schechter NRA case still was before the Supreme Court, a large majority of the operators favored it. Senator Guffey estimated them at 70 per cent. Among those who opposed, however, were James Walter Carter, president of the Carter Coal Company, of West Virginia, who later led the court fight against the act, the United States Steel Corporation, extensive owner of coal lands, the National Manufacturers' Association, inveterate foe of all regulatory measures and, secretly, certain reactionary heads of the American Federation of Labor who feared Lewis and were willing to go to any length, even helping the enemy, in order to knife him.

The Supreme Court's decision wiping out the NRA was both an impetus and a handicap to the Guffey bill.

To the miners the decree made the new bill absolutely essential. Their wage contracts were nearing expiration, and unless new legislation was passed they faced a revival of pay cuts, violence and starvation. Lewis redoubled his efforts to secure action, hammering home upon the White House and its leaders in Congress the seriousness of the crisis confronting the coal industry and the country. On the other hand, the opposition, buoyed up by the Court's verdict, intensified its lobbying against the Guffey bill.

The chief cry against it was unconstitutionality.

Roosevelt had given his private approval to the bill but dodged a public declaration. As the fight grew hotter, however, Lewis put him on the spot with a demand that he climb off the fence. Finally, therefore, Roosevelt sent a letter to the chairman of the House Judiciary Committee declaring that the question of constitutionality was one for the courts to decide and urged adoption of the bill. Under this prodding, Democratic floor leaders reluctantly bestirred themselves, and the bill, after being stripped of the coal-reserve scheme in the Senate, was passed by narrow margins.

The day after the President signed the act the opposition reopened fire with an attack in the courts.

The aggressor was James Walter Carter. Carter is thirty-eight years old, tall, thin, boyish-looking, wears sport coats from Tripler's, speaks with a slight Oxford accent, and, with his father, is the sole owner of the vast $24,000,000 Carter coal properties in West Virginia. Father and son reign over this domain like feudal lords. They have their own company town, Coalwood, a model village, it is true, with cozy modern cottages, gardens, hospital, church, clubhouse, baseball diamond, tennis courts, etc., but ruled with an iron fist. The miners receive part of their wages in scrip, cashable only in the company store, where prices are higher than in adjacent towns. No private stores are allowed in Coalwood. There is no election of town officials. The company superintendent runs the community. Espionage on the private life and morals of the Carter miners is general. The possession of alcoholic beverages of any kind is taboo.

Coalwood is paternalism in its fullest flower, yet it was with the outraged cry of "paternalism" on their lips that the Carters went into the courts and demanded the invalidation of the Guffey Act.

The Carter attack was carefully prepared in advance. While the bill still was in Congress, father and son went to New York and conferred with Frederick H. Wood, of the law firm of Cravath, de Gersdorff, Swaine & Wood. Wood was the lawyer who mysteriously popped up as last-minute counsel for the Schechter brothers in the NRA case. The Carters deny there was any conspiracy in their drive against the Guffey Act. They say that Wood had been their attorney for years and that they paid the entire cost of their suit out of their own pocket. In any event, their strategy was very carefully worked out. The Carter company directors planned to meet and vote to join the code set up by the new law and to pay the tax imposed to administer it. Whereupon young Carter was to file suit to restrain them. Wood meanwhile was to draw up a brief to be held in readiness for this court maneuver.

The program went off like clockwork. The day after the President affixed his signature to the Guffey Act on August 30,

1935, Wood left the general offices of Carter Coal Company, located in Washington just across the street from the Treasury, went before Justice Jesse Adkins, of the District of Columbia Supreme Court, and asked for an injunction to restrain the government from enforcing the law.

The government was not altogether unprepared. It had heard reports that a court attack would be launched against the law before it could be got under way, and Assistant Attorney General John Dickinson, head of the anti-trust division of the Justice Department, a Philadelphian whose ancestor, John Dickinson, was a member of the Constitutional Convention, personally opposed Wood's motion.

Justice Adkins refused to grant an injunction. Instead he ordered a trial and set a date. The trial lasted two weeks. At its conclusion he decreed:

1. That the law was constitutional except in regard to the labor provisions. These were ruled out, leaving intact the price-fixing sections.

2. That the labor and price-fixing provisions were separable. Congress had so specified, and the separation could and should be observed.

In view of the Supreme Court's subsequent decision this last point is important. Knowing that the Court, in the Nebbia milk case, had upheld price fixing, and realizing also that minimum wages in the past had been declared unconstitutional, the drafters of the act had taken pains to specify that the two sections of the act were independent. If one fell before the Court, the other would remain. And so far Justice Adkins proved the wisdom of their strategy.

While the fast-moving Carters got the jump in starting court action, the Adkins decision was not the first on the coal act. The first decree was handed down by Federal Judge Elwood Hamilton of Louisville and was a sweeping victory for the government. Hamilton sustained the law in every respect.

His opinion was rendered in a suit started within a few weeks after that of the Carters by Harlan County, Kentucky, operators, among the most mercenary and merciless in the industry. Their rule of Harlan County is by terror, murder and starvation. They defied and violated the NRA code and fiercely opposed the Guffey bill. When it became law they hustled it to the courts as soon as they could. Their counsel was Charles I. Dawson, a former federal judge who ruled against the Kerr-Smith Tobacco Control Act, then resigned to engage in a lucrative practice as attorney for businessmen warring against the New Deal.

The Hamilton and Adkins decisions started a headlong scramble between Frederick Wood and Charles Dawson to be first to get their cases before the Supreme Court. Each wanted to strut before the footlights of public attention. They made frantic efforts to rush their cases through the lower courts and were furious when Dickinson refused to co-operate. Finally an agreement was reached under which the cases were consolidated and placed on the Supreme Court calendar for argument in March 1936. This was a little more than six months after the law had been enacted and while the Bituminous Coal Commission was still compiling data and statistics on which to base price schedules.

Wood and Dawson divided the time between them, but neither said a word during their lengthy pleas about the disastrous and chaotic history of the coal industry. As far as their arguments were concerned the production of coal was a peaceful, contented and prosperous pursuit that a meddlesome government was forcibly seeking to disrupt with illegal regulation. Dawson expounded weightily on the contention that the coal industry was intra- and not interstate commerce and in support of this claim laid much stress on the Court's 1932 decision wiping out Oklahoma's regulation of ice manufacture. He also attacked the coal law on the ground that it was an illegal delegation of legislative power.

Regarding strikes, bloodshed, bankruptcy, ruinous cutthroat competition, the ex-federal judge was completely silent.

Wood devoted himself to a rehash of the arguments made

against the NRA and the AAA. Sonorously he cited both decisions and, in the same bellowing voice used in attacking the NRA, denounced the administrative tax imposed by the Guffey Act as a device designed to enforce federal regulation and not to raise revenue. Wood's shouting finally became so objectionable that Chief Justice Hughes requested him to speak more quietly.

"I am sorry, your honors," Wood apologized. "I quite frequently forget myself in my zeal."

Wood shifted abruptly from an ear-splitting crescendo to a barely audible pianissimo, and in a few minutes Justice Sutherland, who is somewhat deaf, asked him to speak louder.

Dickinson addressed the Court for three hours, during which the Nine Old Men listened with rapt attention and not a single interruption. This was in marked contrast to the frequent, sometimes caustic, interruptions during other New Deal cases.

Dickinson was assisted in his preparation of the legal phases of his argument by Professor Powell and by Professor Edward S. Corwin of Princeton, author of *The Twilight of the Supreme Court,* and on the technical phases by Fred Tryon, coal expert of the Bureau of Mines. Dickinson's presentation included a vivid and dramatic description of the tragic history of coal, of the vital economic and social considerations that had impelled Congress to enact the Guffey Act. Justice Cardozo laid great stress on these facts in his dissenting opinion. On the legal issues, Dickinson went out of his way to emphasize that the law affected only coal which entered interstate commerce, and particularly he stressed Justice Roberts' decision in the Nebbia case, in which Roberts upheld price fixing.

The Court took the case under advisement March 11. Days passed and nothing happened. As the weeks lengthened into months it was apparent that the justices were embroiled in a fierce wrangle. Finally, on May 18—sixty-eight days later—it announced its decree. The five-one-three decision confirmed all the speculation regarding the Court's dissension.

The majority decision threw out the entire law. Written by

Justice Sutherland, Utah railroad and corporation lawyer, it agreed with Adkins in ruling out the labor provisions. "The labor controversies and evils which it is the object of this act to regulate and minimize," Sutherland declared, "are local controversies and evils affecting local work undertaken to accomplish that local result."

But Sutherland did not go with Adkins all the way. When it came to the separability of the price-fixing and labor clauses, as specified by Congress, Sutherland balked. On this point he scored a new high in judicial arrogance. He ruled that when Congress specified in the Guffey Act that the price-fixing and labor portions were separate and divisible, it had not meant what it said. He pronounced the two features indivisible, and therefore the scuttling of the labor sections doomed the rest of the law. But, while knifing the statute, Sutherland carefully refrained from taking a stand on the legality of price fixing. That might have conflicted with the opinion of his friend, Justice Roberts, in the Nebbia case. Sutherland wanted Roberts' concurrence in throwing out the Guffey bill, and so cannily he said nothing about price fixing.

Thus, the five old men, while stripping the federal government of the power to prohibit the operators from compelling their workers to live in company houses, accept scrip and buy in profiteering company stores, left the door open on the question of the right of the employers to protect their pocketbooks by fixing prices between themselves.

Chief Justice Hughes in an individual opinion concurred in the majority judgment against the labor provisions. But he went the rest of the way with Adkins. Like Adkins, he upheld price fixing and declared that the sections relating to it could be and should be passed upon separately.

The dissenting opinion of Justice Cardozo—on behalf of Stone and Brandeis—raked the majority decision on both flanks, throwing into vivid relief its gross bias.

Where Sutherland was mute regarding the history of coal, Cardozo reviewed the turbulent record of the industry in this language: "Overproduction was at a point where free competition had degraded into anarchy. Prices had been cut so low that profit had become impossible for all except a lucky handful. Wages came down along with prices and with profits. There were strikes with the accompaniment of violence and bloodshed and misery and bitter feeling. . . . In the weeks immediately preceding the passage of this act the country was threatened once more with a strike of ominous proportions. . . ."

Where the five reactionaries coyly pussyfooted on the price-fixing issue, the three liberals, using the complainants as graphic illustrations of the interstate character of the coal industry, vigorously upheld the price-regulating provisions of the law as a valid exercise of the power of Congress to protect and promote interstate commerce.

"In the Carter case," Cardozo declared, "the complainant had admitted that substantially all of the sales of the Carter company are made in interstate commerce. In the other case, the percentages of intrastate sales are, for one of the complaining companies, 25 per cent, for another, 1 per cent, and for most of the others, 2 per cent or 4. Plainly, it is impossible to say either from the statute itself or from any figures laid before us that interstate sales will not be prejudicially affected in West Virginia and Kentucky if intrastate prices are maintained on a lower level. If it is assumed for present purposes that there are other states or regions where the effect may be different, the complainants are not the champions of any right except their own."

And, finally, where the majority first riddled the labor sections and then used this conclusion as an excuse to destroy the entire act, Cardozo, Brandeis and Stone flatly asserted that there was no ground for action on this issue. The majority had set up a straw man and used it as an excuse to destroy the act. With caustic directness Cardozo declared:

"The suits are premature in so far as they seek a judicial declaration as to the validity or invalidity of the regulations in respect of labor. . . . No opinion is expressed either directly or by implication as to those aspects of the case. It will be time enough to consider them when there is the threat or even the possibility of imminent enforcement. If that time shall arrive, protection will be given by clear provisions of the statute against any adverse inference flowing from delay or acquiescence.

"What the code will provide as to wages and hours of labor, or whether it will provide anything, is still in the domain of prophecy. The opinion of the Court begins at the wrong end. To adopt a homely form of words, the complainants have been crying before they are really hurt."

But, as the victorious complainants remarked, while congratulating themselves afterward, they did not cry in vain.

Right may have been on the side of the miners, but might was on the side of the operators. Five reactionary justices bent on legislative murder count for more than three liberals, regardless of how righteous their cause and how irrefutable their logic.

On the day the Court Tories killed the Guffey Act, they reversed a jury verdict convicting Arthur Cutten of violating the Grain Futures Trading Act of 1932. Their decision was based on the technicality that the law was written in the present instead of the past tense. Therefore, they held, the jury verdict was invalid and the notorious Chicago grain speculator was free.

Viewing the day's work of the Court, John L. Lewis remarked:

"It is a tragic and ominous commentary on our form of government when every decision of the Supreme Court seems designed to fatten capital and starve and destroy labor."

CHAPTER XVII

Luck, Politics and Justice

It was September 17, 1932, the seventieth anniversary of the Battle of Antietam. Justice Oliver Wendell Holmes had been shot in the neck in that battle and left for dead at the foot of Mayre's Hill. Now, seventy years later, he was philosophising to Tom Corcoran, his secretary.

"Here I am today, sonny," he said, "ninety-one years old. I've had quite a whack in my time. I've written some opinions that may have counted for something. I've had a little influence on the law.

"But, sonny, do you realize that seventy years ago I was lying on a battlefield with a bullet in my neck? And if that bullet had been one quarter of an inch further to the left, if a breeze had blown, if I hadn't twisted my neck, I wouldn't be here today, and there wouldn't have been any opinions or any dissents.

"It's just luck, sonny, don't fool yourself. People may talk about law and justice, but underneath it all, it's just luck, luck, luck."

Probably not many justices of the Supreme Court now deified through years of homage as the omniscient seers of the nation would admit that any of their decisions are prompted by anything save a mathematical application of the rule of law. But some of the lower federal judges, notably Judge George C. Hutcheson, Jr, of the United States District Court, southern Texas, are more frank.

"I set down boldly," says Judge Hutcheson, "that I, 'even as your other worships do,' invoke and employ hunches in decisions.

"I, after canvassing all the available material at my command, and duly cogitating upon it, give my imagination play and, brooding over the cause, wait for the feeling, the hunch—that intuitive flash of understanding which makes the jump-spark connection between question and decision.

"And more, 'lest I be stoned in the street' for this admission, let me hasten to say to my brothers of the Bench and of the Bar, 'my practice is the same as your other worships'.'"

Entirely aside from the judicial hunch, however, the path of American history is strewn with cases where luck, politics and just plain, downright human nature have influenced important decisions in the life of the nation. If Justice Field had not been shot at in a California railroad station, if Chief Justice Chase had not been consumed with burning presidential ambitions, if Justice Shiras had not been old and in his dotage, if Justice Brandeis' daughter had not been engaged in social welfare, who knows what the result of certain vital cases before the Supreme Court might have been?

Certainly even those who put the Nine Old Men next to God will admit that if luck had not intervened in the Oregon minimum-wage law, the workers of the country would be enjoying minimum wages today.

The first minimum-wage act was passed by Oregon in 1914, was upheld by the Oregon Supreme Court shortly thereafter and came before the Supreme Court of the United States in 1917. Here luck dealt its first blow. Justice Brandeis had been counsel for the minimum-wage advocates and now abstained from voting, making the Court's vote a tie, 4 to 4, which sustained the Oregon law but left the final fate of minimum-wage legislation uncertain. Industrial interests, anxious to defeat the law, hoped that a change of personnel among the Nine Old Men might swing luck their way.

Meanwhile other states had adopted minimum-wage laws,

and every one of their supreme courts—Massachusetts, Minnesota, Arkansas and Washington—upheld its constitutionality unanimously or by large majorities. Meanwhile also Congress adopted a minimum-wage law for the District of Columbia. This was tested in the Circuit Court of Appeals for the District of Columbia on June 6, 1921, and here for the second time the hand of fate intervened. Justice Robb had been thrown from his horse, was absent from the bench, and Justice Stafford of the District of Columbia Supreme Court was designated to sit in his place. He and Justice Smith voted to uphold the minimum-wage law, Justice Van Orsdel dissenting.

But June 9—three days later—counsel for those opposing the District of Columbia minimum-wage law appeared before Justice Robb, who had now recovered, and asked for a rehearing. Justice Robb is a close friend of Justice McReynolds, for years lived in the same apartment house with him, and is famous as one of the few justices as reactionary as McReynolds. Counsel opposed to the minimum-wage law knew, therefore, that it would get sympathetic consideration from Robb, which it did. Robb joined with Van Orsdel, and although the Chief Justice objected, ordered the case reheard.

This, it should be recalled, was in June 1921. If the case had been appealed directly to the Supreme Court it would have been argued during the winter term of 1921 or early 1922, at which time six justices—Taft, Holmes, Brandeis, Clarke, Day and Pitney—all favorable to minimum-wage legislation were on the bench. Even with Brandeis abstaining, five favorable justices remained—sufficient to approve the bill.

But luck had intervened. The case did not come before the Court as normally scheduled. During the time required for the rehearing, Justices Pitney, Clarke and Day all resigned. They were replaced by one justice who favored social legislation—Sanford; and by two vigorous reactionaries—Sutherland and Butler. So finally, when Justice Robb and Van Orsdel finished mauling the Minimum Wage Act in their lower court, it limped up to the Nine Old Men and, on April 9, 1923, Sutherland, one of the newly appointed justices, handed down the majority opinion against it.

Justice Sutherland killed the act, of course, on the ground that it was unconstitutional. But actually, and as Professor Powell pointed out, it was the "malfeasance of chance and the calendar" which wielded the hatchet. In one stroke, five corporation lawyers, their average age sixty-seven, had set at naught the votes of several hundred elected legislators, rejected the solemn judgment of thirty state jurists, and undone the work of decades.

Luck, plus corporation backgrounds, not constitutionality, had done its work.

Luck, the whim of fate, the frailty of human beings, also played an important part in another case, one of the most important in the history of the Court. Congress had passed the Legal Tender Act during the Lincoln administration in order to finance the Civil War, and afterwards—in 1870—the Supreme Court found it unconstitutional. The man who handed down the opinion for the majority was the man who, as Secretary of the Treasury, wrote and administered the act, Salmon P. Chase. Chase, one of the outstanding leaders of that era, had one great human frailty, overweening political ambition. He had served as senator, governor of Ohio, Secretary of the Treasury, chief justice of the Supreme Court, and beyond that he aspired to be President of the United States. Toward this end he had oscillated between the Republican and Democratic parties, having been elected to the Senate by the Democrats, and governor of Ohio by the Republicans. Now, as the country approached the presidential elections of 1872, Chase aspired to the Democratic nomination, in opposition to President Grant, who was sure to be nominated by the Republicans to succeed himself.

It looked like good Democratic politics, therefore, to throw the Legal Tender Act into the teeth of the Republican President who might be his opponent.

Grant, however, filled two vacancies on the Supreme Court on the same day Chase hurled out the legal-tender cases. Thus reinforced, the Court ordered a rehearing. Whereupon Chase filed a secret memorandum with the clerk of the Court criticizing his colleagues for insisting on this rehearing. Learning of this document, they filed a counter memorandum. Subsequently, both sides withdrew the statements, but the memoranda were discovered after Justice Miller died, and reveal in graphic detail how unjudicial, how politics-ridden is the greatest judicial body of the nation.

The cases upon which hinged the constitutionality of the Legal Tender Act were *Hepburn* vs. *Griswold* and *McGlynn* vs. *Magraw*. Only eight justices were then on the Court, and the first vote on *Hepburn* vs. *Griswold* found them divided 4 to 4, which had the effect of affirming the Legal Tender Act. One justice, however, Robert C. Grier, was mentally incompetent, and as his colleagues passed on to the case of *McGlynn* vs. *Magraw,* involving another aspect of the legal-tender question, he discussed it in a way which indicated he had not understood the issue in *Hepburn* vs. *Griswold*. Whereupon Chief Justice Chase pointed out this inconsistency and persuaded him to change his vote. Or, as Justice Miller described it afterwards, "The Chief Justice resorted to all the strategems of the lowest trickery." This change made the vote 5 to 3 against the constitutionality of the Legal Tender Act.

A week later Justice Grier was persuaded to resign, making the final decision 4 to 3 against the act.

How bitter was the feeling between members of the Court—a bitterness probably equaled only by that which exists today—can be gathered from the secret memorandum found in the files of Justice Miller and signed by all the justices supporting the Legal Tender Act. After explaining how the Court first was evenly divided on the *Hepburn* vs. *Griswold* vote, the memorandum stated:

"An attempt was then made to convince an aged and infirm member of the Court that he had not understood the question on which he voted. He said that he understood the Court of Appeals of Kentucky had declared the legal-tender law unconstitutional, and he voted to reverse the judgment. As this was true, the case of *Hepburn* vs. *Griswold* was declared to be affirmed by a Court equally divided, and we passed on to the next case.

"This was the case of *McGlynn* vs. *Magraw,* and involved another aspect of the legal-tender question. In this case the venerable judge referred to, for whose public services and character we entertain the highest respect, made some remarks. He was told that they were inconsistent with his vote in the former case. He was reminded that he had agreed with a certain member of the Court in conversation on propositions differing from all the other judges, and finally his vote was obtained for affirming *Hepburn* vs. *Griswold,* and so the majority, whose judgment is now said to be so sacred, was obtained.

"To all this we submitted. We could do nothing else. In a week from that day every judge on the bench authorized a committee of their number to say to the judge who had reconsidered his vote, that it was their unanimous opinion that he ought to resign.

"These are the facts. We make no comment. We do not say he did not agree to the opinion. We only ask, of what value was his concurrence, and of what value is the judgment under such circumstances?"

After the present Nine Old Men pass on to join John Marshall and Roger B. Taney, wherever they may be, it will be interesting to read whatever notes they took during the bitter debates over the New Deal and to know what elements of luck, politics and human frailty influenced the vital decisions of today.

Luck and prejudice played an important part in another decision which rocked the country, the decision of 1895 invalidating the income tax. Justice Jackson was sick when the act first came up for Supreme Court consideration, due to which fact the vote was 4 to 4. Had he been present he would have voted emphatically to uphold the law, and the eighteen years required to amend the Constitution would have been saved. But because of the stalemate resulting from his absence, a re-argument was ordered. And here again the hand of fate intervened. Justice Shiras had voted to support the tax during the first consideration of the law. But now he switched. This swung the decision from a 5–4 vote upholding the bill to a 5–4 vote against it. Justice Jackson, now recovered, wrote a vigorous dissent:

"This decision," he said, "is the most disastrous blow ever struck at the constitutional power of Congress." His dissenting colleagues were equally severe, Justice Brown stating that "the decision involves nothing less than a surrender of the taxing power to the moneyed class."

It required eighteen long years and the tremendous task of pushing a constitutional amendment through thirty state legislatures before the work of those two slips of chance were overcome.

Justice Field, who led the attack against the income tax, filed a bitter opinion in which he said:

"The present assault upon capital is but the beginning. It will be but the stepping-stone to others, larger and more sweeping, till our political contests will become a war of the poor against the rich; a war constantly growing in intensity and bitterness."

Justice Field was then nearly eighty years old. Born during the close of the naval war with Great Britain when the nation was a handful of struggling states huddled round the Atlantic seaboard, he now held up the development of a modern, swift-moving industrial nation about to turn the corner into the twentieth century. Old and senile beyond his years, he slept during arguments, did not always comprehend the private discussions of his colleagues, and became furious when a committee of his fellow justices suggested his retirement. There was no other way to remove him.

He was to remain until as late as 1897, a relic of an age that was past, an unyielding bulwark against change.

Age is not the only factor that can thwart popular change, and when it comes to matters of life and death, luck is all-important. During the fifty-one years that have passed since the Court finally transferred the Fourteenth Amendment from the protection of slaves to the protection of property, Republican Presidents have appointed twenty-one justices during their thirty-two years in office while Democratic Presidents have appointed eight justices in their nineteen years. Had the Democrats appointed at the same rate as the Republicans, they would have had twelve justices instead of eight, giving them four or possibly five of the present Court. But mathematics does not apply where justice is concerned. During the twenty-one years of Republican rule there were thirteen deaths and eight resignations. Republican justices resigned only when Republican Presidents were in power and could fill their shoes, as for instance the fatal resignations of Pitney and Day during the early part of the Harding administration which brought the nullification of the Minimum Wage Act.

But during the nineteen years of Democratic rule there was only one resignation. With the exception of Charles Evans Hughes, who resigned to run against a Democratic President, Republican justices did not resign with Democratic Presidents in the White House. Only Death removed them. Day and Pitney waited until Woodrow Wilson had left and Harding was safely inaugurated before turning in their resignations, and the present reactionaries are grimly waiting for Father Time to mow them down rather than resign while Franklin Roosevelt can appoint their successors.

Had the Democrats had resignations in proportion to their nineteen years in office, the law of mathematics now could have given them practically five justices, or more than one half the bench. But luck and politics, not mathematics, govern appointments to the Supreme Court.

Theodore Roosevelt has been the only President frankly to

admit that the Supreme Court was and should be political. But every other President, though silent on the point, has carried it out in practice. Almost invariably they have appointed members of their own party to the bench until they had a majority and then rewarded supposedly "safe" members of the opposite party. How political have been most appointments is obvious from one glance down the list of chief justices. John Jay resigned as chief justice to run for governor of New York, but lost to George Clinton. His successor, John Rutledge, was a South Carolina politician and governor of the state. John Marshall was Secretary of State in John Adams' cabinet, an active arch-Federalist, and was appointed chief justice for the open and avowed purpose of perpetuating Federalist ideas after Adams' defeat. Taney was an active Maryland politician and a member of Jackson's cabinet before attaining the chief justiceship. Chase had been a senator, governor, Secretary of the Treasury and was one of the most active politicians of his day, seeking both Democratic and Republican presidential nominations. Waite was active in Whig, later in Republican, politics. White was a senator from Louisiana. Taft had been a cabinet officer and President of the United States. Hughes was governor of New York, Secretary of State, and Republican nominee for the presidency. Only one chief justice in the history of the nation—Melville W. Fuller—lacked a political background. His background was that of counsel to Marshall Field, Armour & Company and the Chicago, Burlington & Quincy Railroad.

Fate also has been particularly kind to some Presidents, niggardly to others. Harding, who lived only two years in office, and whose administration was one of the most scandalous in recent history, appointed four justices—Taft, Sutherland, Butler and Sanford. Taft, who remained in the White House only one term and was more disastrously defeated than any other President, appointed six justices. On the other hand, McKinley, a popular President, appointed only one, while Wilson, who served for eight years, appointed only three.

In other words, justice has no relation whatsoever to popular will. Administrations may come and go, the temper of the people may reverse itself, economic conditions may be revolutionized, the Nine Old Men sit on. John Marshall sat for thirty-four years. He saw Jefferson, Madison, Monroe, John Quincy Adams come and go. All were of liberal Democratic faith. He was an arch-Federalist. Finally came Andrew Jackson. The country had changed. Democratic Presidents had packed the Court against him. But he hung on—until death.

Roger B. Taney, who succeeded him as chief justice, saw nine Presidents enter the White House—Van Buren, Harrison, Tyler, Polk, Fillmore, Pierce, Buchanan, Abraham Lincoln. They came and went, political and economic tides shifted. But he did not. He served as chief justice for twenty-eight years. Old and out of tune with the times, he helped plunge the country into the bloodiest war in our history, dying penniless and discredited. Later, Melville W. Fuller served as chief justice for twenty-two years, saw five Presidents come and go—Cleveland, Benjamin Harrison, McKinley, Theodore Roosevelt, Taft.

In all, three chief justices of the Supreme Court in eighty-four long years! Eighty-four years—forty-one newly elected Houses of Representatives, sixteen newly elected Senates, twenty newly elected Presidents and only three chief justices of the United States! In 147 years of our history, there have been seventy-four newly elected Congresses, thirty-two elected Presidents and only ten chief justices. Protected, secure from the approval or disapproval of the ballot box, the Nine Old Men sit on. It is easier to change the ruling head of the European monarchal system, which we shook off, than the Supreme Court's decree.

On the gallery floor of the Library of Congress is a glass case in which rests a parchment, yellowed with age. Guarding it all day long stands George McNamara, a Tipperary Irishman. Occasionally he strolls to the open balcony doors to look out at the new Supreme Court Building shimmering in the sun. Below, in the street, PWA workers are busy ripping up street-car tracks which the founding fathers never dreamed would mar the serenity of their land when they drafted the document which McNamara guards. But the street-car tracks have served their turn, and now buses are to run over an open roadway.

McNamara glances on beyond them to the Capitol. There, across the Plaza, is the Congress which enacted legislation to help the workers in the street. There, across the street, is the Supreme Court which may annul that legislation. And inside its glass case is the Constitution, yellow and faded, but still reaching out from the past to mold the destinies of the men in the street, and the Supreme Court across the way, and the Congress across the Plaza.

A layer of yellow gelatine covers the glass case, filtering out harmful actinic rays and giving the parchment a peculiar saffron color. It is written in the fine script of Gouverneur Morris in the days before typewriters or shorthand reporters, and after eighty-five days of discussion during which the founding fathers almost despaired of agreement.

"I almost despair of seeing a favorable issue to the proceed ings of the convention," George Washington wrote a friend during those eighty-five days in Philadelphia, "and I do therefore regret that I have had any agency in the business."

"No man's ideas are more remote from the plan than my own," said Alexander Hamilton after the Constitution finally was drafted, "but . . . it is the best the present situation and circumstances of the country will permit."

"I confess there are several parts of the Constitution which I do not at present approve," remarked Benjamin Franklin before he affixed his signature to the new parchment, "but I am not sure that I shall never approve them."

Today the crowds stream past the glass shrine and the yellow parchment, some throwing themselves on their knees before it, some asking to see the signature of Christopher Columbus, some the signature of Colonel Lindbergh. And McNamara, who stands guardian all day long, sometimes looks at his sacred charge and says:

"Strange to hear so much about it. I say to myself almost